**Preclassic Maya Pottery at Cuello, Belize**

ANTHROPOLOGIAL PAPERS OF
THE UNIVERSITY OF ARIZONA
NUMBER 47

# Preclassic Maya Pottery at Cuello, Belize

Laura J. Kosakowsky

THE UNIVERSITY OF ARIZONA PRESS
TUCSON, ARIZONA
1987

*About the author*

LAURA J. KOSAKOWSKY began her career in archaeology as an undergraduate at Stanford University, receiving a Bachelor of Arts degree in anthropology in 1976. She worked at a number of sites in California, the American Southwest, England, and Italy before attending the University of Arizona, where she specialized in Maya archaeology. She spent part of each ensuing year living and working in the Central American nation of Belize, and completed her doctoral degree in 1983 on the ceramics from the site of Cuello. Since that time she has returned to Belize to do postdoctoral research on the ceramics from the site of Nohmul. Dr. Kosakowsky has served as an Instructor and Research Associate in the Department of Anthropology at the University of Arizona and has authored and co-authored several publications on Maya archaeology.

*Cover:* Fragment of Muxanal Red-on-cream: San Lazaro Variety pottery depicting a human face in profile, excavated from the Lopez-Mamom levels at Cuello, Belize in 1976. (Photo by Norman Hammond, mezzotint image reversed for cover design; sherd from the Duncan Pring collections.)

THE UNIVERSITY OF ARIZONA PRESS

Copyright © 1987
The Arizona Board of Regents
All Rights Reserved

This book was set in 10/12 Linotype CRTronic Times Roman
Manufactured in the U.S.A.

Library of Congress Cataloging-in-Publication Data

Kosakowsky, Laura J.
 Preclassic Maya pottery at Cuello, Belize.

 (Anthropological papers of the University of Arizona; no. 47)
 Bibliography: p.
 Includes index.
 1. Cuello Site (Belize)  2. Mayas—Pottery.
3. Indians of Central America—Belize—Pottery.
4. Excavations (Archaeology)—Belize.  5. Indians of Central America—Belize—Antiquities.  6. Mayas—Antiquities.  7. Belize—Antiquities.  I. Title.
II. Series.
F1435.1.C84K67  1987     972.82′6     87-16249

ISBN 0-8165-1017-2 (alk. paper)

British Library Cataloguing in Publication data are available.

# Contents

| | |
|---|---|
| PREFACE | vii |
| 1. THE SITE OF CUELLO | 1 |
|     Summary of the 1980 Excavations | 1 |
| 2. CERAMIC ANALYSIS | 7 |
|     Definition of Terms | 7 |
|     Comparisons with the Cuello Ceramic Analysis by Duncan Pring | 9 |
| 3. SWASEY CERAMIC COMPLEX | 13 |
|     Type Descriptions (Swasey? Ceramic Sphere) | 13 |
| 4. BLADEN CERAMIC COMPLEX | 23 |
|     Type Descriptions (Xe? Ceramic Sphere) | 23 |
|     Mortuary Vessels | 38 |
|     Differentiating Features Between the Swasey and Bladen Ceramic Complexes | 40 |
| 5. LOPEZ CERAMIC COMPLEX | 41 |
|     Type Descriptions (Mamom Ceramic Sphere) | 41 |
| 6. COCOS CERAMIC COMPLEX | 54 |
|     Type Descriptions (Chicanel Ceramic Sphere) | 55 |
|     Mortuary Vessels | 83 |
| 7. THE CUELLO CERAMIC SEQUENCE | 88 |
|     Early Ceramic Complexes in the New World | 88 |
|     Ceramic Development at Cuello | 89 |
| REFERENCES | 93 |
| INDEX | 95 |
| ABSTRACT | 101 |

## FIGURES

| | | |
|---|---|---|
| 1.1. | Northern Belize, showing the location of Cuello and other major archaeological sites | viii |
| 1.2. | Site plan of Cuello, showing the location of the Platform 34 area | 2 |
| 1.3. | Location of excavation units on Platform 34, Cuello | 2 |
| 1.4. | South Square, Early Preclassic | 3 |
| 1.5. | South Square, Middle and Late Preclassic | 4 |
| 1.6. | North Square, Late Preclassic | 5 |
| 1.7. | North Square, Late Preclassic | 6 |
| 2.1. | Key to color symbols used in ceramic illustrations | 8 |
| 3.1. | Copetilla Unslipped: Copetilla Variety | 14 |
| 3.2. | Patchchacan Pattern-burnished: Patchchacan Variety | 15 |
| 3.3. | Consejo Red: Consejo Variety | 16 |
| 3.4. | Backlanding Incised: Backlanding Variety | 17 |
| 3.5. | Backlanding Incised: Grooved-incised Variety | 18 |
| 3.6. | Pettville Red-and-cream pottery | 18 |
| 3.7. | Consejo Ceramic Group pottery (Swasey) | 19 |
| 3.8. | Machaca Ceramic Group pottery | 20 |
| 3.9. | Chicago Orange: Chicago Variety | 21 |
| 4.1. | Copetilla Unslipped: Gallon Jug Variety | 24 |
| 4.2. | Consejo Red: Estrella Variety | 25 |
| 4.3. | Barquedier Grooved-incised: Barquedier Variety | 25 |
| 4.4. | Fireburn Red-and-cream pottery | 27 |
| 4.5. | Cudjoe Composite pottery | 28 |
| 4.6. | Consejo Ceramic Group pottery (Bladen) | 29 |
| 4.7. | Machaca Black: Wamil Variety | 30 |

| | | | | |
|---|---|---|---|---|
| 4.8. | Chacalte Incised: Yo Creek Variety | 30 | 6.5. | Sierra Red: Sierra Variety | 59 |
| 4.9. | Quamina Cream: Quamina Variety | 31 | 6.6. | Whole vessels of Sierra Red: Sierra Variety, buckets and jars | 60 |
| 4.10. | Tower Hill Red-on-cream: Tower Hill Variety | 32 | 6.7. | Whole vessels of Sierra Red: Sierra Variety, plates and dishes | 61 |
| 4.11. | Tower Hill Red-on-cream: Unnamed variety (resist) | 33 | 6.8. | Whole vessels of Sierra Red: Sierra Variety, bowls | 62 |
| 4.12. | Quamina Ceramic Group pottery | 34 | 6.9. | Sierra Red: Big Pond Variety | 63 |
| 4.13. | Chicago Orange: Nago Bank Variety | 34 | 6.10. | Society Hall Red: Society Hall Variety | 64 |
| 4.14. | Cotton Tree Incised: Cotton Tree Variety | 36 | 6.11. | Whole vessels of Society Hall Red: Society Hall Variety, buckets and jars | 65 |
| 4.15. | Honey Camp Orange-brown: Honey Camp Variety | 37 | 6.12. | Whole vessels of Society Hall Red: Society Hall Variety, dishes and bowls | 66 |
| 4.16. | Copper Bank Incised: Copper Bank Variety | 38 | 6.13. | Society Hall Red: Bound to Shine Variety | 67 |
| 4.17. | Whole vessels from Burial Feature 219 | 38 | 6.14. | Society Hall Red: Unnamed variety (dichrome) | 68 |
| 4.18. | Whole vessels from Burial Feature 251 | 39 | 6.15. | Laguna Verde Incised: Grooved-incised Variety | 69 |
| 5.1. | Richardson Peak Unslipped: Richardson Peak Variety (Lopez) | 42 | 6.16. | Laguna Verde Incised: Laguna Verde Variety | 70 |
| 5.2. | Joventud Red: Palmasito Variety | 43 | 6.17. | Lagartos Punctated: Lagartos Variety | 71 |
| 5.3. | Guitara Incised: Grooved-incised Variety | 44 | 6.18. | Repollo Impressed: Variety Unspecified | 72 |
| 5.4. | Guitara Incised: Grooved-incised Variety | 45 | 6.19. | Union Appliquéd: Variety Unspecified | 72 |
| 5.5. | Joventud Ceramic Group pottery | 45 | 6.20. | Puletan Red-and-unslipped: Puletan Variety | 73 |
| 5.6. | Joventud Ceramic Group pottery, modeled and incised | 46 | 6.21. | Puletan Red-and-unslipped: Unnamed variety | 75 |
| 5.7. | Chunhinta Ceramic Group pottery | 47 | 6.22. | Sierra Ceramic Group pottery, with modeling | 76 |
| 5.8. | Pital Ceramic Group pottery | 48 | 6.23. | Polvero Ceramic Group pottery | 76 |
| 5.9. | Muxanal Red-on-cream: San Lazaro Variety | 50 | 6.24. | Polvero Ceramic Group pottery, with modeling | 77 |
| 5.10. | Muxanal Ceramic Group pottery | 51 | 6.25. | Flor Cream: Variety Unspecified | 79 |
| 5.11. | Chicago Orange: Warrie Camp Variety | 52 | 6.26. | Matamore Dichrome: Matamore Variety | 80 |
| 6.1. | Richardson Peak Unslipped: Richardson Peak Variety (Cocos) | 55 | 6.27. | Escobal Red-on-buff: Variety Unspecified | 81 |
| 6.2. | Sapote Striated: Variety Unspecified | 56 | 6.28. | Chicago Ceramic Group pottery | 82 |
| 6.3. | Sierra Red: Ahuacan Variety | 57 | 6.29. | Whole vessels from the mass burial | 84 |
| 6.4. | Ahchab Red-and-buff: Variety Unspecified | 58 | 6.30. | Whole vessels from Feature 128 | 86 |
| | | | 6.31. | Whole vessels from the Stela cache | 87 |

**TABLES**

| | | | | |
|---|---|---|---|---|
| 1.1. | Divisions of the Preclassic period | 1 | | Bladen Ceramic Complex | 23 |
| 2.1. | Alphabetical listing of Cuello ceramic varieties, types, groups, wares, and complexes, with the Pring equivalent | 10 | 4.2. | Major discriminating features of pottery varieties in the Swasey and Bladen ceramic complexes | 40 |
| 3.1. | Classification of pottery in the Swasey Ceramic Complex | 13 | 5.1. | Classification of pottery in the Lopez Ceramic Complex | 41 |
| 4.1. | Classification of pottery in the | | 6.1. | Classification of pottery in the Cocos Ceramic Complex | 54 |

# Preface

The site of Cuello in Belize was first discovered in 1973 during reconnaissance work by the British Museum-Cambridge University Corozal Project, under the direction of Norman Hammond. The pottery recovered from the entire survey of northern Belize was initially analyzed by Duncan Pring for his doctoral dissertation at the University of London, England (Pring 1977). His results provided a regional sequence for northern Belize and pottery from test pits revealed the presence of an Early Preclassic (Formative) occupation at Cuello. More detailed chronological refinements for that site could not be made then, however, because of the lack of extensive excavation and the limited ceramic sample. My own affiliation with the project began in 1978 when excavations were conducted from March through June, and research continued during January through March in 1979 and 1980. During that time we were fortunate to live in a camp constructed at the edge of the site.

The general aim of the project from 1978 to 1980 was to learn more about the Early Preclassic community that lived at Cuello. Most of the 1978 season was spent on defining the extent of Platform 34, clearing the small superincumbent pyramid, Structure 35, and digging through the Late Preclassic material that was known to overlie the earlier levels. Ceramics from the 1978 excavations confirmed the chronology for the Late Preclassic in northern Belize that had been established by Pring.

In 1979 the total area of excavation on Platform 34 was enlarged. Excavation once again centered on digging deeper into Platform 34 to uncover the Early Preclassic settlement. The later building phases of Structure 35 were removed to reveal a well-preserved Late Preclassic pyramid dating to about A.D. 200 to 300. The 1979 season provided larger quantities of pottery recovered from stratigraphic deposits of the Early, Middle, and Late Preclassic periods, and my examination of the material suggested that refinement of the Cuello ceramic sequence was indeed possible.

In 1980 major excavation was confined to two 10-by-10-meter squares on Platform 34. These stratified deposits provided the best sample of ceramics to date from the Early, Middle, and Late Preclassic periods, and this collection is the pottery used to redefine the Cuello ceramic chronology presented in this volume.

After 1980 and the initial sorting of ceramics that was done on site, the pottery was shipped to Tucson, Arizona where I was working on my doctoral degree in the Department of Anthropology, University of Arizona. The laboratory analysis and development of the typology was conducted from 1980 to 1982 and formed the basis of my doctoral dissertation (Kosakowsky 1983).

The excavations and ceramic research from Cuello have shown the presence of Early Preclassic occupation in the Maya Lowlands by 2000 B.C. At Cuello, the inhabitants were already practicing maize agriculture, erecting plaster-surfaced buildings, and producing large quantities of pottery, which suggest an early, indigenous, sedentary settlement in the Maya Lowlands.

*Acknowledgments*

Principal funding for the Cuello Project was provided by the National Geographic Society (Grants 1856, 1967, 2077, and 2156), the Wenner-Gren Foundation, the British Museum, Rutgers University, and the University of Arizona. Additional support for ceramic research came from the University of Arizona. T. Patrick Culbert, William Longacre, William Rathje, Mary Ellen Morbeck, and Raymond H. Thompson, all of the Department of Anthropology at the University of Arizona, supervised various stages of the research and writing.

Many colleagues in Belize archaeology contributed to my understanding of the Cuello ceramics, although they are in no way responsible for any omissions or mistakes in the text. I would like to acknowledge the help of Norman Hammond, Duncan Pring, Joe Ball, Fred Valdez, Jr., R. E. W. Adams, Robin Robertson, Elizabeth Graham, David Pendergast, Harry Shafer, Tom Hester, Charlie Miksicek, Becky Mcswain, Richard Wilk, Juliette Gerhardt, Sara Donaghey, Muriel Kirkpatrick, and Carol Gifford, editor of the *Anthropological Papers*. Special thanks are extended to fellow archaeologists Anne Pyburn and Laura Levi for helping with the actual analysis and providing helpful insights. The government of Belize and the Department of Archaeology graciously granted the necessary permits to allow the transfer of pottery from Belize to Tucson for further study.

Many of the ceramic illustrations in this volume are the fine work of the Cuello Project illustrators: Sue Bird, Louise Belanger, and Paul Stempen.

Appreciation is expressed to the University of Arizona Press, directed by Stephen Cox, for making this unique material available to other scholars, and I would like to thank especially John Bancroft, Production Manager, and Cal Cook, Designer, for the production of this volume.

Finally, without the support for many years of my entire family, Ruth and Abe Kosakowsky, Susan Kosakowsky, Louise Mandelbaum, and, before his death, Richard Mandelbaum, and my husband, Henry Truebe, this monograph would never have been finished. This one is for you, Henry, and our children, Sarah and Brian.

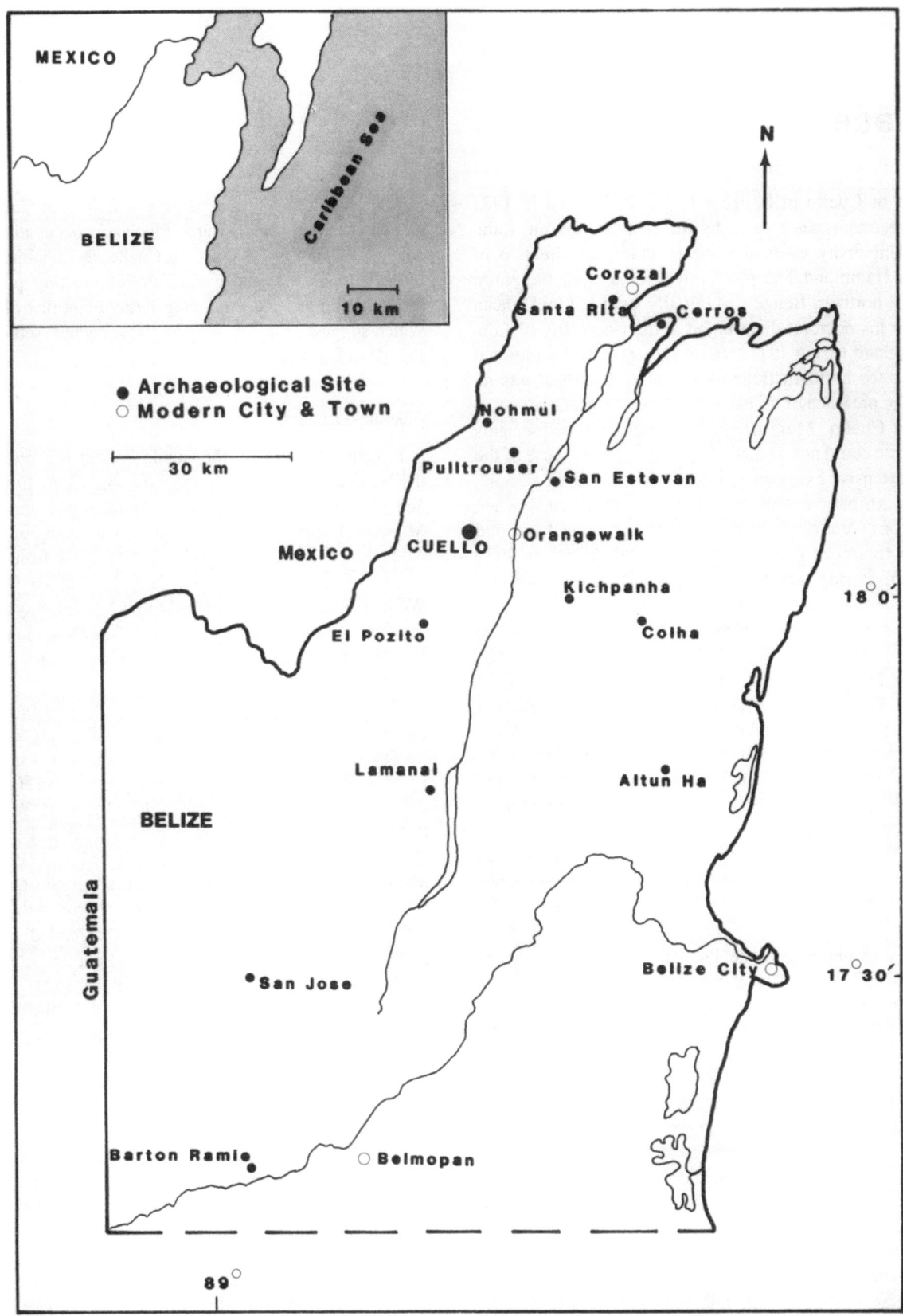

Figure 1.1 Northern Belize, showing the location of Cuello and other major archaeological sites.

CHAPTER ONE

# The Site of Cuello

In the beginning of this century, Maya archaeology was concerned with a single most important problem: in order to define prehistoric cultures objectively, the archaeologists needed some knowledge of and control over the reckoning of time. Traditionally pottery studies and the development of ceramic typologies have played a key role in setting up these time-space frameworks. Pottery-making was a craft that was in a state of constant flux, and it was obvious that pottery styles gradually changed and were replaced through time. This underlying premise to ceramic analysis has been retained as Maya archaeology has continued to develop and as Maya scholars have become interested in addressing more difficult questions concerning prehistoric behavior.

Many archaeologists now are interested in the processes that lead to the development of complex societies, and the Maya area is fertile ground for such studies. The discovery of early radiocarbon dates at the pottery producing site of Cuello gave us an opportunity to examine more closely the period of time leading up to Classic Maya society, and excavations in well-stratified deposits at the site provided an exceptional pottery collection for setting up an early chronology and for understanding more about the earliest Maya.

The site of Cuello, located in the northern part of the Central American nation of Belize (Fig. 1.1), was discovered and investigated during archaeological surveys in 1973 and 1974 (Hammond 1975). Belize is situated south of the Yucatan Peninsula between the latitudes 15°53′ N to 18°30′ N and longitudes 87°15′ W to 89°15′ W. Belize shares borders with Mexico to the north, with Guatemala to the south and west, and with the Caribbean Sea to the east. Elevations in Belize are from sea level to 150 meters, and the northern part of the country is especially low.

The overall climate is subtropical with a mean annual humidity of 80 percent and average annual temperature of 22° C in winter and 28° C in summer. Annual rainfall in the north is approximately 1,350 mm, with a dry season from January through April or May.

The landform in northern Belize is part of the Yucatan Peninsula, consisting of a low lying shelf of limestone that yields soft siliceous (sandy) soils. The original vegetation that developed in these soils was subtropical broad-leaved forests. Subsequently, however, the land has been used intensively for sugar cane farming and cattle grazing and most, if not all, of the higher vegetation is now gone.

Cuello is west of the modern town of Orangewalk, located in the middle of a cow pasture and surrounded by sugar cane

**Table 1.1. Divisions of the Preclassic Period**

| Preclassic Period | Date |
|---|---|
| Late | 400 B.C.–A.D. 250 |
| Middle | 1000–400 B.C. |
| Early | 2000–1000 B.C. |

and corn fields. The site was named after the family who owns the land and manages a rum distillery on the site.

The focus of excavation from 1978 to 1980 was on the massive Platform 34 (see Fig. 1.2), which stands some 4 m high and is clearly visible on the ground in open pasture. The Cuello site area is actually much larger and includes a small ceremonial precinct about 300 m northeast of Platform 34. The precinct has two plazas, each dominated by 9-m-high pyramids. In addition, there is a settlement area surrounding the ceremonial precinct that has been only partially mapped.

The first excavations at Cuello (Hammond 1975) quickly demonstrated the site's potential for contributing to an understanding of the earliest Preclassic period of Maya society. The sequence of architecture and pottery showed that the upper layers had been constructed in the Late Preclassic, over both Middle Preclassic occupation and an even earlier component of the Preclassic called the Swasey phase (Hammond 1975, 1976; Pring 1977). Radiocarbon samples provided chronological divisions of the Preclassic period (Early, Middle, Late) that corresponded with the major ceramic complexes first identified at Cuello (Table 1.1). Although archaeological research took place at the site for a number of seasons (Hammond 1975, 1976, 1978), the 1980 excavations provided the best controlled collection of ceramics and it forms the basis of this study.

## SUMMARY OF THE 1980 EXCAVATIONS

The major Preclassic component at Cuello consists of a sequence of building levels preserved by the construction of a platform (34) with a small superincumbent pyramid (Structure 35), dating to the end of the Late Preclassic (Fig. 1.2). The excavations in 1980 took place in two 10–square–meter areas to the east of Structure 35 (Fig. 1.3). The south area (grid squares 20/30, 25/30, 25/35, 20/35) was excavated completely from surface to bedrock, and the north area (grid squares 40/30, 45/30, 40/35, 45/35) was dug to the base of the Late Preclassic deposits.

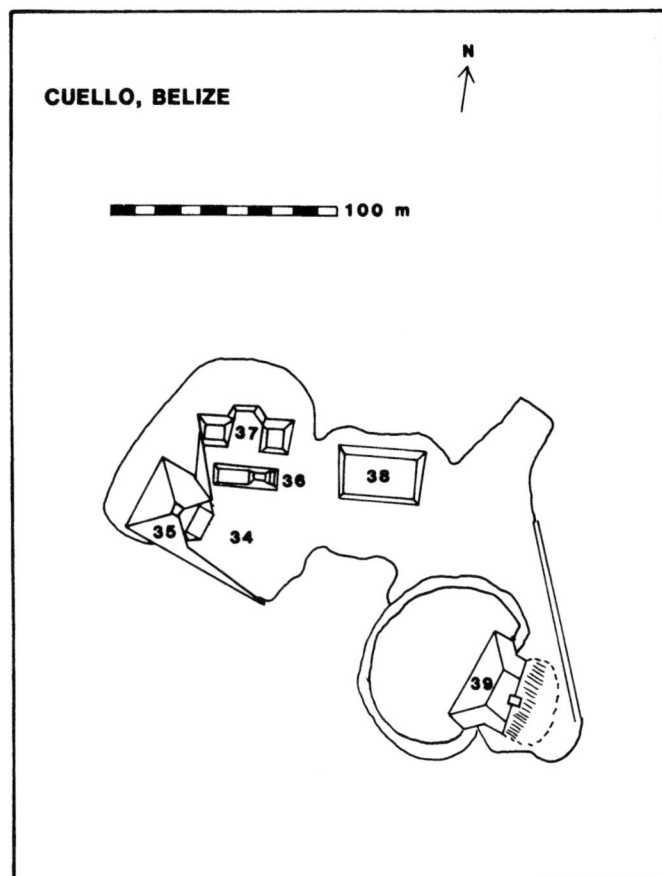

Figure 1.2. Site plan of Cuello, showing the location of the Platform 34 area.

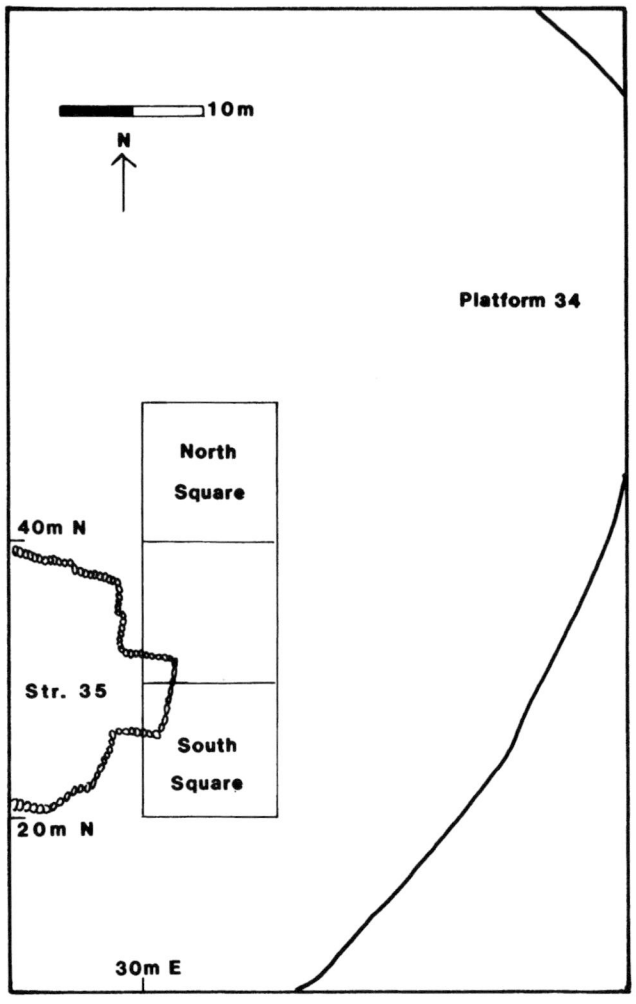

Figure 1.3. Location of excavation units on Platform 34, Cuello.

## South Area

Although lacking any structural architectural features such as floors or fill material, the earliest evidence for occupation at the site consists of a series of three postholes cut through soil into bedrock and refuse deposited directly on the old ground surface. This material may be as old as 2000 B.C., though radiocarbon dates have yet to be determined. The earliest structure exposed (but not excavated), Feature 262 (Fig. 1.4a), is subcircular in plan with a slightly projecting eastern portion. The sections of the postholes that cut through the floor indicate a single plaster floor was laid directly on the old ground surface, with just a thin layer of limestone rubble for fill beneath it, sometime about 1800 B.C. Furthermore, the positions of the post holes in the floor of Feature 262 show that several successive superstructures may have been constructed.

To the north of Feature 262 and coeval with it is Feature 82, a circular building that was partially excavated in 1976 and 1979 (Fig. 1.4a). Feature 82 was not well preserved, but it revealed construction techniques similar to Feature 262 with a rubble base below a plaster floor some 6 m in diameter. The architectural features of both structures are like the typical modern Maya habitation of pole and thatch.

Constructed partially above the earlier Feature 262 and dating to about 1600 B.C. is Feature 250, a curved substructure roughly 10 m by 5 m with a superstructure of timbers set into regularly placed postholes (Fig. 1.4b). An unusual aspect of this low platform is an access step added to the north side of the building during the second phase of construction. During the final building phase, entry was gained to the structure by way of a T–shaped ramp that sloped down into the interior. The ramp was flanked by screens of a perishable material set in narrow slots and upright posts. Although Hammond (1980) suggests that this elaborate entryway represents a public or ceremonial function for Feature 250, the associated ceramics and other refuse appear to result from everyday household use.

Directly over this building, with five successive construction phases dating between 1300 B.C. and 1000 B.C., is Feature 220, the final Early Preclassic building excavated (Fig. 1.4c). This structure was 11.5 m long and 6 m wide, and the pattern of numerous postholes and the wear on the floors suggest that it underwent a number of successive con-

# The Site of Cuello 3

structions and refloorings after the initial building. Several human graves were cut into the structure and often into each other as well. Across the courtyard from this building, to the north, is another structure (Feature 59) excavated in 1976, and to the east is Feature 230, both similar in construction to Feature 220.

The pattern of occupation during the Early Preclassic at Cuello may be described as pole and thatch habitations representing a small village complex. Although the excavations frequently revealed a grouping of house platforms and structures around a central courtyard, the exact size of the settlement during the Early Preclassic is difficult to estimate based on the small areas uncovered. The ceramics from the Early Preclassic analyzed in this study rarely represent refuse from more than two to four structures and the constructional fill from public areas between them. The botanical remains recovered (Miksicek 1978; Hammond and Miksicek 1981) suggest that small-scale maize and squash agriculture, as well as the gathering of plants and hunting of animals, formed the major subsistence base, and support the idea of at least a part-time habitation function for these structures. Ceremonial activities certainly took place at the village in the form of human burial offerings and caches of vessels and their contents. This is not to suggest, however, that only a narrow range of activities took place on a daily basis at Cuello.

The settlement pattern of small platforms around a central courtyard continued into the Middle Preclassic at Cuello. The northern and western sides of the courtyard group were excavated in 1976, 1978, and 1979, indicating, through the destruction of the earlier buildings, an expansion to the north of the central patio area at the beginning of the Middle Preclassic about 1000 B.C. The 1980 excavations then exposed portions of the southern and western buildings of the courtyard, thus delimiting the southwestern edge of the patio area.

The southern building (Feature 200, Fig. 1.5a) was 11 m long, and its initial construction took place sometime about 1000 B.C. using the destroyed core of the Early Preclassic building below it, Feature 220. Feature 200 was built 2 m south of the front facade of the earlier structure, indicating an expansion at the southern edge of the courtyard at about the same time as the northern expansion detected earlier. Feature 200 was successively resurfaced during the Middle Preclassic and was penetrated by a number of human burials that confirmed the dates of construction.

Sometime between 500 and 400 B.C. Feature 200 was severely destroyed. The timber superstructure burned and fell into the courtyard, leaving scorch marks on the plaster floor. The western building in the Middle Preclassic courtyard group was refloored and refaced throughout the phase and in its last period of construction received annexes to the north and south, lengthening it from 7 m to 10 m.

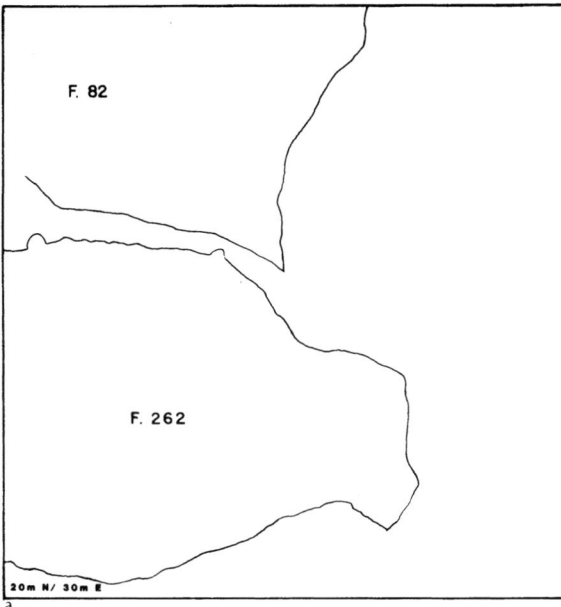
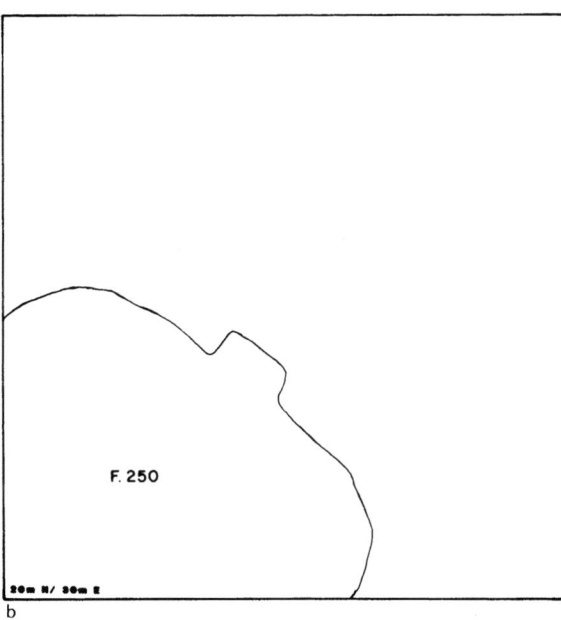
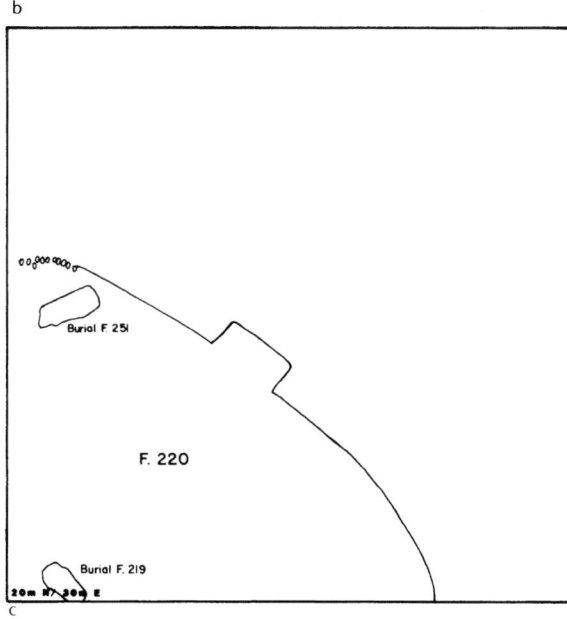

Figure 1.4. South Square, Early Preclassic: *a*, 1800 B.C.; *b*, 1600 B.C.; *c*, 1300 to 1000 B.C.

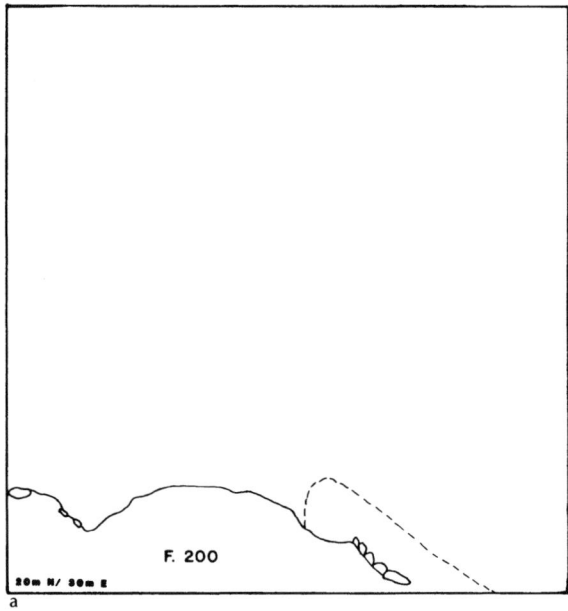

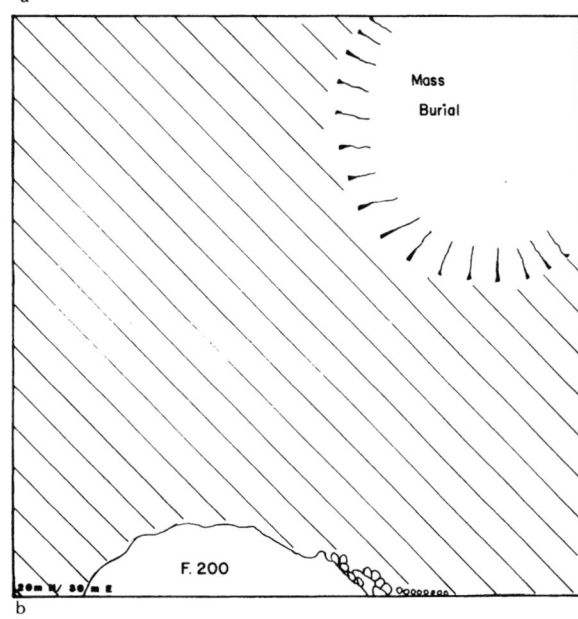

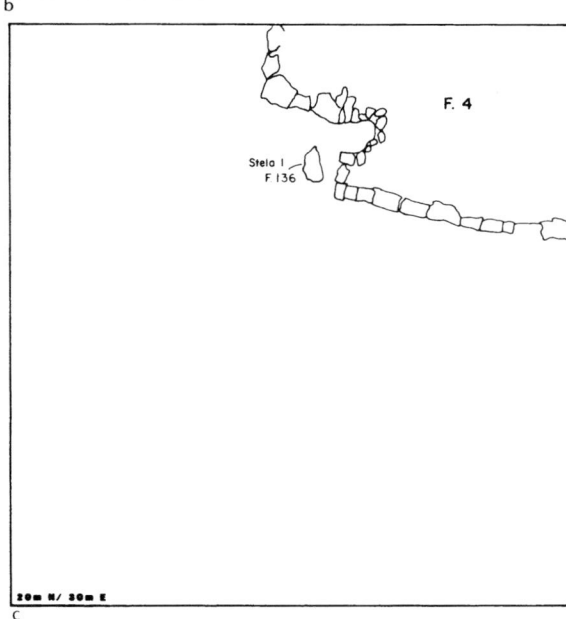

Figure 1.5. South Square: *a*, Middle Preclassic, 1000 to 500 B.C.; *b*, Middle to Late Preclassic transition, 400 B.C.; *c*, Late Preclassic, A.D. 250.

At the end of the Middle Preclassic, about 400 B.C., the entire courtyard group was buried underneath a rubble infill that formed a broad open surface (Platform 34). In conjunction with this architectural transformation was the interment of a large number of persons with associated grave goods. The mass burial (Fig. 1.5*b*) occurred sometime around 400 to 300 B.C. and included articulated as well as dismembered individuals. A shallow saucerlike depression 1 m deep was left in the top of the rubble layer and in it a number of individuals were laid along with grave goods. Preliminary analysis of the bones suggests that as many as 20 to 25 individuals are represented. Clearly the mass burial, including some possible human sacrificial victims (one skull had a sharp-edged hole in it), and the covering of the Middle Preclassic courtyard group represent a change in the style of living and the ideology of the inhabitants at Cuello, although what sparked the reorientation remains unclear.

Throughout the Late Preclassic, 400 B.C. to A.D. 250, this portion of the village was an open, plaster-floored plaza area. It is possible that the locations of the center of the buried Middle Preclassic courtyard group and the mass burial remained known throughout the Late Preclassic, because a number of subsequent human burials were laid directly over the mass burials at various times during the Late Preclassic. Some time during the Late Preclassic a small pyramid (Structure 35; see Fig. 1.3), facing east, was constructed on the western edge of the platform area. The pyramid underwent a number of reconstructions during the Late Preclassic. In the middle of the Late Preclassic and associated with one of the rebuilding episodes of the pyramid, an unmarked stela with associated cache vessels was erected in the open plaza area in front of the pyramid.

Late in the Late Preclassic the final addition to the plaza was a small platform structure, Feature 4, which nearly covered the stela and lay directly over the earlier mass burial in the center of the plaza (Fig. 1.5*c*). Feature 4 was demolished sometime in the fourth century A.D., when the final phase of pyramid construction included the addition of a long, projecting eastern staircase.

The Late Preclassic stepped pyramid was resurfaced in the Early Classic, but there was minimal use of Platform 34 beyond that time.

## North Area

Although the 1980 excavations in the north area of Platform 34 tied into the building sequence at the beginning of the Late Preclassic, excavations in 1976 demonstrated the presence of a late Middle Preclassic rectangular building,

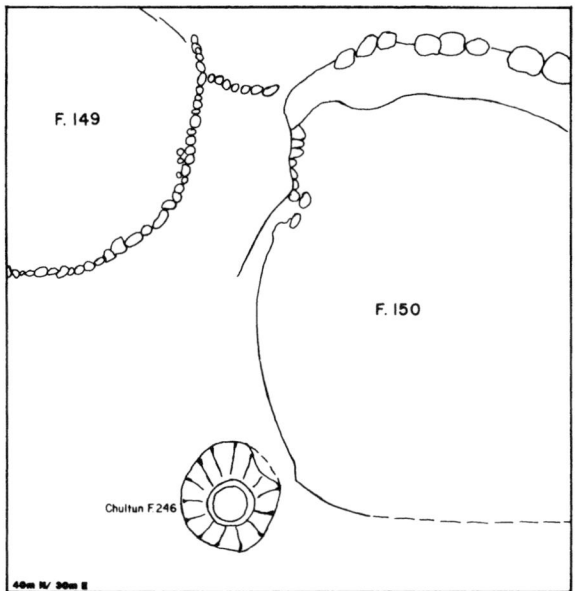
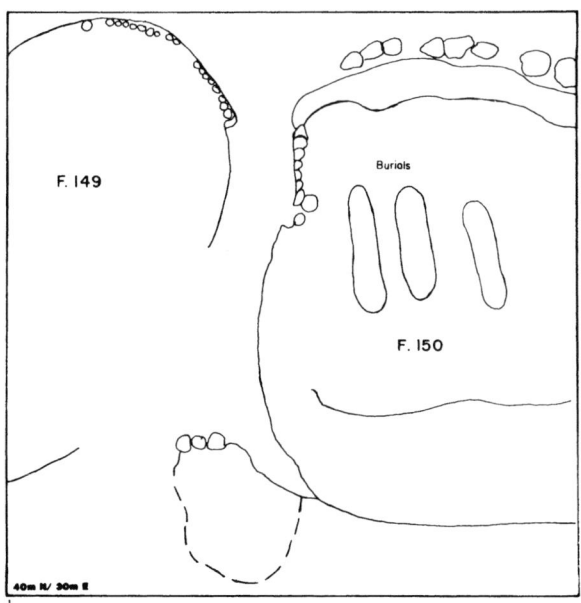
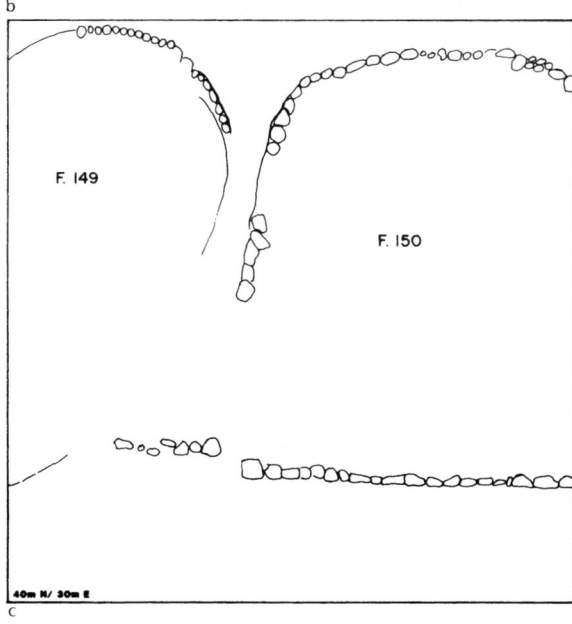

11 m long and about 5 m wide. The building apparently had standing masonry walls, some of the earliest such walls in this area of Mesoamerica.

In addition, the 1980 excavations revealed a chultun dating to about 400 to 300 B.C. that had been dug through the continuous plaster floors and fills of the preceding Middle and Early Preclassic phases (see Feature 246; Fig. 1.6a). The shaft was not eroded and the types of ceramics present suggest that the single chamber chultun was used only for a short time prior to its abandonment and filling in with rubbish.

The chultun was sealed by the earliest construction phase of two subcircular buildings: Feature 149 that was located west of the excavation area and Feature 150, a larger building on the east (Fig. 1.6b, c). Both buildings were first constructed on a continuous plaster surface that spanned the excavation area and that was bordered on the north by a retaining wall. Both buildings had complex architectural histories, each with three major rebuildings. The superstructures were of perishable, substantial timbers set into postholes.

In its early phase Feature 150 contained three extended burials, and in its later phase of reconstruction the circular front was converted into a rectangular shape (Fig. 1.6c). Both buildings (Features 149 and 150) faced south, and in their final phase the two were joined by the addition of a new front and the infilling of the narrow alley between them to form a single platform, Feature 151 (Fig. 1.7a, b).

At various times throughout the Late Preclassic, the successive marl layers used to expand Platform 34 in the north area were penetrated by human burials. These burials were of seated individuals with crossed legs set in circular shafts. Most burials (approximately a dozen in all, spanning the entire end of the Late Preclassic) were closely spaced though they were not encroaching on each other, suggesting the burials may have been marked in some fashion. Almost all were accompanied by one or two Late Preclassic vessels.

Within these same layers were a number of pits characteristically lined with vertical stone slabs and large pieces of broken pottery. These pits are similar to the shielded hearth areas often utilized by the Maya in southern Belize today; however, not all the pits showed evidence of burning.

The final architectural features in the north area excavation were two structures, one a substantial limestone block foundation, Feature 16 (Fig. 1.7c), and the other an apsidal structure. Burials associated with each structure suggest they date to the terminal part of the Late Preclassic, probably the third century A.D. A part of the apsidal feature was destroyed in the beginning of the Early Classic period by the final phase of construction of the pyramid.

Figure 1.6 North Square: a, Late Preclassic, 400 to 300 B.C.; b, c, Late Preclassic.

Chapter 1

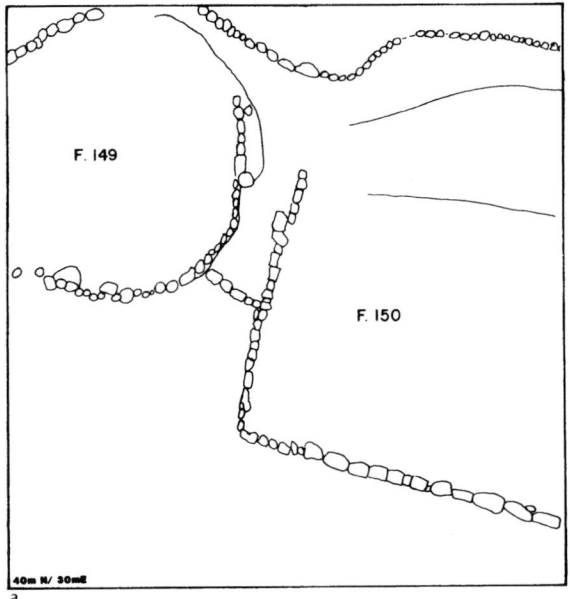

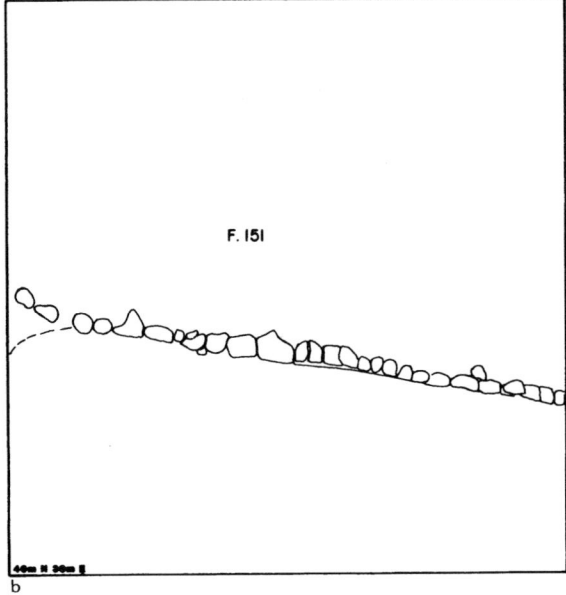

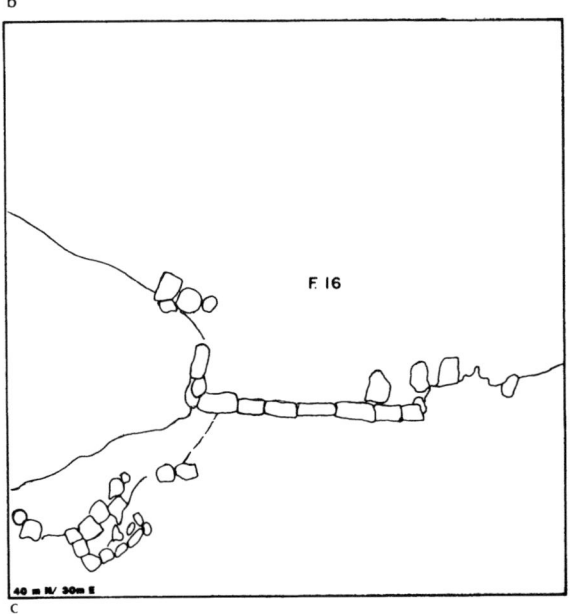

The 1980 excavations provided a generally uninterrupted ceramic sequence from the beginning of the Early Preclassic to the end of the Late Preclassic. This sequence represents only a small portion of the entire area occupied by the site of Cuello, namely two 10–square–meter excavations centered solely on Platform 34. Clearly then, the analysis of artifacts from this area represents only a partial view of the entire range of activities and inhabitants that occupied the site.

Figure 1.7. North Square: *a, b,* Late Preclassic; *c,* Late Preclassic, A.D. 250.

CHAPTER TWO

# Ceramic Analysis

The 1980 excavations at Cuello produced approximately 120,000 sherds from Platform 34. Initial sorting of this material was done in the site laboratory in Belize. In general, sorting was based on the gross surface characteristics of sherds, in keeping with the type-variety system of classification for Maya ceramics (Willey, Culbert, and Adams 1967; Gifford 1960, 1976).

The initial sorting process involved a system of "highgrading," whereby all sherds were examined within their stratigraphic units and all nondiagnostic body sherds were classified by ceramic group, counted, and discarded. These tabulations are on file in the Arizona State Museum Library, University of Arizona. The remaining sherds, including all rims, appendages, and diagnostic body sherds, were bagged and labeled according to stratigraphic units and shipped to Tucson for further analysis at the University of Arizona. The sample size was thus reduced by about half to approximately 60,000 sherds.

The final sorting process identified the range of variability in the Cuello collection by separating all 60,000 sherds into type and variety categories, where possible. The number of sherds studied in order to fully describe type characteristics was large, but only rim sherds and whole vessels were used in the frequency counts within types, were measured for rim diameters and vessel thickness, and were included in the sample on which Munsell colors were taken. Therefore, the total counts listed under each type or variety description are considerably smaller than the actual number of sherds examined. Sorting problems that arose are described under the corresponding type. In general, previously established types and varieties from other sites in the Maya area have been used to describe the Cuello material where appropriate.

Stratigraphic units were kept intact, and type and vessel form counts were made for each stratigraphic unit in order to demonstrate the temporal integrity of the proposed ceramic complexes (Kosakowsky 1983). The building sequence of Platform 34 was divided into 14 architectural phases, corresponding to changes in the platform floors and the various surrounding structures. Architectural phases I and II correspond to the Swasey Ceramic Complex, III to the Bladen Ceramic Complex, IV to the Lopez Ceramic Complex, and V through XIV to the Cocos Ceramic Complex. The Cocos complex is further subdivided into an Early Facet (architectural phase Va), a Middle Facet (architectural phases Vb–X), and a Late Facet (architectural phases XI–XIV).

I have chosen to work within the tenets of the type-variety classification system and to adhere to the definitions of the different levels of analysis as strictly as possible (Willey, Culbert, and Adams 1967; Gifford 1960, 1976). Much debate has focused on the utility of classification systems for ordering archaeological data and on the type-variety system in particular (see Brew 1946: 44–46; Ford 1954: 42–54; Wright 1967; Sabloff and Smith 1969; Dunnell 1971). Suffice it to say that I believe the advent of a standardized type description format has made it easier for others to recognize a ceramic type when the archaeologist clearly states the sorting criteria utilized. Type descriptions and the typology itself are therefore open-ended and, as new information becomes known, new type names or changes in old types may be added. The flexibility of the system has been especially advantageous in this analysis because it required combining the previous analytical units and nomenclature used by Pring (1977) with the new and more detailed classifications based on the larger ceramic sample recovered in 1980.

One of the greatest benefits of the type-variety system is that the standardization of ceramic description throughout the Maya Lowlands allows the ceramicist to make intersite comparisons with greater ease. It is now possible to recognize and describe distinctive ceramic attribute clusters with a wide geographic range and limited chronological spread.

## DEFINITION OF TERMS

In order to provide comparability among ceramic analyses from site to site in the Maya Lowlands, the type-variety descriptions in Chapters Three through Six follow the format established by earlier scholars and, in particular, are patterned after the definitions used by Sabloff (1975) at Seibal.

*TYPE:* Name.

*VARIETY:* The principles of the type-variety system are used to name types and varieties (Smith, Willey, and Gifford 1960). In accordance with Pring, actual names are taken from villages and towns in northern Belize. In general, Pring adopted a narrow range of variation for the varietal unit and gave new varietal names to several Cuello units as local variants of wider spread types. He also recognized varieties, such as Sierra Red: Sierra Variety for the Cuello monochrome type, where they were indistinguishable from other Late Preclassic varieties at other sites. Insofar as possible, I have followed Pring's original Cuello typology and divergences are noted in Table 2.1 at the end of this chapter. I also have chosen to leave certain varieties undesignated where sample sizes are small. These include both "unspecified" and "unnamed" varieties of types.

A Variety Unspecified is a local Cuello variety of a type previously identified at some other Maya site, but because of the small sample at Cuello the actual varietal designation was uncertain.

An Unnamed variety is a separate second variety of a type that is newly identified and newly named at Cuello. Because of the small sample of the unnamed variety and the similarities between it and the named variety, it is possible that further research and larger samples will indicate the two units should be combined into a single variety. I chose to split them into separate varieties for the time being to ascertain any possible cultural meaning for the observed differences but to leave the smaller of the two samples unnamed.

*ESTABLISHED AS A TYPE OR VARIETY:* This section lists the first establishment of the type or variety according to priority of publication. When a Cuello type coincides with a previously described type in chronological or areal extent, then it is included in the already established type; if not, a new variety is identified. If the sample size is too small to warrant a new type designation, the material is included within the major type of each group or within an unnamed type or variety of the group. This section usually also indicates the numbers of sherds and whole vessels used to define the type by me and occasionally by Pring.

*GROUP:* Types are incorporated into larger groupings of related types that have significance for broad regional comparisons.

*WARE:* Wares are broadly defined on the basis of technological similarity. Pring (1977) originally identified two new northern Belize wares for the Swasey Ceramic Complex, Belize Glossy and Corozal Orange, now called Rio Nuevo Glossy and Fort George Orange, respectively.

*COMPLEX:* Ceramic complexes are defined following the format of the type-variety system (Willey, Culbert, and Adams 1967). Individual names were chosen by Pring (1977) from stretches of water in northern Belize, and I have followed his example in naming the Bladen Ceramic Complex.

*SPHERE AFFILIATION:* Broad regional associations among ceramic complexes are identified by tying the complex into a ceramic sphere. Where information from sites other than Cuello is lacking or in preparation, I have indicated tentative sphere affiliation as "Swasey?"

*FREQUENCY:* The frequency of each type within the entire ceramic complex is listed as a percentage. While all of the selected 60,000 rim, base, and diagnostic body sherds were classified into types and varieties where possible, only the rim sherds and whole vessels were extensively examined and measured. When it was necessary to use body sherds for the description of certain characteristics, their quantity is indicated under *Established as a type or variety,* but for consistency and comparability the percentages listed under *Frequency* are based only on rim sherds and whole vessels.

*ILLUSTRATIONS:* Most of the illustrations in this volume were drawn at one-third scale for whole vessels and for sherd material. A 5 cm scale indicates size; some figures were reduced slightly for publication and a few were drawn larger to show detail. The conventions for slip color that were established by Smith (1955) for Uaxactun have been used for the Cuello ceramics (Fig. 2.1).

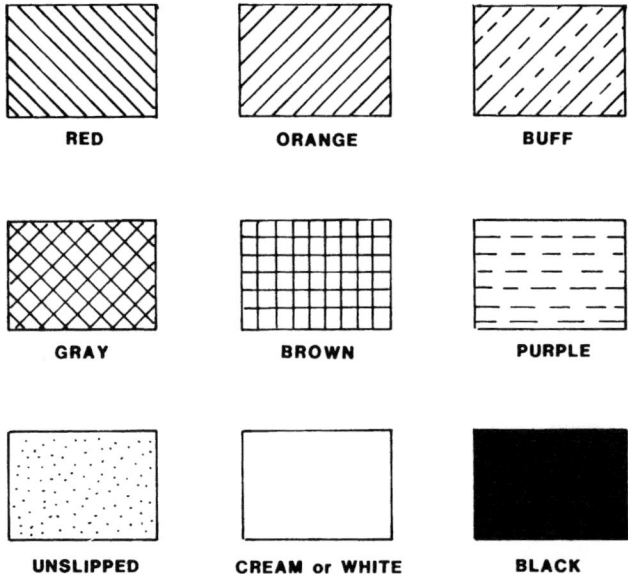

Figure 2.1. Key to color symbols used in ceramic illustrations.

*PRINCIPAL IDENTIFYING ATTRIBUTES:* Following Sabloff (1975), those attributes that most clearly identify the types are listed.

*PASTE, TEMPER, AND FIRING:* Paste texture, color, firing, and size of clay inclusions were studied, including both macroscopic observation as well as the use of a 10X hand lens. For sample sizes of 30 sherds or less, all sherds were examined; for larger samples, approximately 30 percent of the sherds were examined. In accordance with Pring (1977), dilute hydrochloric acid was used to determine the presence of carbonate inclusions. The Munsell color of unslipped sherds also was recorded.

*SURFACE FINISH AND DECORATION:* Descriptions of the surface finish, color, and nature of the decoration are included. Munsell colors are used to describe the surface and were recorded on all sherds brought to Tucson for the Swasey and Bladen ceramic complexes and on 30 percent of each variety of the Lopez and Cocos complexes, which are better known from other sites. The Munsell color was determined under fluorescent lights in a laboratory setting.

*FORM:* Vessel forms are described following the terms used by Sabloff (1975). Diameter measurements are of vessel orifices unless otherwise stated and are from outer edge to outer edge of rims. Vessel thickness is the average wall thickness, avoiding any extremes on the surface of the vessel. I measured approximately 30 percent of large sherd samples and all sherds of types with small sample sizes, unless the sherd was too small to get an accurate measurement.

*INTRASITE DISTRIBUTION:* The distribution of the type within the site is discussed, along with any spatial or ceramic changes through time that were noted. For my ceramic samples, location is restricted to either the North or South Square excavation areas in Platform 34.

*INTERSITE DISTRIBUTION:* In this section I describe comparative material from other sites in the Maya Lowlands, either from published reports or from personal observation of the material. In all cases the comparisons with Tikal pottery involve personal communication with T. Patrick Culbert. I have studied type collections from the sites of Tikal, Seibal, Altar de Sacrificios, Barton Ramie, Santa Rita, Uaxactun, Colha, Nohmul, and Cerros. In addition, I have examined all the ceramics currently housed in the Department of Archaeology of the government of Belize in Belmopan that were excavated from northern Belize sites.

## COMPARISONS WITH THE CUELLO CERAMIC ANALYSIS BY DUNCAN PRING

The initial research on Cuello ceramics was conducted in the late 1970s by Duncan Pring for a doctoral dissertation at the University of London. Site excavation at Cuello and the pottery sample recovered from it were limited, and that material was combined with pottery from four other sites included in the project survey of northern Belize: Nohmul, San Estevan, Colha, and Santa Rita. From these collections Pring (1977) put together a "regional" sequence based on "regional" ceramic complexes rather than on site-specific complexes. The original identification of the Swasey and Lopez complexes, however, was made with pottery only from Cuello and the Cocos complex was defined largely with ceramics from Santa Rita, although Cocos material was present at the other four sites as well (Hammond 1975; Pring 1977).

The 1980 excavations at Cuello provided a large enough sample to determine finer chronological divisions, and I undertook a more detailed ceramic analysis based solely on the pottery from that site. For the purposes of the current work and after some consultation with Pring, his complex names have been adopted for the site of Cuello specifically. In the future, new names will be chosen for the other northern Belize sites in keeping with the definitions of the type-variety classification system (Willey, Culbert, and Adams 1967; Gifford 1960, 1976). Differences detected in the typology developed by Pring and by my research (Kosakowsky 1983) have caused some confusion for other scholars. Table 2.1 at the end of this chapter and the following explanation outline the major differences between the Pring Cuello typology and mine.

All of Pring's original ware units have been retained, but certain ware names have been changed because his initial designations conflicted with names previously used for other sites. Hence, his Belize Glossy Ware has been renamed Rio Nuevo Glossy Ware and his Corozal Orange Ware is now Fort George Orange Ware.

Pring identified three ceramic complexes for the Preclassic period at Cuello: Swasey, lasting approximately one thousand years from 2000 to 1000 B.C.; Lopez (Mamom), from 1000 to 400 B.C.; and Cocos (Chicanel), from 400 B.C. to A.D. 250. The larger sample from the 1980 excavations provided an opportunity to further divide these three complexes. A new ceramic complex for the period of time originally identified as terminal Swasey has been separated and named the Bladen Ceramic Complex. As currently defined, then, Swasey now encompasses the period from 2000 to 1500 B.C., Bladen (Xe sphere) extends from 1500 to 1000 B.C., and Lopez (Mamom sphere) remains as defined by Pring. The Cocos (Chicanel sphere) Ceramic Complex also is the same time period as originally defined, but a late facet of it has been identified based on observable ceramic changes during the last hundred years or so of that complex.

In the Middle Preclassic Lopez Ceramic Complex there is largely a one-to-one correspondence between Pring's inventory and mine, except several types that Pring found in very small quantities were not represented in the current sample and were dropped from the typology. These included the following Pring types: in the Joventud Ceramic Group—Melinda Punctated, Resaca Impressed, Patos Appliquéd, Bobo Red-and-unslipped, and Pinol Black-on-red; and in the Pital Ceramic Group—Barranco Red-on-cream. Sherds from both the Jocote Ceramic Group and the Machiquila Ceramic Group were not identified in the 1980 sample, and it is likely that the sherds Pring classified as part of the buff Machiquila Ceramic Group fit within the range of variation I defined for the orange Chicago Ceramic Group and the cream Pital Ceramic Group.

The inventory for the Late Preclassic Cocos Ceramic Complex involved some redefinition of types. It is difficult to classify unslipped sherds based on surface characteristics, and there is an overall ceramic homogeneity of unslipped types in the Mamom and Chicanel ceramic spheres throughout the Maya Lowlands. For these reasons, Pring (1977) decided to use a new name for the Cuello unslipped type of these time periods, Richardson Peak Unslipped. He left the variety of that type unspecified, but to mark the similarity he included the type in the same ceramic groups as the unslipped types from other sites. Because he was the first to sort and name the type, its variety in essence was the established variety and it should have been designated Richardson Peak Variety. In keeping with the classificatory system, therefore, I have changed this unspecified variety to Richardson Peak. If future comparisons indicate this type is like one of the other previously defined unslipped types, Richardson Peak may be subsumed in it and, pending those comparisons, the group also is listed as Richardson Peak.

The red-on-buff Escobal Ceramic Group was left unchanged, as was the black Polvero Ceramic Group, but the following Pring types were not found in the 1980 sample: Blackadore Punctated, Gallo Impressed, and Corriental Appliqué. In the Matamore Ceramic Group, the Shipyard Variety of Matamore Dichrome was not represented in the current sample. The buff Cockscomb Ceramic Group was not recognized and, as in the Middle Preclassic, it is likely that sherds similar to those Pring identified as buff have been placed in the orange Chicago Ceramic Group. The cream Flor Ceramic Group has been added to the revised typology, although it was not in Pring's inventory. The red Sierra Ceramic Group required the greatest redefinition, as shown in Table 2.1.

A few minor name changes also have been made to the classification scheme presented in Kosakowksy (1983). Users of that former Cuello typology should note that Barquedier has been changed to Barquedier Grooved-incised: Barquedier Variety, Fireburn Red-on-cream to Fireburn Red-and-cream, Pettville Red-on-cream to Pettville Red-and-cream, and Ahchab Red-on-buff to Ahchab Red-and-buff, a change that is being made with this type by Culbert in the Tikal pottery analysis also. Throughout the Cuello sequence most of these typological refinements are based on the large increase in our knowledge of northern Belize ceramics since the late 1970s.

**Table 2.1. Alphabetical Listing of Cuello Ceramic Varieties, Types, Groups, Wares, and Complexes, with the Pring Equivalent**

| Kosakowsky (1983) | Pring (1977) |
|---|---|
| (Richardson Peak Ceramic Group, pending comparisons with other unslipped groups) | Achiotes Ceramic Group (?) |
| Ahchab Red-and-buff: Variety Unspecified | (Not represented) |
| Ahuacan Variety (Sierra Red) | (Not represented) |
| Backlanding Incised: Backlanding Variety | Backlanding Incised |
| Backlanding Incised: Grooved-incised Variety | (Same) |
| Barquedier Grooved-incised: Barquedier Variety | (Not represented) |
| (Not represented) | Barranco Red-on-cream |
| Big Pond Variety (Sierra Red) | (Same) |
| (Not represented) | Blackadore Punctated |
| Bladen Ceramic Complex | (Not differentiated from Swasey) |
| (Not represented) | Bobo Red-and-unslipped |
| Bound to Shine Variety (Society Hall Red) | (Sierra Red: Xaibe Variety) |
| (In Backlanding Incised: Grooved-incised Variety) | Calcutta Incised: Grooved-incised Variety |
| (In Other Consejo Ceramic Group: Unspecified) | Canquin Black-on-red |
| Chacalte Incised: Chacalte Variety | (Same) |
| Chacalte Incised: Yo Creek Variety | (Cowpen Incised?) |
| (Not represented) | Chacchinic Red-on-orange-brown: Variety Unspecified |
| Chicago Ceramic Group | (Same) |
| Chicago Orange: Chicago Variety | (Same) |
| Chicago Orange: Chucun Variety | (Same) |
| Chicago Orange: Chucun Variety (Black-rimmed) | (Not represented) |
| Chicago Orange: Nago Bank Variety | (Not represented) |
| Chicago Orange: Warrie Camp Variety | (Same) |
| Chucun Variety (Chicago Orange) | (Same) |
| Chucun Variety (Black-rimmed) | (Not represented) |
| Chunhinta Black: Chunhinta Variety | (Same) |
| Chunhinta Ceramic Group | (Same) |
| (In Chicago Orange) | Cockscomb Buff |
| (In Chicago Ceramic Group) | Cockscomb Ceramic Group |
| Cocos Ceramic Complex | (Same) |
| Consejo Ceramic Group | (Same) |
| Consejo Red: Consejo Variety | (Same) |
| Consejo Red: Estrella Variety | (Not represented) |
| Consejo Red: Unnamed Variety | (Not represented) |
| Copetilla Ceramic Group | (Same) |
| Copetilla Unslipped: Copetilla Variety | (Same) |
| Copetilla Unslipped: Gallon Jug Variety | (Not represented) |

**Table 2.1.**
*(continued)*

| Kosakowsky (1983) | Pring (1977) |
|---|---|
| Copper Bank Incised: Copper Bank Variety | (Not represented) |
|   (Name changed to Fort George Orange Ware) | Corozal Orange Ware |
|   (Not represented) | Corriental Appliquéd |
| Cotton Tree Incised: Cotton Tree Variety |   (Some Cowpen Incised) |
|   (In Cotton Tree Incised and Chacalte Incised: Yo Creek Variety) | Cowpen Incised: Cowpen Variety |
| Cudjoe Composite: Cudjoe Variety |   (Formerly Estero Red-and-unslipped) |
| Cudjoe Composite: Unnamed Variety | (Not represented) |
| Deprecio Incised: Grooved-incised Variety | (Deprecio Incised: Variety Unspecified) |
| Desvario Chamfered: Desvario Variety | (Same) |
| Escobal Ceramic Group | (Same) |
| Escobal Red-on-buff: Variety Unspecified | (Same) |
|   (Name changed to Cudjoe Composite) | Estero Red-and-unslipped: Estero Variety |
| Estrella Variety (Consejo Red) | (Not represented) |
| Fireburn Red-and-cream: Fireburn Variety | (Not represented) |
| Fireburn Red-and-cream: Unnamed Variety | (Not represented) |
| Flor Ceramic Group | (Not represented) |
| Flor Cream: Variety Unspecified | (Not represented) |
| Flores Waxy Ware | (Same) |
| Fort George Orange Ware | (Formerly Corozal Orange Ware) |
|   (Not represented) | Gallo Impressed |
| Gallon Jug Variety (Copetilla Unslipped) | (Not represented) |
| Guitara Incised: Grooved-incised Variety | (Same) |
|   (Not represented) | Guitara Incised: Guitara Variety |
| Honey Camp Ceramic Group | (Not represented) |
| Honey Camp Orange-brown: Honey Camp Variety | (Not represented) |
|   (Not represented) | Jocote Ceramic Group |
| Joventud Ceramic Group | (Same) |
| Joventud Red: Palmasito Variety | (Same) |
| Lagartos Punctated: Lagartos Variety | (Same) |
| Laguna Verde Incised: Grooved-incised Variety | (Same) |
| Laguna Verde Incised: Laguna Verde Variety | (Same) |
|   (Name changed to San Lazaro Variety) | Lazaro Variety (Muxanal Red-on-cream) |
| Lechugal Incised: Grooved-incised Variety | (Same) |
|   (In Cudjoe Composite: Cudjoe Variety) | London Red-and-unslipped: Variety Unspecified |
| Lopez Ceramic Complex | (Same) |
| Machaca Black: Machaca Variety | (Same) |
| Machaca Black: Wamil Variety | (Not represented) |
| Machaca Ceramic Group | (Same) |
|   (In Chicago Orange and Pital Cream) | Machiquila Buff |
|   (In Chicago and Pital ceramic groups) | Machiquila Ceramic Group |
| Matamore Ceramic Group | (Same) |
| Matamore Dichrome: Matamore Variety | (Same) |
|   (Not represented) | Melinda Punctated |
| Muxanal Ceramic Group | (Same) |
| Muxanal Red-on-cream: San Lazaro Variety | Muxanal Red-on-cream: Lazaro Variety |
| Nago Bank Variety (Chicago Orange) | (Not represented) |
|   (Not represented) | Ossory Red-on-orange |
|   (Richardson Peak Ceramic Group, pending comparisons with other unslipped groups) | Paila Ceramic Group |
| Palmasito Variety (Joventud Red) | (Same) |
| Paso Caballo Waxy Ware | (Same) |
| Paso Danto Incised: Variety Unspecified | (Same) |
|   (Not represented) | Patos Appliquéd |
| Patchchacan Pattern-burnished: Patchchacan Variety | (Formerly Yotolin Pattern-burnished: Variety Unspecified) |
| Pettville Red-and-cream: Pettville Variety | (Not respresented) |

**Table 2.1.**
*(continued)*

| Kosakowsky (1983) | Pring (1977) |
|---|---|
| Pettville Red-and-cream: Unnamed Variety | (Not represented) |
| Pital Ceramic Group | (Same) |
| Pital Cream: Variety Unspecified | (Same) |
| Polvero Black: Polvero Variety | (Same) |
| Polvero Ceramic Group | (Same) |
| Puletan Red-and-unslipped: Puletan Variety | (Same) |
| Puletan Red-and-unslipped: Unnamed Variety | (Not represented) |
| Quamina Ceramic Group | (Same) |
| Quamina Cream: Quamina Variety | (Same) |
| (In Consejo Red: Consejo Variety) | Ramgoat Red: Ramgoat Variety |
| (Not represented) | Repasto Black-on-red |
| Repollo Impressed: Variety Unspecified | (Same) |
| (Not represented) | Resaca Impressed |
| Richardson Peak Unslipped: Richardson Peak Variety (Cocos) | Richardson Peak Unslipped: Variety Unspecified (Cocos) |
| Richardson Peak Unslipped: Richardson Peak Variety (Lopez) | Richardson Peak Unslipped: Variety Unspecified (Lopez) |
| Rio Nuevo Glossy Ware | (Formerly Belize Glossy Ware) |
| San Lazaro Variety (Muxanal Red-on-cream) | (Formerly Lazaro Variety) |
| Sapote Ceramic Group | (Same) |
| Sapote Striated: Variety Unspecified | (Same) |
| (Not represented) | Shipyard Variety (Matamore Dichrome) |
| Sierra Ceramic Group | (Same) |
| Sierra Red: Ahuacan Variety | (Not represented) |
| Sierra Red: Big Pond Variety | (Same) |
| Sierra Red: Sierra Variety | (Same) |
| Society Hall Red: Bound to Shine Variety | (Formerly Sierra Red: Xaibe Variety) |
| Society Hall Red: Society Hall Variety | (Formerly Sierra Red: Xaibe Variety) |
| Society Hall Red: Unnamed Variety (dichrome) | (Not represented) |
| (In Chicago Orange and Machaca Black) | Stopper Brown |
| (In Chicago and Machaca ceramic groups) | Stopper Ceramic Group |
| Swasey Ceramic Complex | (Same) |
| (In Chicago Orange) | Tiger Buff |
| (In Chicago Ceramic Group) | Tiger Ceramic Group |
| Tower Hill Red-on-cream: Tower Hill Variety | (Same) |
| Tower Hill Red-on-cream: Unnamed Variety (resist) | (Not represented) |
| Uaxactun Unslipped Ware | (Same) |
| Union Appliquéd: Variety Unspecified | (Same) |
| Wamil Variety (Machaca Black) | (Not represented) |
| Warrie Camp Variety (Chicago Orange) | (Same) |
| Yo Creek Variety (Chacalte Incised) | (Not represented) |
| (Name changed to Patchchacan Pattern-burnished) | Yotolin Pattern-burnished: Variety Unspecified |

CHAPTER THREE

# Swasey Ceramic Complex

The Swasey Ceramic Complex spans a period of time from about 2000 to 1500 B.C. The selected sample intensively analyzed from temporally pure Swasey levels consists of 360 rim sherds and 11 body sherds. The complex is composed of 4 major ceramic groups with 10 types and varieties, and the relative frequencies of the groups are shown in Table 3.1. As indicated, 91.1 percent of Swasey Ceramic Complex pottery is slipped, with only one unslipped group, Copetilla, dating to this time period. Of the slipped pottery, approximately 25.2 percent is decorated with incising (5.8%), groove-incising (3.3%), dichrome slips (16.1%), or in some fashion such as modeling (one or two examples), punctating, and black smudging. In addition, the unslipped pottery is occasionally decorated with pattern-burnishing (0.3%).

This complex originally was identified by Pring (1977), and the present work redefines it as stratigraphically sandwiched between bedrock and the succeeding Bladen Ceramic Complex in the South Square excavations of Platform 34 (grid squares 20/30, 25/30, 25/35, 20/35). It thus comprises the first half of the Early Preclassic and a new ceramic sphere, Swasey, is tentatively defined herein because this material has now been found at a number of sites in northern Belize.

## TYPE DESCRIPTIONS
### (Swasey? Ceramic Sphere)

*TYPE:* Copetilla Unslipped.
*VARIETY:* Copetilla.

*ESTABLISHED AS A TYPE OR VARIETY:* Pring (1977). Pring's description was based on 400 sherds that included 75 rims or large sherds indicating vessel form. This description is based on 31 rim sherds.
*GROUP:* Copetilla.
*WARE:* Unspecified.
*COMPLEX:* Swasey.
*SPHERE AFFILIATION:* Swasey?
*FREQUENCY:* 8.6 percent of the Swasey Ceramic Complex rim sherds.
*ILLUSTRATION:* Figure 3.1.
*PRINCIPAL IDENTIFYING ATTRIBUTES:* Jar forms with thickened rims and square lips; bottle forms; smoothed surfaces; wide range of surface colors.
*PASTE, TEMPER, AND FIRING:* In accordance with Pring, there is a wide range of paste color and texture. Paste color ranges from dark gray (5YR 4/1) through light gray (5YR 6/1), and reddish pale brown (10YR 7/2–7/4). The color centers on 5YR 7/4 pink, and 7.5YR 7/4 pink, with 43 percent of the type comprising those two Munsell colors. This type overlaps in color with Chicago Orange, and in cases where the slip is well-smoothed, these two types are often difficult to differentiate. The paste is almost always oxidized throughout (90%), although a few sherds possess a darker core. Paste texture ranges from fine grained to medium, with some coarse grained, and most sherds have carbonate inclusions.
*SURFACE FINISH AND DECORATION:* The variation in surface colors is a reflection of the wide range in paste colors indicated originally by Pring (1977). Fire-clouding on vessel

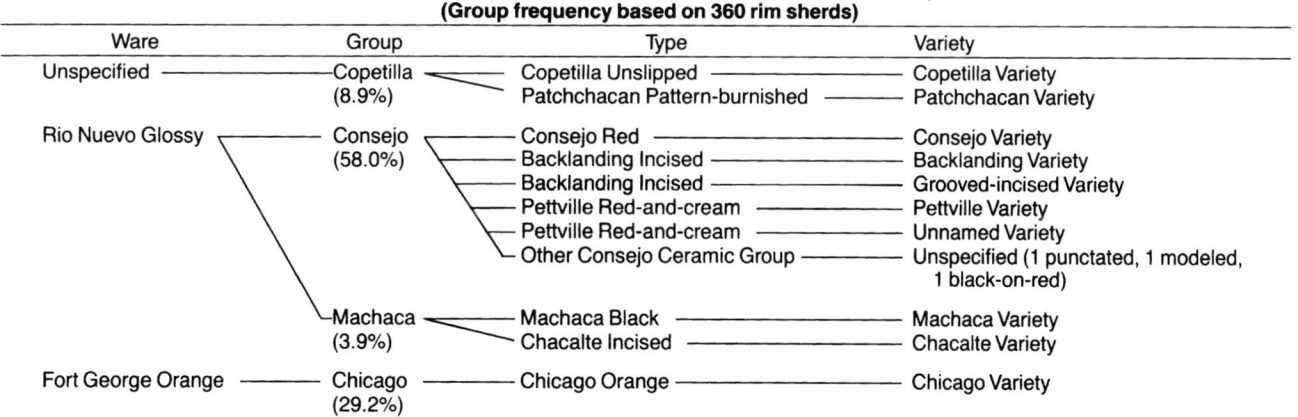

Table 3.1. Classification of Pottery in the Swasey Ceramic Complex
(Group frequency based on 360 rim sherds)

| Ware | Group | Type | Variety |
|---|---|---|---|
| Unspecified | Copetilla (8.9%) | Copetilla Unslipped | Copetilla Variety |
| | | Patchchacan Pattern-burnished | Patchchacan Variety |
| Rio Nuevo Glossy | Consejo (58.0%) | Consejo Red | Consejo Variety |
| | | Backlanding Incised | Backlanding Variety |
| | | Backlanding Incised | Grooved-incised Variety |
| | | Pettville Red-and-cream | Pettville Variety |
| | | Pettville Red-and-cream | Unnamed Variety |
| | | Other Consejo Ceramic Group | Unspecified (1 punctated, 1 modeled, 1 black-on-red) |
| | Machaca (3.9%) | Machaca Black | Machaca Variety |
| | | Chacalte Incised | Chacalte Variety |
| Fort George Orange | Chicago (29.2%) | Chicago Orange | Chicago Variety |

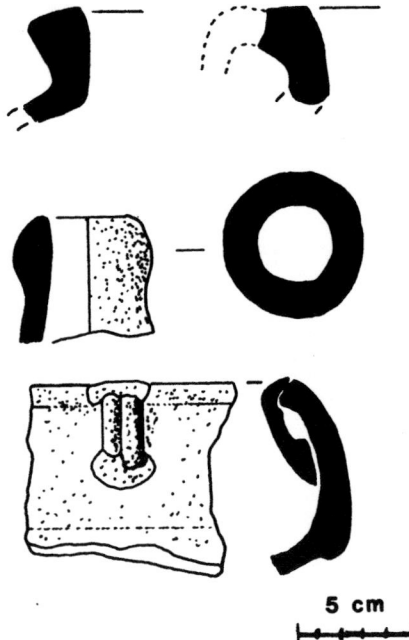

Figure 3.1. Copetilla Unslipped: Copetilla Variety.

surfaces is common. Surfaces are usually well-smoothed, causing confusion between this type and Chicago Orange, as noted above. A conscious attempt was made not to inflate the size of this category with slip-eroded sherds, although some may have been included mistakenly. As in Pring (1977), the ware for this group has been left unspecified because the current sample size is too small to suggest ware affiliations.

*FORMS*

1. Short to medium flaring and vertical necked jars with exteriorly and interiorly thickened rims and square lips (28.6%). Rim diameter, 12–30 cm; wall thickness, 0.5–1.8 cm (taken at medial point of neck); neck height, 1.0–3.8 cm.
2. Long necked jars with direct rims and round or square lips (28.6%). Rim diameter, 20–25 cm; wall thickness, 0.5–1.2 cm; neck height, 2.8–5.0 cm.
3. Vertical or slightly tapered bottle with exteriorly folded rim and pointed or beveled-out lip (14.3%). Rim diameter, 2.2–3.2 cm; wall thickness, 0.5–1.8 cm.
4. Vertical or slightly flaring sided dish or bowl with direct rim and round or square lip (10.7%). Rim diameter, 15–30 cm; wall thickness, 0.5–1.0 cm.
5. Incurving-recurving sided dish or bowl with direct or thickened rim and round lip (7.1%). Rim diameter, 12–30 cm; wall thickness, 0.5–0.8 cm.
6. Incurving sided bowl with restricted orifice, thickened rim, and round lip (7.1%). Rim diameter, 15–20 cm; wall thickness, 0.5 cm.
7. Outcurving sided dish or bowl with thickened rim and square lip (3.6%). Rim diameter, 20 cm; wall thickness, 0.7 cm.

*APPENDAGES: Handles.* Three handles were found on sherds of this type. Two are double cylinder strap handles, and one is a quadruple cylinder strap handle. This style of handle, diagnostic of the Swasey Ceramic Complex material and perhaps continuing into the Bladen Ceramic Complex, is made of two, or sometimes three or four, cylinders of clay joined together on the same plane and then attached to the surface of the vessel. The attachment of the handle is crude, with the upper part usually joined to the rim and the lower part to the neck-body juncture. The cylinders normally form a straight handle, although in the case of the quadruple cylinder handle, they are curved.

*INTRASITE DISTRIBUTION:* The type is defined on the basis of sealed levels of the Swasey phase material in the lower levels of the South Square excavations (grid squares 20/30, 25/30, 25/35/, 20/35). Copetilla pottery continues throughout the Swasey Ceramic Complex without any apparent changes.

*INTERSITE DISTRIBUTION:* Pring (1977) has identified the presence of this type at the sites of El Pozito, San Estevan, Nohmul, and Santa Rita in northern Belize. However, there appears to be little resemblance between this type and other unslipped types in the Maya Lowlands. It has a distinctly different surface finish from the major unslipped ware, Achiotes Unslipped, at Seibal and Altar de Sacrificios (Sabloff 1975; Adams 1971). The double cylinder handle is depicted on unslipped storage jars from San Jose in the San Jose I period (Thompson 1939, Fig. 221) and on unslipped types at Uaxactun in Period Ia (Ricketson and Ricketson 1937, Fig. 152*d*); the Swasey material, however, predates both of these examples. The square-lipped jar form seems rare from other sites. Pring (1977) has suggested that similar forms occur at Tres Zapotes and Altamira, but the similarities are faint at best. For distribution of the bottle form, see the Intersite Distribution section for Patchchacan Pattern-burnished.

*TYPE:* Patchchacan Pattern-burnished.
*VARIETY:* Patchchacan.
*ESTABLISHED AS A TYPE OR VARIETY:* Present work. This pottery was originally identified as an Unspecified Variety of Yotolin Pattern-burnished by Pring (1977). The Cuello sherds predate the presence of Yotolin Pattern-burnished at Mani Cenote (Brainerd 1958) by more than 1,000 years. Recent examination of the Cuello collection by Will Andrews indicates that the Cuello pottery is probably not the same as the Mani Cenote type. Because of the chronological disparity between the presence of pattern-burnishing at Cuello and in the Yucatan, I have chosen to classify the Cuello pattern-burnished pottery as a new type. Pring's (1977) description of this pottery was based on 26 body sherds. This description is based on 1 rim sherd and 8 body sherds.
*GROUP:* Copetilla.
*WARE:* Unspecified.

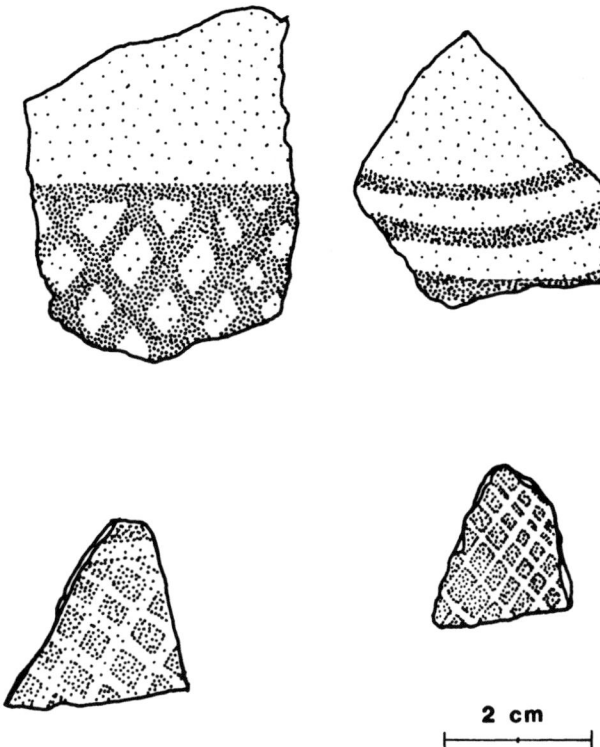

Figure 3.2. Patchchacan Pattern-burnished: Patachchacan Variety.

COMPLEX: Swasey.
SPHERE AFFILIATION: Swasey?
FREQUENCY: 0.3 percent of the Swasey Ceramic Complex rim sherds (body sherds not included in the frequency percentage).
ILLUSTRATION: Figure 3.2.
PRINCIPAL IDENTIFYING ATTRIBUTES: Unslipped, smoothed surfaces; pattern-burnishing consisting of thin lines or cross-hatching; bottle or jar forms.
PASTE, TEMPER, AND FIRING: Paste color is slightly more restricted in range than Copetilla Unslipped, centering on 10R 6/1 and 6/2, light gray and light brownish gray, with the burnishing resulting in a slighter darker color, 10R 4/1 and 4/2, dark gray and dark brownish gray. The paste shows differential firing, with the outer surface usually a darker color than the inner. Paste texture ranges from fine to medium to coarse grained. All sherds have carbonate inclusions, and a few have crushed mica.
SURFACE FINISH AND DECORATION: Surface color is in accordance with paste color, as described above. The entire surface of the pot is well-smoothed, and decoration consists of thin banding (2 examples) or, more commonly, triangular or rectangular areas of cross-hatching (7 examples) with alternate areas left unburnished to form a checkerboard effect. The width of the burnishing marks is fine, about 0.2 cm wide.
FORMS: The one rim sherd (not illustrated) is from a bottle with an exteriorly folded rim and pointed lip. The neck of the bottle is undecorated, suggesting that some sherds of this type may have been sorted with the unslipped type. Decoration extends downward from the neck-body juncture. The body sherds from this sample, in agreement with Pring (1977), are of a curvature and thickness as to suggest jar or bottle forms.
APPENDAGES: None noted.
INTRASITE DISTRIBUTION: The type is defined on the basis of the Swasey phase material in the lower levels of the South Square excavations (grid squares 20/30, 25/30, 25/35, 20/35). The sample size is too small to hazard any suggestions about changes throughout the complex, although sherds of this type seem to be most numerous in the lowest levels.
INTERSITE DISTRIBUTION: Brainerd (1958) discovered pattern-burnished pottery at Mani, Yucatan that belonged to a then previously unknown ceramic horizon. The only vessel form that Brainerd (1958) identified was the bottle.
Coe and Diehl (1980) mention latticework burnishing in the Ojochi complex at San Lorenzo (1450–1350 B.C.). Meggars, Evans, and Estrada (1965: 122) identify a pottery type known as Machalilla Burnished Line in coastal Ecuador that is modally similar. Pattern-burnishing may also occur during the Monte Alban I phase at Monte Alban (Sorenson 1955: 49). However, the Cuello material predates the other examples of pattern-burnishing in Mesoamerica. According to Andrews (1986), Yotolin Pattern-burnished water bottles of the Mani Cenote type are found among the earliest levels of Loltun Cave, but they specifically date to the Middle Preclassic period at that site and no earlier. For a more complete discussion of the intersite distribution of Patchchacan Pattern-burnished, see Yotolin Pattern-burnished in Pring (1977).

TYPE: Consejo Red.
VARIETY: Consejo.
ESTABLISHED AS A TYPE OR VARIETY: Pring (1977). Pring's description was based on about 450 sherds, including 100 rims or large sherds indicating vessel form. This description is based on 125 rim sherds.
GROUP: Consejo.
WARE: Rio Nuevo Glossy.
COMPLEX: Swasey.
SPHERE AFFILIATION: Swasey?
FREQUENCY: 34.7 percent of the Swasey Ceramic Complex rim sherds.
ILLUSTRATION: Figure 3.3.
PRINCIPAL IDENTIFYING ATTRIBUTES: Lustrous to glossy bright red slip; well-smoothed surfaces with a thin white or buff underslip or wash; incurved-recurved sided bowls or dishes with direct rims; vertical sided bowls or dishes with direct rims; a high percentage of the direct rims have square lips.

16  Chapter 3

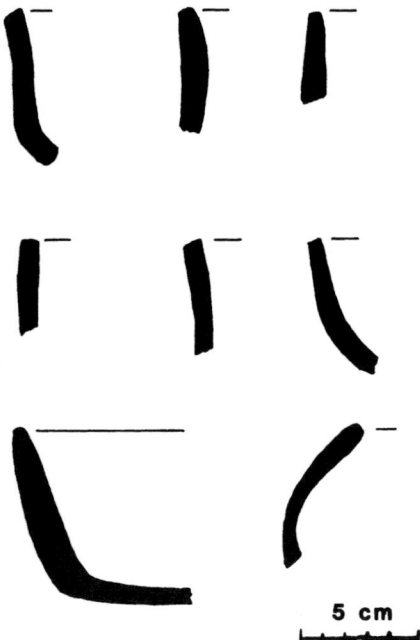

Figure 3.3. Consejo Red: Consejo Variety

*PASTE, TEMPER, AND FIRING:* Paste color ranges from dark brown and gray to a light colored buff, orange, and pink. Differential firing is almost always the case, with dark gray or black cores. All sherds have carbonate inclusions and paste texture ranges from fine to medium grained.

*SURFACE FINISH AND DECORATION:* Consejo pottery is characterized by a glossy red slip over a creamy white, pale buff, or orange underslip or wash. The underslip is very thin and on some sherds it is difficult to detect its presence. The surface of the vessel is generally so well smoothed that in some cases it may give the appearance of an underslip where in fact there is none. Pring (1977) originally identified two monochrome red types, Ramgoat Red and Consejo Red, the former lacking the underslip present in the latter. After further examination of more material, it appears that this distinction is spurious and almost impossible to identify. All Swasey monochrome red sherds from Cuello have been placed in the Consejo Ceramic Group.

Consejo Red is homogenous in color, centering on 10R 4/8 red (60%), with the rest of the sherds ranging from 10R 5/8 red to 2.5YR 4/8 and 5/8 red. Brush marks are visible on some sherds, suggesting the glossiness derives from the slip rather than from postslip burnishing and from the smoothness of the vessel surfaces to which the slip is applied.

The slip weathers in a characteristic fashion, eroding rather than flaking. Another feature of sherds of this type is the presence of tiny white rootlet marks that leave the white underslip visible. Fire clouding occurs but is rare.

*FORMS*
1. Incurved-recurved sided dish or bowl with direct or slightly exteriorly folded rim and round or square lip (31.6%). Rim diameter, 20–35 cm; wall thickness, 0.5–0.9 cm.
2. Vertical or slightly flaring sided dish or bowl with direct rim and round or square lip (21%). Most bases are flat. Rim diameter, 15–40 cm; wall thickness, 0.5–0.8 cm.
3. Slightly outcurving sided dish or plate with direct or exteriorly folded rim and round lip (17.5%). Rim diameter, 28–45 cm; wall thickness, 0.5–0.8 cm.
4. Incurving sided bowl or dish with restricted orifice, direct or interiorly folded rim, and round or pointed lip (12.3%). Rim diameter, 10–25 cm; wall thickness, 0.4–0.8 cm.
5. Incurving sided bowl with short vertical neck or collar, direct rim, and round lip (7.9%). Rim diameter, 18–30 cm; wall thickness, 0.4–0.8 cm.
6. Flaring sided dish with direct or slightly exteriorly thickened rim and round or square lip (5.3%). Bases are generally flat. Rim diameter, 15–40 cm; wall thickness, 0.5–0.9 cm.
7. Medium flaring or outcurving necked jar with exteriorly folded or direct rim and round lip (2.6%). Rim diameter, 10–18 cm; wall thickness, 0.5–0.9 cm; neck height, 0.8–2.5 cm.
8. Slightly tapered bottle neck with exteriorly folded rim and round or pointed lip (1.8%). Rim diameter, 3.2–3.7 cm; wall thickness, 0.5–0.7 cm.

*APPENDAGES:* None noted.

*INTRASITE DISTRIBUTION:* The type is defined on the basis of sealed levels of the Swasey phase material in the lower levels of the South Square excavation (grid squares 20/30, 25/30, 25/35, 20/35). It continues throughout the Swasey phase with an apparent increase in round lips and decrease in square lips. Consejo Red extends into the following Bladen Ceramic Complex, demonstrating continuity, although later in time it becomes more consistent in color (a dark vermilion).

*INTERSITE DISTRIBUTION:* The type has been identified by Pring (1977) at San Estevan, Nohmul, Santa Rita, and El Pozito in northern Belize. I have studied material from the site of Colha and identified small amounts of this type from that site (Kosakowsky and Valdez 1982).

Examination of the material from Becan by Pring (1977: 106) showed that there were small quantities of this type as far north as the Yucatan.

Similar early material is lacking from other sites. At Altar de Sacrificios, the Xe Ceramic Complex monochrome red, Abelino, has a thin slip over a buff undersurface, and while it is distinctly more glossy than the later Mamom material, it is not as glossy as Consejo Red and tends to be lighter in color (Adams 1971). The early monochrome red from the Real (Xe) Ceramic Complex at Seibal is obviously similar to the Abelino Red from Altar de Sacrificios. At Dzibilchaltun the monochrome reds from the Nabanche complex also tend to be glossier than the later Preclassic material, but otherwise they have little similarity to Consejo Red.

There is some likeness in vessel form to the Real material at Seibal (Sabloff 1975) and the Xe material from Altar de Sacrificios (Adams 1971).

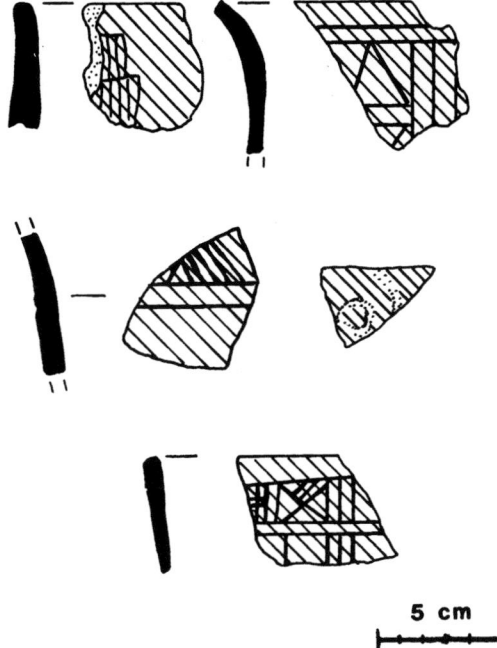

Figure 3.4. Backlanding Incised: Backlanding Variety.

*TYPE:* Backlanding Incised.
*VARIETY:* Backlanding.
*ESTABLISHED AS A TYPE OR VARIETY:* Established as a type by Pring (1977); established as a variety, present work. This description is based on 13 rim sherds and 2 body sherds.
*GROUP:* Consejo.
*WARE:* Rio Nuevo Glossy.
*COMPLEX:* Swasey.
*SPHERE AFFILIATION:* Swasey?
*FREQUENCY:* 3.6 percent of the Swasey Ceramic Complex rim sherds (body sherds not included in the frequency percentage).
*ILLUSTRATION:* Figure 3.4.
*PRINCIPAL IDENTIFYING ATTRIBUTES:* Glossy red slip, same as Consejo Red; shallow postslip incising in a variety of designs over the exteriors of vessels; vertical to slightly flaring sided dishes or bowls with direct rims.
*PASTE, TEMPER, AND FIRING:* Same as Consejo Red: Consejo Variety.
*SURFACE FINISH AND DECORATION:* Slip characteristics are the same as Consejo Red: Consejo Variety. Decoration consists of postslip incising in the form of one or two shallow horizontal fine lines below the rim on the exterior of vessels or more elaborate designs on the body exterior. The designs are usually geometric, although they occasionally appear to take the form of elaborate doodling.
*FORMS*
1. Vertical to slightly flaring sided bowl or dish with direct or occasionally exteriorly everted rim and square or round lip (33.3%). Rim diameter, 15–38 cm; wall thickness 0.5–0.9 cm.
2. Incurved-recurved sided dish or bowl with direct rim and round or square lip (25%). Rim diameter, 20–28 cm; wall thickness, 0.5–0.8 cm.
3. Outcurving sided bowl with direct or slightly interiorly thickened rim and round or square lip (25%). Rim diameter, 15–36 cm; wall thickness, 0.5–0.7 cm.
4. Incurving sided bowl or dish with a generally unrestricted orifice, direct or interiorly thickened rim, and round or square lip (16.7%). Rim diameter, 15–25 cm; wall thickness, 0.5–0.7 cm.
*APPENDAGES:* None noted.
*INTRASITE DISTRIBUTION:* See Consejo Red: Consejo Variety; sherds tend to be most numerous in the earlier levels.
*INTERSITE DISTRIBUTION:* For general relationships, see Consejo Red: Consejo Variety. It is not known whether this particular variety of Blacklanding Incised is found at other sites in northern Belize, although the Grooved-incised Variety has been identified elsewhere. Postslip incising occurs on the monochrome red sherds from the Xe Ceramic Complex at Altar de Sacrificios (Adams 1971) and the Real Ceramic Complex at Seibal (Sabloff 1975), and it bears some similarity to the Cuello material. However, the incised type at both these sites, Pico de Oro Incised, is later in date than the Swasey Backlanding Incised.

*TYPE:* Backlanding Incised.
*VARIETY:* Grooved-incised.
*ESTABLISHED AS A TYPE OR VARIETY:* Pring (1977). Pring's description was based on 25 sherds and 3 whole vessels. This description is based on 12 rim sherds.
*GROUP:* Consejo.
*WARE:* Rio Nuevo Glossy.
*COMPLEX:* Swasey.
*SPHERE AFFILIATION:* Swasey?
*FREQUENCY:* 3.3 percent of the Swasey Ceramic Complex rim sherds.
*ILLUSTRATION:* Figure 3.5.
*PRINCIPAL IDENTIFYING ATTRIBUTES:* Glossy red slip, same as Consejo Red; shallow preslip, groove-incising around the exterior of vessels; incurved-recurved sided dishes and bowls with direct rims.
*PASTE, TEMPER, AND FIRING:* Same as Consejo Red: Consejo Variety.
*SURFACE FINISH AND DECORATION:* Slip characteristics are the same as Consejo Red: Consejo Variety. Decoration consists of preslip groove-incising that is cut in narrow horizontal channels, usually around the exterior of the vessel just below the rim. These channels tend to occur in two or three parallel lines. Occasionally, the channels also are cut near the base of the vessel. These channels are so shallow that they are barely perceptible, as first described by Pring (1977).
*FORMS*
1. Incurved-recurved sided bowl or dish with direct rim

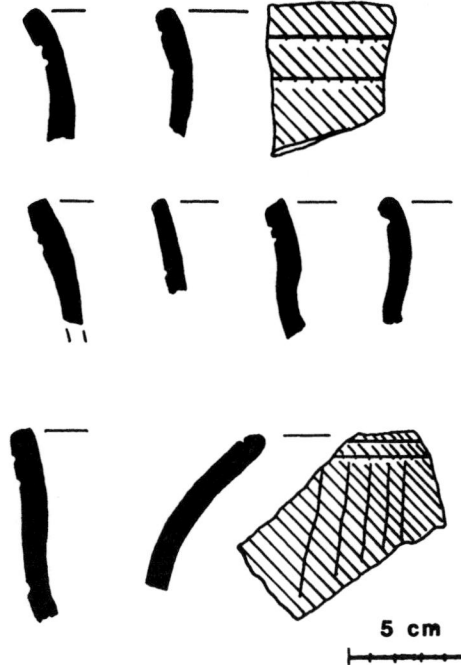

Figure 3.5. Backlanding Incised: Grooved-incised Variety.

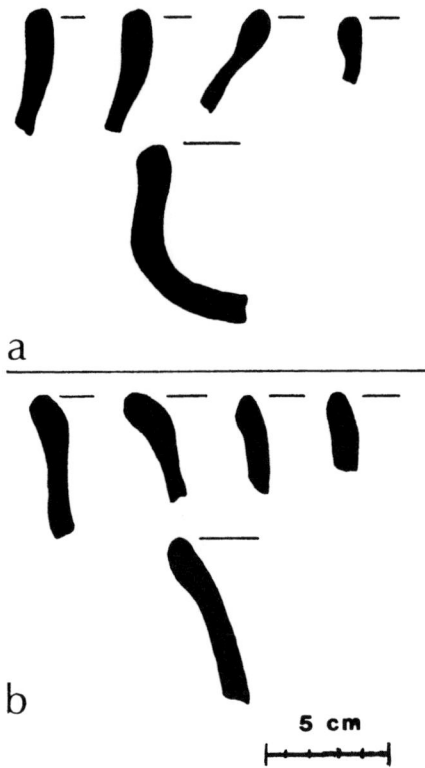

Figure 3.6. Pettville Red-and-cream pottery: a, Pettville Variety; b, Unnamed variety.

and commonly a square lip, although there are a number of round lips (45.5%). Rim diameter, 18–30 cm; wall thickness, 0.5–0.8 cm.

2. Vertical to slightly flaring sided dish or bowl with direct rim and square lip (27.3%). Rim diameter, 15–35 cm; wall thickness, 0.5–0.9 cm.

3. Incurving sided bowl with a slightly restricted orifice, direct or interiorly thickened rim, and round or square lip (18.2%). Rim diameter, 15–25 cm; wall thickness, 0.5–0.7 cm.

4. Outcurving sided dish or bowl with direct or slightly interiorly thickened rim and round lip (9%). Rim diameter, 24 cm; wall thickness, 0.5 cm.

APPENDAGES: None noted.

INTRASITE DISTRIBUTION: See Consejo Red: Consejo Variety; sherds tend to be more numerous in the later levels of the Swasey Ceramic Complex.

INTERSITE DISTRIBUTION: For general comments, see Consejo Red: Consejo Variety. Pring (1977) has identified sherds of this variety in the type collection from the site of Becan, Campeche. The monochrome red incised type from Seibal and Altar de Sacrificios, Pico de Oro Incised, includes a variety with faint horizontal incising on both the exterior and interior of vessels (Sabloff 1975; Adams 1971). In the Eb Ceramic Complex at Tikal, according to T. Patrick Culbert, Haleb Red-on-cream has preslip horizontal groove-incising. All these examples postdate the Swasey material.

TYPE: Pettville Red-and-cream.
VARIETY: Pettville.

ESTABLISHED AS A TYPE OR VARIETY: Present work. This description is based on 40 rim sherds.
GROUP: Consejo.
WARE: Rio Nuevo Glossy.
COMPLEX: Swasey.
SPHERE AFFILIATION: Swasey?
FREQUENCY: 11.1 percent of the Swasey Ceramic Complex rim sherds.
ILLUSTRATION: Figure 3.6a.
PRINCIPAL IDENTIFYING ATTRIBUTES: Glossy red slip, similar to Consejo Red, but occurring only on the exterior of vessels; interior of vessels are a glossy cream or buff; incurving bowls or incurved-recurved bowls or dishes with round lips.
PASTE, TEMPER, AND FIRING: Same as Consejo Red: Consejo Variety.
SURFACE FINISH AND DECORATION: Slip characteristics are the same as Consejo Red: Consejo Variety. Decoration involves leaving the *interior* of vessels with the underslip showing, thus creating a dichrome effect. The red is the same color as Consejo Red: Consejo Variety and the cream centers on 5YR 7/4 pink, 5YR 6/4 light reddish brown, and 5YR 7/3 pink. Pring (1977) mentions that a number of sherds of this variety were found and placed within the Consejo Variety of Consejo Red because the sample size was too small to suggest a separate type or variety. However, I feel that the

sample size is sufficient and that the sherds are distinctive enough to warrant their inclusion in a separate variety.

*FORMS*

1. Incurved-recurved sided dish or bowl with direct or slightly interiorly thickened rim and round lip (41%). Rim diameter, 20–30 cm; wall thickness, 0.5–0.8 cm.
2. Vertical to slightly flaring sided dish with direct rim and round or square lip (30.8%). Rim diameter, 15–35 cm; wall thickness, 0.5–0.9 cm.
3. Incurving sided bowl with short vertical collar, restricted orifice, direct or interiorly folded rim, and round lip (28.2%). Rim diameter, 10–24 cm; wall thickness, 0.5–0.7 cm.

*APPENDAGES:* None noted.

*INTRASITE DISTRIBUTION:* See Consejo Red: Consejo Variety. Sherds tend to be more numerous in the *earlier* levels of the Swasey Ceramic Complex.

*INTERSITE DISTRIBUTION:* For general relationships, see Consejo Red: Consejo Variety. This variety bears only a faint resemblance, at best, to Toribio Red-on-cream in the Xe Ceramic Complex at Altar de Sacrificios (Adams 1971), which has a cream exterior and red-slipped interior on jar forms only. An Unnamed Red-and-white Dichrome in the Real Ceramic Complex at Seibal has a white exterior and red interior but shares a similar flaring sided vessel form with the Swasey type (Sabloff 1975). Haleb Red-on-cream from the Eb Ceramic Complex at Tikal bears little resemblance, according to Culbert.

*TYPE:* Pettville Red-and-cream.
*VARIETY:* Unnamed.
*ESTABLISHED AS A TYPE OR VARIETY:* Present work. This description is based on 18 rim sherds.
*GROUP:* Consejo.
*WARE:* Rio Nuevo Glossy.
*COMPLEX:* Swasey.
*SPHERE AFFILIATION:* Swasey?
*FREQUENCY:* 5.0 percent of the Swasey Ceramic Complex rim sherds.
*ILLUSTRATION:* Figure 3.6b.
*PRINCIPAL IDENTIFYING ATTRIBUTES:* Glossy red slip, similar to Consejo Red, but occurring only on the interior of vessels; exterior of vessels are a glossy cream or buff; vertical to slightly flaring sided dishes or bowls with direct or interiorly thickened rims and square lips.
*PASTE, TEMPER, AND FIRING:* Same as Consejo Red: Consejo Variety.
*SURFACE FINISH AND DECORATION:* Slip characteristics are the same as Consejo Red: Consejo Variety. Decoration involves leaving the *exterior* of the vessel with the cream to buff underslip showing, while the interior of the vessel is red, thus creating a dichrome effect opposite to the Pettville Variety. The red is the same color as Consejo Red: Consejo Variety. The cream centers on 5YR 7/4 pink, 5YR 7/3 pink, and 5YR 6/4 light reddish yellow. Pring (1977) mentions that

a number of sherds of this variety were identified and placed within Consejo Red because of a small sample size. I have chosen to upgrade these sherds into another variety of the newly established type, Pettville Red-and-cream. I have not named this variety because the sample size is still relatively small and this pottery may yet be recombined with the Pettville Variety if further research does not support the establishment of a separate variety.

*FORMS*

1. Vertical to slightly flaring sided bowl or dish with direct or interiorly thickened rim and square, or occasionally round, lip (81%). Rim diameter, 15–40 cm; wall thickness, 0.5–0.9 cm.
2. Incurving sided bowl with short vertical collar, slightly restricted orifice, interiorly folded rim, and round lip (13%). Rim diameter, 10–25 cm; wall thickness, 0.5–0.7 cm.
3. Incurved-recurved sided dish or bowl with direct rim and round or square lip (6.%). Rim diameter, 28 cm; wall thickness, 0.5 cm.

*APPENDAGES:* None noted.

*INTRASITE DISTRIBUTION:* See Consejo Red: Consejo Variety. Sherds tend to be most numerous in the *later* Swasey levels.

*OTHER CONSEJO CERAMIC GROUP POTTERY:* Unspecified.

One sherd within the Consejo Ceramic Group has an unslipped exterior and red-slipped interior. In addition, the exterior of the vessel is decorated with small punctations (Fig. 3.7a). Pring (1977) identified a red-and-unslipped incised type within the Consejo Ceramic Group. However, I feel this one sherd is too small to classify accurately. Another sherd possesses some modeling but is too small to identify the design that was intended. Finally, one sherd has some evidence of intentional black line smudging on it (Fig. 3.7b); it may be Canquin Black-on-red (Pring 1977), but I have not placed it within any particular type. These unclassified sherds appear in the later levels of the Swasey Ceramic Complex and, in fact, a red-and-unslipped type has been identified in the Bladen Ceramic Complex (Chapter 4).

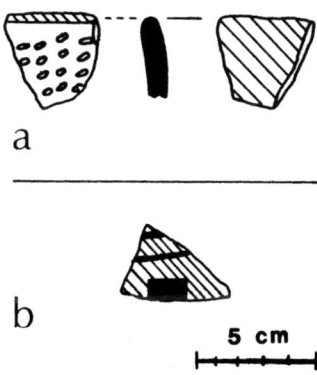

Figure 3.7. Consejo Ceramic Group pottery, unspecified: *a*, red-and-unslipped with punctations; *b*, with black line smudging.

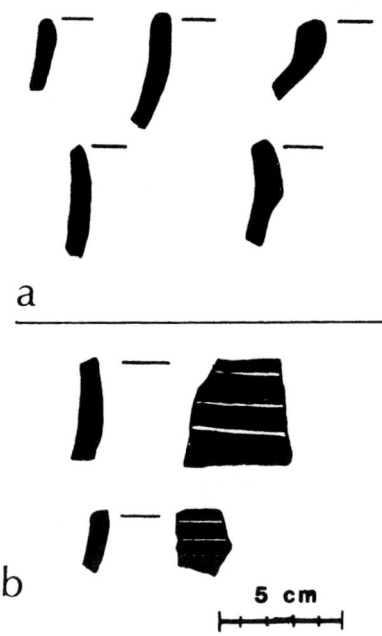

Figure 3.8. Machaca Ceramic Group pottery: *a*, Machaca Black: Machaca Variety; *b*, Chacalte Incised: Chacalte Variety.

*TYPE:* Machaca Black.
*VARIETY:* Machaca.
*ESTABLISHED AS A TYPE OR VARIETY:* Pring (1977). Pring's description was based on 160 sherds, including 10 rims or large sherds indicating vessel form. This description is based on 6 rim sherds.
*GROUP:* Machaca.
*WARE:* Rio Nuevo Glossy.
*COMPLEX:* Swasey.
*SPHERE AFFILIATION:* Swasey?
*FREQUENCY:* 1.7 percent of the Swasey Ceramic Complex rim sherds.
*ILLUSTRATION:* Figure 3.8*a*.
*PRINCIPAL IDENTIFYING ATTRIBUTES:* Dark brown to gray or black glossy slip; vertical to slightly flaring or outcurving sided dishes or bowls with direct rims and square or pointed lips.
*PASTE, TEMPER, AND FIRING:* Paste color ranges from brown to dark gray, although it is mostly the latter. Differential firing is common. Carbonate inclusions are present in all sherds. Paste texture is fine to medium grained.
*SURFACE FINISH AND DECORATION:* The type is characterized by a well-smoothed paste fired to a gray color and covered with a thin black slip, which Pring (1977) has identified correctly as being glossy when well preserved though it is very prone to weathering. The slip color ranges from 5YR 2/1 black, to 2.5YR N3/ very dark gray, 7.5YR N3/ very dark gray, 10R 3/1 very dark gray, and 10R 4/1 dark gray. Pring (1977) originally suggested there was a sorting problem between the buff sherds and the black. However, his Tiger Buff type did not appear to be present in my collections and I sorted the lighter black or gray sherds into the orange Chicago Ceramic Group that contains vessels with extensive fire-clouding in a black, gray, or buff color. I made a conscious effort to sort all questionable material into the Chicago Group, keeping the Machaca Ceramic Group small in size and therefore more "pure" or restricted in definition.
*FORMS*
1. Vertical to slightly outcurving or flaring sided bowl or dish with direct rim and square or pointed lip (50%). Rim diameter, 18–26 cm; wall thickness, 0.5–0.8 cm.
2. Incurved-recurved sided bowl or dish with direct rim and square or round lip (33.3%). Rim diameter, 20–32 cm; wall thickness, 0.5–0.8 cm.
3. Incurving sided bowl with restricted orifice, interiorly thickened rim, and round lip (16.7%). Rim diameter, no measurement; wall thickness, 0.5 cm.
*APPENDAGES:* None noted.
*INTRASITE DISTRIBUTION:* The type is defined on the basis of sealed levels of the Swasey phase material in the lower levels of the South Square excavations (grid squares 20/30, 25/30, 25/35, 20/35). Machaca Black continues throughout the Swasey Ceramic Complex without any apparent changes.
*INTERSITE DISTRIBUTION:* No known comparisons. Crisanto Black, the Early Formative monochrome black type from Seibal and Altar de Sacrificios, is duller and occurs on different vessel forms (Sabloff 1975; Adams 1971).

*TYPE:* Chacalte Incised.
*VARIETY:* Chacalte.
*ESTABLISHED AS A TYPE OR VARIETY:* Pring (1977). Pring's description was based on 2 sherds. This description is based on 8 rim sherds, one of which consists of five adjoining pieces from the same vessel.
*GROUP:* Machaca.
*WARE:* Rio Nuevo Glossy.
*COMPLEX:* Swasey.
*SPHERE AFFILIATION:* Swasey?
*FREQUENCY:* 2.2 percent of the Swasey Ceramic Complex rim sherds.
*ILLUSTRATION:* Figure 3.8*b*.
*PRINCIPAL IDENTIFYING ATTRIBUTES:* Slip color and texture the same as Machaca Black; decoration with postslip, fine-line incising in geometric patterns; incurved-recurved sided dishes or bowls.
*PASTE, TEMPER, AND FIRING:* Same as Machaca Black: Machaca Variety.
*SURFACE FINISH AND DECORATION:* Slip characteristics are the same as Machaca Black: Machaca Variety. Decoration consists of postslip, fine-line incising that extends in horizontal lines around the exterior of vessels below the rim; some vessels are additionally decorated with diagonal parallel lines.

*FORMS*
1. Incurved-recurved sided dish or bowl with direct rim and square lip (87.5%). Rim diameter, 16–28 cm; wall thickness, 0.5–0.8 cm.
2. Vertical sided dish or bowl with direct rim and square or pointed lip (12.5%). Rim diameter, 22 cm; wall thickness, 0.6 cm.
*APPENDAGES:* None noted.
*INTRASITE DISTRIBUTION:* Same as Machaca Black: Machaca Variety.
*INTERSITE DISTRIBUTION:* Although there are no specified comparisons for this time period, Chompipi Incised, the monochrome black incised type from both Seibal and Altar de Sacrificios, bears a faint resemblance (Sabloff 1975; Adams 1971).

*TYPE:* Chicago Orange.
*VARIETY:* Chicago.
*ESTABLISHED AS A TYPE OR VARIETY:* Pring (1977). Pring's description was based on 30 sherds, half of which were rims or large sherds indicating vessel form. This description is based on 105 rim sherds.
*GROUP:* Chicago.
*WARE:* Fort George Orange.
*COMPLEX:* Swasey.
*SPHERE AFFILIATION:* Swasey?
*FREQUENCY:* 29.2 percent of the Swasey Ceramic Complex rim sherds.
*ILLUSTRATION:* Figure 3.9.
*PRINCIPAL IDENTIFYING ATTRIBUTES:* A thin nonlustrous pale orange slip or wash of the same color as the paste; wide range of surface colors caused by differential firing; jar forms with outflaring or outcurving necks; double cylinder strap handles.
*PASTE, TEMPER, AND FIRING:* Paste color ranges from buff or tan to a pale orange. Differential firing is present with a dark gray core and lighter edges. All sherds have carbonate inclusions. Paste texture is generally medium.
*SURFACE FINISH AND DECORATION:* The type is characterized by a pale, thin, nonlustrous slip or wash that generally reflects the same color as the paste. Slip color ranges from 5YR 6/1 light gray, through 5YR 6/6 reddish yellow, to 5YR 7/1 light gray, through 5YR 7/6 reddish yellow, and 7.5YR 7/2 pinkish gray, to 7.5YR 7/4 pink. However, 49 percent of the sherds are 5YR 7/4 pink. The slip is generally badly weathered.

Originally, Pring (1977) identified both a buff and an orange group. On closer examination I have chosen to lump together the sherds from these two groups because they overlap in vessel form and site distribution. Apparently some of the material, when incompletely oxidized, tends to a more buff color than the completely oxidized sherds that turn a pale pinkish orange. While this may have been an intentional

Figure 3.9. Chicago Orange: Chicago Variety.

distinction manufactured by the potters, the overlap seems too great to warrant separation into distinct types. An additional sorting problem arose because the slip erodes easily and completely, and therefore a number of Chicago Orange sherds may have been placed inadvertently in the unslipped type, Copetilla. As stated previously, throughout the sorting procedure a conscious attempt was made to recognize this problem and, in general, Chicago Orange has a finer paste texture than the unslipped type, helping to distinguish between the two.

Pring (1977) describes Tiger Buff as having a more lustrous, durable slip than Chicago Orange; however, I was unable to identify any such material and have combined all buff-orange sherds with orange sherds in the same type, Chicago Orange.

*FORMS*
1. Long necked jar with outflaring or outcurving neck, thickened or direct rim, and square lip (33.3%). Rim diameter, 18–28 cm; wall thickness, 0.8–1.0 cm; neck height, 2.8–4.5 cm.
2. Short necked jar with outflaring or outcurving neck, thickened or direct rim, and square lip (23.8%). Rim diameter, 15–22 cm; wall thickness, 0.6–0.9 cm; neck height, 1.5–2.5 cm.
3. Incurved-recurved sided bowl or dish with direct rim and square lip (20%). Rim diameter, 15–20 cm; wall thickness, 0.5–0.8 cm.
4. Vertical to slightly flaring sided dish or bowl with direct rim and square or round lip (13.3%). Rim diameter, 16–25 cm; wall thickness, 0.5–0.8 cm.

5. Incurving sided bowl with a generally unrestricted orifice, direct or interiorly thickened rim, and round or square lip (5.7%). Rim diameter, 12–20 cm; wall thickness, 0.5–0.8 cm. Three sherds of this form have shallow horizontal grooving in parallel lines around the exterior of the vessel, giving the appearance of mock-chamfering.

6. Vertical or slightly tapered bottle neck with exteriorly folded rim and round or pointed lip (2.9%). Rim diameter, 2.5–2.9 cm; wall thickness, 0.5–0.7 cm.

*APPENDAGES: Handles*. Eight handles were found on jar forms of Chicago Orange. Five are double cylinder strap handles (see Copetilla Unslipped for a description of this handle style). In addition, one triple cylinder handle and two quadruple cylinder handles occur. Such handles are apparently diagnostic of the Swasey Ceramic Complex material.

*Spouts*. There are four unsupported spouts that are round in cross section; median spout length is 5.5 cm.

*Foot*. There is one hollow round foot, but it is not clear to what vessel form it may belong.

*INTRASITE DISTRIBUTION:* The type is defined on the basis of sealed levels of the Swasey phase material from the lower levels of the South Square excavations (grid squares 20/30, 25/30, 25/35, 20/35). Chicago Orange continues throughout the Swasey Ceramic Complex without any apparent changes other than an increased emphasis on round lips on bowl and dish forms.

*INTERSITE DISTRIBUTION:* Pring (1977) has identified this type at the site of El Pozito in northern Belize. Additionally, Fred Valdez, Jr. and I have identified Chicago Orange at the site of Colha (Kosakowsky and Valdez 1982). For a comparison of the intersite distribution of vessel forms, see the corresponding section for Copetilla Unslipped.

CHAPTER FOUR

# Bladen Ceramic Complex

The Bladen Ceramic Complex spans the period from about 1500 B.C. to about 1000 or 900 B.C. The selected sample intensively analyzed from Bladen levels consists of 1,302 rim sherds, 12 body sherds, and 13 whole vessels. The complex is composed of 6 major ceramic groups with 16 types and varieties and the relative frequencies of the groups are given in Table 4.1. Copetilla is the only unslipped group, so that 97.8 percent of Bladen pottery is slipped, a slightly higher percentage than in the earlier Swasey complex. Of the slipped pottery, 36.1 percent is decorated with incising (3.2%), groove-incising (20.4%), dichrome slips (11.2%), or by other means (1.3%) such as resist painting, punctating, and modeling.

The Bladen Ceramic Complex is defined on the basis of this work; originally this pottery formed the terminal part of the Swasey Ceramic Complex identified by Pring (1977). Bladen material is stratigraphically sandwiched between the preceding Swasey phase and the succeeding Lopez phase in the South Square excavations of Platform 34 (grid squares 20/30, 25/30, 25/35, 20/35). It thus comprises the terminal half of the Early Preclassic and has been placed tentatively in the Xe Ceramic Sphere.

## TYPE DESCRIPTIONS
### (Xe? Ceramic Sphere)

*TYPE:* Copetilla Unslipped.
*VARIETY:* Gallon Jug.
*ESTABLISHED AS A TYPE OR VARIETY:* Established as a type by Pring (1977); established as a variety, present work. This description is based on 29 rim sherds and 1 whole vessel.
*GROUP:* Copetilla.
*WARE:* Unspecified.
*COMPLEX:* Bladen.
*SPHERE AFFILIATION:* Xe?
*FREQUENCY:* 2.2 percent of the Bladen Ceramic Complex rim sherds.
*ILLUSTRATIONS:* Figures 4.1, 4.18f.
*PRINCIPAL IDENTIFYING ATTRIBUTES:* Jar forms with thickened rims and round or square lips; bottle forms; wide range of surface colors (see below); loop handles.
*PASTE, TEMPER, AND FIRING:* For general description, see Copetilla Unslipped: Copetilla Variety in the Swasey Ceramic Complex (Chapter Three). Paste color, as in the

**Table 4.1. Classification of Pottery in the Bladen Ceramic Complex**
**(Group frequency based on 1302 rim sherds)**

| Ware | Group | Type | Variety |
|---|---|---|---|
| Unspecified | Copetilla (2.2%) | Copetilla Unslipped | Gallon Jug Variety |
| Rio Nuevo Glossy | Consejo (55.6%) | Consejo Red | Estrella Variety |
|  |  | Barquedier Grooved-incised | Barquedier Variety |
|  |  | Fireburn Red-and-cream | Fireburn Variety |
|  |  | Fireburn Red-and-cream | Unnamed Variety |
|  |  | Cudjoe Composite | Cudjoe Variety |
|  |  | Cudjoe Composite | Unnamed Variety |
|  |  | Other Consejo Ceramic Group | Unspecified (1 modeled, 1 fingernail incised, 1 punctated, 2 black-on-red) |
|  | Machaca (1.6%) | Machaca Black | Wamil Variety |
|  |  | Chacalte Incised | Yo Creek Variety |
|  | Quamina (1.3%) | Quamina Cream | Quamina Variety |
|  |  | Tower Hill Red-on-cream | Tower Hill Variety |
|  |  | Tower Hill Red-on-cream | Unnamed Variety (resist) |
|  |  | Other Quamina Ceramic Group | Unspecified (1 gadrooned, 2 grooved-incised, 3 fine-line incised) |
| Fort George Orange | Chicago (24.1%) | Chicago Orange | Nago Bank Variety |
|  |  | Cotton Tree Incised | Cotton Tree Variety |
| Unspecified | Honey Camp (15.2%) | Honey Camp Orange-brown | Honey Camp Variety |
|  |  | Copper Bank Incised | Copper Bank Variety |

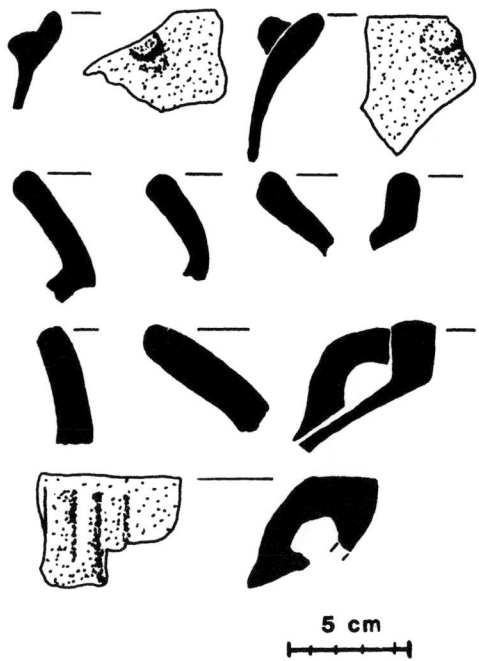

Figure 4.1. Copetilla Unslipped: Gallon Jug Variety.

Swasey type, ranges from dark gray (5YR 4/1) through light gray (5YR 6/1), reddish browns (5YR 6/3–6/6), pink (5YR 7/1–7/6, 7.5YR 7/4), to pale brown (10YR 7/2–7/4). Unlike the Swasey variety, the Gallon Jug Variety does not tend to be well-smoothed in all cases. In paste texture, temper, and firing, it follows Copetilla Unslipped: Copetilla Variety.

*SURFACE FINISH AND DECORATION:* For general description, see Copetilla Unslipped: Copetilla Variety in the Swasey complex.
  FORMS
1. Short to medium outcurving and flaring necked jars with thickened or direct rims and round or square lips (58.6%). Rim diameter, 12–32 cm; wall thickness, 0.7–2.0 cm; neck height, 1.0–3.5 cm.
2. Short vertical necked jar with thickened rim and square or round lip (21.2%). Rim diameter, 10–26 cm; wall thickness, 0.5–1.2 cm; neck height, 0.6–1.4 cm.
3. Long outflaring necked jar with direct or slightly thickened rim and square or round lip (13.8%). Rim diameter, 14–34 cm; wall thickness, 0.5–1.2 cm; neck height, 3.0–4.2 cm.
4. Vertical or slightly tapered bottle with exteriorly folded rim and pointed or beveled out lip (6.4%). Rim diameter, 2.2–3.2 cm; wall thickness, 0.5–1.8 cm. (It is possible that this bottle form is actually a Swasey complex shape that does not occur in the Bladen Ceramic Complex. However, the presence of the bottle form in the subsequent Mamom sphere strongly suggests continuity of use throughout the Bladen complex.)
  *APPENDAGES: Handles.* The majority of handles (9 out of 16) are loop handles with incisions. There are 5 double cylinder strap handles (described in the appendage section of Copetilla Unslipped: Copetilla Variety, Chapter Three). One loop handle is composed of three cylinders, and one is composed of two cylinders twisted together.
  *INTRASITE DISTRIBUTION:* The type is defined on the basis of sealed levels of the Bladen phase material (late Early Preclassic) in the South Square excavations (grid squares 20/30, 25/30, 25/35, 20/35). Gallon Jug Variety continues throughout the Bladen Ceramic Complex without any apparent changes.
  *INTERSITE DISTRIBUTION:* For general discussion see Copetilla Unslipped: Copetilla Variety in the Swasey Ceramic Complex (Chapter Three). The Gallon Jug Variety of Copetilla Unslipped shares a generally unsmoothed surface with major unslipped types of the Xe Ceramic Sphere such as Achiotes Unslipped from Altar de Sacrificios and Seibal (Adams 1971; Sabloff 1975). In addition, the Unnamed Appliquéd variety listed under "Other Achiotes Group" at Seibal (Sabloff 1975: 60) has nubbinlike modeled adornos similar to some examples of the Gallon Jug Variety of Copetilla Unslipped.

*TYPE:* Consejo Red.
*VARIETY:* Estrella.
*ESTABLISHED AS A TYPE OR VARIETY:* Established as a type by Pring (1977); established as a variety, present work. This description is based on 311 rim sherds and 2 whole vessels.
*GROUP:* Consejo.
*WARE:* Rio Nuevo Glossy.
*COMPLEX:* Bladen.
*SPHERE AFFILIATION:* Xe?
*FREQUENCY:* 23.8 percent of the Bladen Ceramic Complex rim sherds.
*ILLUSTRATIONS:* Figures 4.2, 4.18d.
*PRINCIPAL IDENTIFYING ATTRIBUTES:* Lustrous to glossy bright red slip; well-smoothed surfaces with a thin white or buff underslip or wash; incurved-recurved sided bowls or dishes with direct rims; a high percentage of direct rims have round lips; a high percentage of all vessel forms have flat bases.
  PASTE, TEMPER, AND FIRING: See Consejo Red: Consejo Variety in the Swasey Ceramic Complex (Chapter Three).
  *SURFACE FINISH AND DECORATION:* See Consejo Red: Consejo Variety. However, unlike the Consejo Variety, Estrella Variety has a surface color centered on 10R 4/8 red to the virtual exclusion of all other colors (98 percent of all sherds examined).
  *FORMS*
1. Incurved-recurved sided bowl or dish with direct or slightly exteriorly thickened rim and round lip (47.1%). Rim diameter, 20–36 cm; wall thickness, 0.5–0.9 cm.
2. Incurving sided bowl with an unrestricted orifice, direct rim, and rounded or pointed lip (16.6%). Rim diameter, 14–28 cm; wall thickness, 0.5–0.8 cm.
3. Vertical or slightly flaring sided bowl or dish with direct

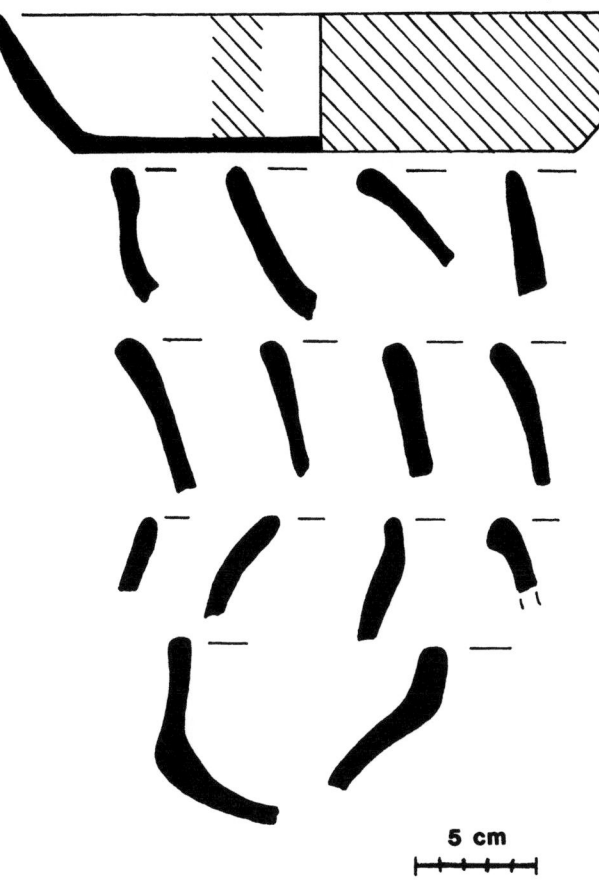

Figure 4.2. Consejo Red: Estrella Variety.

rim and round lip (15.3%). Rim diameter, 18–38 cm; wall thickness, 0.5–0.8 cm.
4. Outcurving sided bowl or dish with direct or slightly exteriorly folded rim and round lip (12.4%). Rim diameter, 18–32 cm; wall thickness, 0.5–0.8 cm.
5. Incurving sided bowl with short vertical neck or collar, direct or slightly exteriorly folded rim, and round or pointed lip (4.5%). Rim diameter, 16–30 cm; wall thickness, 0.5–0.8 cm.
6. Flaring sided dish with direct or slightly exteriorly thickened rim and round lip (1.3%). Rim diameter, 18–32 cm; wall thickness, 0.5–0.8 cm.
7. Slightly tapered bottle neck with exteriorly folded rim and round or pointed lip (1.3%). Rim diameter, 2.5–3.8 cm; wall thickness, 0.5–0.8 cm.
8. Incurving sided bowl with restricted orifice (tecomate), direct or interiorly folded rim, and round or pointed lip (0.9%). Rim diameter, 10–25 cm; wall thickness, 0.5–0.8 cm.
9. Short outcurving necked jar with direct rim and round lip (0.6%). Rim diameter, 10–22 cm; wall thickness, 0.5–0.8 cm; neck height, 0.8–2.0 cm.

*APPENDAGES: Handles.* There are three handles, two associated with incurving bowls and one with a jar form. The former are single loop, horizontal handles, and the latter is a single loop vertical handle.

*Spout.* There is one spout, round in cross section and fairly crude. It is approximately 6 cm in length but is broken before its base.

*Feet.* There are two round, hollow feet, each about 4.5 cm in diameter and 6 cm in height. It is not known to what form they belonged, although the identification of similar feet on monopod bottles from Mani cenote (Brainerd 1958) may suggest a similar form.

*INTRASITE DISTRIBUTION:* The type is defined on the basis of sealed levels of the Bladen phase material (late Early Preclassic) in the South Square excavations (grid squares 20/30, 25/30, 25/35, 20/35). Estrella Variety continues throughout the Bladen Ceramic Complex, with an increased emphasis on outcurving sided dishes in the later levels.

*INTERSITE DISTRIBUTION:* See Consejo Red: Consejo Variety (Chapter Three). The type has been identified in the Bolay Ceramic Complex at Colha (Kosakowsky and Valdez 1982).

*TYPE:* Barquedier Grooved-incised.
*VARIETY:* Barquedier.
*ESTABLISHED AS A TYPE OR VARIETY:* Present work. This description is based on 267 rim sherds and 1 whole vessel.
*GROUP:* Consejo.
*WARE:* Rio Nuevo Glossy.
*SPHERE AFFILIATION:* Xe?
*FREQUENCY:* 20.4 percent of the Bladen Ceramic Complex rim sherds.
*ILLUSTRATION:* Figure 4.3.
*PRINCIPAL IDENTIFYING ATTRIBUTES:* Glossy red slip, same as Consejo Red; shallow preslip, groove-incising around the exterior of vessels; incurved-recurved sided dishes and bowls with direct rims.

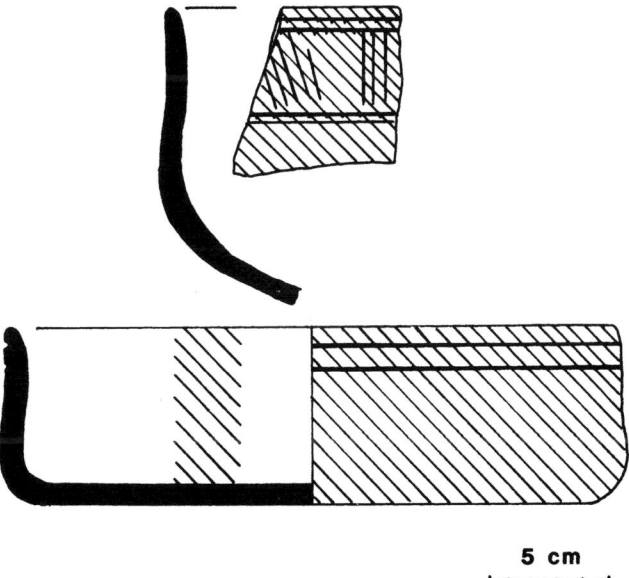

Figure 4.3. Barquedier Grooved-incised: Barquedier Variety.

*PASTE, TEMPER, AND FIRING:* Same as Consejo Red: Consejo Variety in the Swasey Ceramic Complex (Chapter Three) and Consejo Red: Estrella Variety in the Bladen Ceramic Complex (above).

*SURFACE FINISH AND DECORATION:* Same as Backlanding Incised: Grooved-incised Variety in the Swasey Ceramic Complex. For Munsell color, see Consejo Red: Estrella Variety. Barquedier Grooved-incised has similar decoration to Backlanding Incised, but it is decorated with diagonal parallel groove-incisions on the exteriors of vessels in addition to the horizontal parallel channels.

*FORMS*
1. Incurved-recurved sided bowl or dish with direct rim and round lip (67.4%). Rim diameter, 18–32 cm; wall thickness, 0.5–0.8 cm.
2. Vertical to slightly flaring sided bowl or dish with direct or slightly exteriorly thickened rim and round lip (15.2%). Rim diameter, 16–38 cm; wall thickness, 0.5–0.9 cm.
3. Incurving sided bowl with an unrestricted orifice, direct or slightly interiorly thickened rim, and round lip (13.3%). Rim diameter, 16–30 cm; wall thickness, 0.5–0.8 cm.
4. Incurving sided bowl with short vertical neck or collar, interiorly thickened rim, and round lip (1.9%). Rim diameter, 15–26 cm; wall thickness, 0.5–0.8 cm.
5. Outcurving sided bowl or dish with direct or exteriorly folded rim and round lip (1.1%). Rim diameter, 18–42 cm; wall thickness, 0.5–0.8 cm.
6. Flaring sided bowl or dish with direct or slightly outflared everted rim and round lip (1.1%). Rim diameter, 18–38 cm; wall thickness, 0.5–0.8 cm.

*APPENDAGES:* None noted.

*INTRASITE DISTRIBUTION:* The type is defined on the basis of sealed levels of the Bladen phase material (late Early Preclassic) in the South Square excavations (grid squares 20/30, 25/30, 25/35, 20/35). Barquedier Grooved-incised continues throughout the Bladen Ceramic Complex without any apparent changes.

*INTERSITE DISTRIBUTION:* See Backlanding Incised: Grooved-incised Variety in the Swasey Ceramic Complex (Chapter Three). Barquedier Grooved-incised is modally similar to the red incised types of the Real Ceramic Complex at Seibal (Sabloff 1975) and the Xe Ceramic Complex at Altar de Sacrificios (Adams 1971). Furthermore, it is similar in form to Pinola Creek Incised: Variety Unspecified in the Jenney Creek Ceramic Complex at Barton Ramie (Gifford 1976, Fig. 30*j–n*), although Barquedier Grooved-incised predates the Barton Ramie type.


*TYPE:* Fireburn Red-and-cream.
*VARIETY:* Fireburn.
*ESTABLISHED AS A TYPE OR VARIETY:* Present work. This description is based on 75 rim sherds. The name Fireburn was initially used by Pring (1977) for an unrelated Protoclassic vessel from Nohmul. However, that name subsequently was discarded and it is being used for this type.

*GROUP:* Consejo.
*WARE:* Rio Nuevo Glossy.
*COMPLEX:* Bladen.
*SPHERE AFFILIATION:* Xe?
*FREQUENCY:* 5.7 percent of the Bladen Ceramic Complex rim sherds.
*ILLUSTRATION:* Figure 4.4*a*.

*PRINCIPAL IDENTIFYING ATTRIBUTES:* Glossy red slip, same as Consejo Red: Estrella Variety but occurring only on the exterior of vessels; vessel interiors are a glossy cream or buff; incurved-recurved sided bowls or dishes; a high percentage of forms have round lips.

*PASTE, TEMPER, AND FIRING:* Same as Consejo Red: Consejo Variety and Consejo Red: Estrella Variety.

*SURFACE FINISH AND DECORATION:* For general description, see Pettville Red-and-cream: Pettville Variety in the Swasey Ceramic Complex (Chapter Three). In keeping with Consejo Red: Estrella Variety, the Munsell color of the red slip centers on 10R 4/8 red (95%), and the cream is the same as Pettville Red-and-cream.

*FORMS*
1. Incurved-recurved sided bowl or dish with direct or exteriorly folded rim and round lip (47.6%). Rim diameter, 15–30 cm; wall thickness, 0.5–0.9 cm.
2. Vertical sided bowl or dish with direct rim and round or occasionally square lip (13.3%). Rim diameter, 15–35 cm; wall thickness, 0.5–0.8 cm.
3. Incurving sided bowl with generally unrestricted orifice, direct or interiorly thickened rim, and round lip (12.2%). Rim diameter, 16–34 cm; wall thickness, 0.5–0.8 cm.
4. Incurving sided bowl with short vertical collar, restricted orifice, direct or interiorly folded or thickened rim, and round lip (9.8%). Rim diameter, 12–28 cm; wall thickness, 0.5–0.8 cm.
5. Outcurving sided bowl or dish with direct or exteriorly folded rim and round lip (9.8%). Rim diameter, 18–38 cm; wall thickness, 0.5–0.8 cm.
6. Incurving sided bowl with restricted orifice (tecomate), direct or interiorly folded or thickened rim, and round lip (4.9%). Rim diameter, 10–14 cm; wall thickness, 0.5–0.8 cm.
7. Short outcurving necked jar with direct rim and round lip (2.4%). Rim diameter, 10–14 cm; wall thickness, 0.5–0.8 cm; neck height, 1.8–2.4 cm.

*APPENDAGES:* None noted.

*INTRASITE DISTRIBUTION:* The type is defined on the basis of sealed levels of the Bladen phase material (late Early Preclassic) in the South Square excavations (grid squares 20/30, 25/30, 25/35, 20/35). Fireburn Red-and-cream continues throughout the Bladen Ceramic Complex without any apparent changes.

*INTERSITE DISTRIBUTION:* For general discussion, see Pettville Red-and-cream: Pettville Variety in the Swasey Ceramic Complex (Chapter Three). It is worth noting that the Bladen type Fireburn Red-and-cream is modally similar to the red-on-cream types of the Xe Ceramic Sphere at Altar

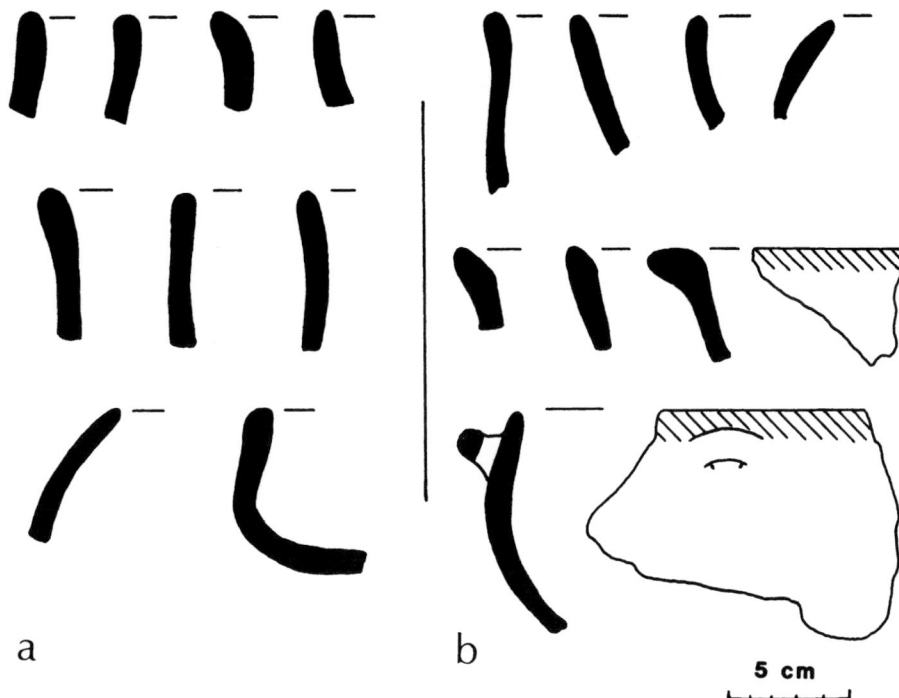

Figure 4.4. Fireburn Red-and-cream pottery: *a*, Fireburn Variety; *b*, Unnamed variety.

de Sacrificios (Adams 1971) and at Seibal (Sabloff 1975), as well as the red-on-cream type of the Eb Ceramic Complex at Tikal. In vessel form it is similar to Muxanal Red-on-cream: Variety Unspecified of the Ah Pam Ceramic Complex at Yaxha-Sacnab (Rice 1979), although the Cuello type predates it.

*TYPE:* Fireburn Red-and-cream.
*VARIETY:* Unnamed.
*ESTABLISHED AS A TYPE OR VARIETY:* Present work. This description is based on 64 rim sherds. See Fireburn Red-and-cream: Fireburn Variety for a discussion of the type name. No varietal name was assigned because further research may warrant recombining this variety with the Fireburn Variety.
*GROUP:* Consejo.
*WARE:* Rio Nuevo Glossy.
*COMPLEX:* Bladen.
*SPHERE AFFILIATION:* Xe?
*FREQUENCY:* 4.9 percent of the Bladen Ceramic Complex rim sherds.
*ILLUSTRATION:* Figure 4.4b.
*PRINCIPAL IDENTIFYING ATTRIBUTES:* Glossy red slip, same as Consejo Red: Estrella Variety but occurring only on the interior of vessels; exterior of vessels are a glossy cream or buff; incurved-recurved sided bowls or dishes; a high percentage of round and everted lips.
*PASTE, TEMPER, AND FIRING:* Same as Consejo Red: Consejo Variety and Consejo Red: Estrella Variety.
*SURFACE FINISH AND DECORATION:* For general description, see Pettville Red-and-cream: Unnamed Variety in the Swasey Ceramic Complex (Chapter Three). In keeping with Consejo Red: Estrella Variety, the Munsell color of the red slip centers on 10R 4/8 red (92%), and the color of the cream slip is the same as Pettville Red-and-cream.

*FORMS*
1. Incurved-recurved sided bowl or dish with direct or interiorly thickened rim and round lip (45.5%). Rim diameter, 22–34 cm; wall thickness, 0.5–0.8 cm.
2. Incurving sided bowl with generally unrestricted orifice, direct or interiorly thickened rim, and round lip (30%). Rim diameter, 21–30 cm; wall thickness, 0.5–0.8 cm.
3. Outcurving sided bowl or dish with exteriorly thickened and everted or direct rim and round lip (17.5%). Rim diameter, 18–40 cm; wall thickness, 0.5–0.9 cm.
4. Vertical sided bowl or dish with direct or exteriorly thickened rim and round lip (3.5%). Rim diameter, 16–30 cm; wall thickness, 0.5–0.8 cm.
5. Flaring sided bowl or dish with direct or exteriorly or interiorly thickened rim and round lip (3.5%). Rim diameter, 15–42 cm; wall thickness, 0.5–0.8 cm.

*APPENDAGES: Handle.* There is one horizontally molded loop handle attached to an incurving sided bowl.
*INTRASITE DISTRIBUTION:* The type is defined on the basis of sealed levels of the Bladen phase material (late Early Preclassic) in the South Square excavations (grid squares 20/30, 25/30, 25/35, 20/35). This Unnamed variety of Fireburn continues throughout the Bladen Ceramic Complex without any apparent changes.
*INTERSITE DISTRIBUTION:* For general discussion, see Pettville Red-and-cream: Pettville Variety and Unnamed variety in the Swasey Ceramic Complex (Chapter Three). As in the Fireburn Variety of this type, the Unnamed variety is

modally similar to the red-on-cream type of the Xe Ceramic Sphere at Altar de Sacrificios (Adams 1971) and at Seibal (Sabloff 1975), as well as the red-on-cream type of the Eb Ceramic Complex at Tikal. In vessel form it is similar to Muxanal Red-on-cream: Variety Unspecified in the Ah Pam Ceramic Complex at Yaxha-Sacnab (Rice 1979), although the Cuello type predates it.

*TYPE:* Cudjoe Composite.
*VARIETY:* Cudjoe.
*ESTABLISHED AS A TYPE OR VARIETY:* Pring (1977); originally named Estero Red-and-unslipped. Because the name Estero had been used previously by Matheny (1970), I renamed the type Bomba Red-and-unslipped: Bomba Variety in my dissertation (Kosakowsky 1983). Subsequently I learned that the name Bomba had been used at Colha by Fred Valdez, Jr. and the final permanent type name is Cudjoe Composite because all sherds are also incised. Pring's description was based on 4 sherds and 1 whole vessel. This description is based on 2 body sherds.
*GROUP:* Consejo.
*WARE:* Rio Nuevo Glossy.
*COMPLEX:* Bladen.
*SPHERE AFFILIATION:* Xe?
*FREQUENCY:* These 2 body sherds are not included in the frequency percentages of rim sherds.
*ILLUSTRATION:* Figure 4.5a.
*PRINCIPAL IDENTIFYING ATTRIBUTES:* Slip color and texture of vessel interior same as Consejo Red; exterior vessel surface is unslipped; secondary decoration on exterior surface is incising.
*PASTE, TEMPER, AND FIRING:* Same as Consejo Red: Consejo Variety.
*SURFACE FINISH AND DECORATION:* Vessel interior is slipped red and has the same characteristics (color and texture) as Consejo Red: Consejo Variety in the Swasey Ceramic Complex (Chapter Three). The slip usually continues over the rim of the vessel onto the exterior. Secondary decoration consists of deeply incised lines in a band of horizontal chevrons around the entire vessel.
*FORMS:* Slightly outcurving sided dish with exteriorly folded rim, and round lip. Wall thickness, 0.5–0.7 cm.
*APPENDAGES:* None noted.
*INTRASITE DISTRIBUTION:* The type is defined on the basis of sealed levels of the Bladen phase material (late Early Preclassic) in the South Square excavations (grid squares 20/30, 25/30, 25/35, 20/35). Cudjoe continues throughout the Bladen Ceramic Complex without any apparent changes. Pring (1977) placed this type in the Swasey Ceramic Complex, and noted that it occurred in the earlier levels of the Swasey phase. I disagree with Pring, however, and after examination of a larger sample I feel that this type actually occurs in the later Early Preclassic levels. Therefore, I have placed it in the Bladen Ceramic Complex.

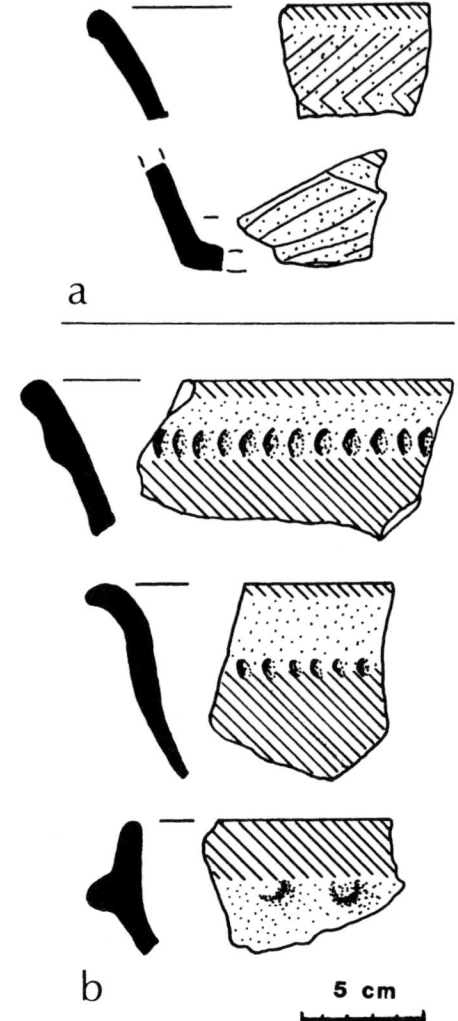

Figure 4.5. Cudjoe Composite pottery: *a*, Cudjoe Variety (rim sherd from Pring collections); *b*, Unnamed variety.

*INTERSITE DISTRIBUTION:* Pring (1977) mentions the possible occurrence of this type at El Pozito in northern Belize. There are no other known comparisons of similar types. In form and decoration there is a vague similarity to Chacchinic Red-on-orange-brown at Barton Ramie (Gifford 1976, Fig. 21*j*) and to Yalmanac Impressed: Unspecified Variety at Seibal (Sabloff 1975), although these postdate the Cuello type.

*TYPE:* Cudjoe Composite.
*VARIETY:* Unnamed.
*ESTABLISHED AS A TYPE OR VARIETY:* Established as a type by Pring (1977); originally named Estero Red-and-unslipped. (See Cudjoe Composite: Cudjoe Variety for a discussion of the name changes concerning this type.) Established as a variety, and type renamed, present work. No varietal name was given because the sample size is small. This description is based on 4 rim sherds.

*GROUP:* Consejo.
*WARE:* Rio Nuevo Glossy.
*COMPLEX:* Bladen.
*SPHERE AFFILIATION:* Xe?
*FREQUENCY:* 0.3 percent of the Bladen Ceramic Complex rim sherds.
*ILLUSTRATION:* Figure 4.5b.
*PRINCIPAL IDENTIFYING ATTRIBUTES:* Slip color and texture of vessel interior and area just over the rim exteriorly are the same as Consejo Red; exterior vessel surface is largely unslipped; secondary decoration on the exterior surface with punctation or modeling.
*PASTE, TEMPER, AND FIRING:* Same as Consejo Red: Consejo Variety.
*SURFACE FINISH AND DECORATION:* Vessel interior is slipped red and has the same characteristics (color and texture) as Consejo Red: Consejo Variety in the Swasey Ceramic Complex (Chapter Three). In all cases the slip continues over the rim of the vessel onto the exterior. In two cases a band around the midsection of the vessel is left unslipped, and the basal area of the vessel is slipped red as on the interior surface. In two cases secondary decoration of the unslipped area is by deep fingernail punctations in a single line around the vessel. In the other two cases, decoration is by modeling; however, the sherds are too small to determine the design intended.

In all probability, sherds of this Unnamed variety will be placed within Cudjoe Variety when a larger sample is available for analysis. Pring (1977) suggests the possibility that different forms of secondary decoration occur on the unslipped surfaces. All this material eventually may be combined into one type, but for now I have chosen to keep them separate.

*FORMS*
1. Incurved-recurved to outcurving sided bowl or dish with direct rim and round lip. The two sherds with punctation are this form. Rim diameter, 18 and 24 cm; wall thickness, 0.5 and 0.6 cm.
2. Incurving sided bowl with slightly restricted orifice, interiorly thickened or direct rim, and round lip. The two sherds with modeled decoration are of this form. Rim diameter, no measurements; wall thickness, 0.7 and 0.8 cm.
*APPENDAGES:* None noted.
*INTRASITE DISTRIBUTION:* See Cudjoe Composite: Cudjoe Variety.
*INTERSITE DISTRIBUTION:* See Cudjoe Composite: Cudjoe Variety.

*OTHER CONSEJO CERAMIC GROUP POTTERY:* Unspecified.
*WARE:* Rio Nuevo Glossy.
*COMPLEX:* Bladen.
*SPHERE AFFILIATION:* Xe?
*FREQUENCY:* 0.5 percent of the Bladen Ceramic Complex rim sherds; this description is based on 6 rim sherds.

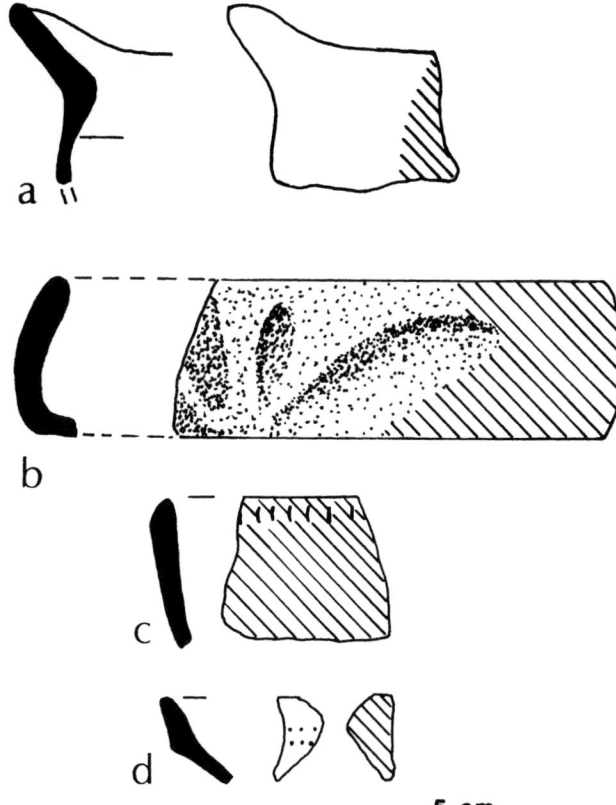

Figure 4.6. Consejo Ceramic Group pottery, unspecified, with modeling, fingernail incisions, and punctations.

*ILLUSTRATION:* Figure 4.6.
*PASTE, TEMPER, AND FIRING:* Same as Consejo Red: Estrella Variety.
*SURFACE FINISH AND DECORATION:* For general discussion, see Consejo Red: Estrella Variety.
*FORMS:* The sample sizes of these examples are too small to warrant identifying separate types, although future research may suggest such a division.
1. One sherd is an incurving sided bowl with an unusual modeled spout (Fig. 4.6a). In addition, there is a modeled sherd that has an unidentifiable decoration on it, also on an incurving sided bowl (Fig. 4.6b). This latter sherd is red slipped on the interior and only partially red slipped on the exterior.
2. One sherd is from an incurving sided bowl, red slipped on both surfaces, with fingernail incisions around the exterior of the rim (Fig. 4.6c).
3. One sherd is from an incurving sided bowl with a sharp medial break, red slipped interior, and cream exterior. It is secondarily decorated on the exterior with a number of rows of punctate holes (Fig. 4.6d).
4. Two sherds are decorated with black-line irregular smudging and may or may not belong to Canquin Black-on-red (Pring 1977). In addition, since one sherd of this type may

have been found in the lower Swasey levels, the two Bladen examples may be placed more appropriately within the Swasey Ceramic Complex. Both belong to incurved-recurved sided bowls.

*TYPE:* Machaca Black.
*VARIETY:* Wamil.
*ESTABLISHED AS A TYPE OR VARIETY:* Established as a type by Pring (1977); established as a variety, present work. This description is based on 9 rim sherds.
*GROUP:* Machaca.
*WARE:* Rio Nuevo Glossy.
*SPHERE AFFILIATION:* Xe?
*FREQUENCY:* 0.7 percent of the Bladen Ceramic Complex rim sherds.
*ILLUSTRATION:* Figure 4.7.
*PRINCIPAL IDENTIFYING ATTRIBUTES:* Dark gray to black glossy slip; incurved-recurved sided bowls or dishes.
*PASTE, TEMPER, AND FIRING:* Same as Machaca Black: Machaca Variety in the Swasey Ceramic Complex (Chapter Three).
*SURFACE FINISH AND DECORATION:* Same as Machaca Black: Machaca Variety in the Swasey Ceramic Complex.
*FORMS*
1. Incurved-recurved sided bowl or dish with direct or slightly exteriorly thickened rim and round lip (60%). Rim diameter, 16–30 cm; wall thickness, 0.5–0.7 cm.
2. Vertical to slightly flaring sided bowl or dish with direct or exteriorly thickened rim and round lip (40%). Rim diameter, 18–28 cm; wall thickness, 0.5–0.7 cm.
*APPENDAGES:* None noted.
*INTRASITE DISTRIBUTION:* The type is defined on the basis of sealed levels of the Bladen phase material (late Early Preclassic) in the South Square excavations (grid squares 20/30, 25/30, 25/35, 20/35). Wamil Variety continues throughout the Bladen Ceramic Complex without any apparent changes.
*INTERSITE DISTRIBUTION:* For general discussion, see Machaca Black: Machaca Variety in the Swasey Ceramic Complex (Chapter Three). The Bladen Wamil Variety, however, is modally similar to the monochrome black types in the Real Ceramic Complex at Seibal (Sabloff 1975) and the Xe Ceramic Complex at Altar de Sacrificios (Adams 1971).

*TYPE:* Chacalte Incised.
*VARIETY:* Yo Creek.
*ESTABLISHED AS A TYPE OR VARIETY:* Established as a type by Pring (1977); established as a variety, present work. This description is based on 12 rim sherds and 1 body sherd.
*GROUP:* Machaca.
*WARE:* Rio Nuevo Glossy.
*COMPLEX:* Bladen.
*SPHERE AFFILIATION:* Xe?
*FREQUENCY:* 0.9 percent of the Bladen Ceramic Complex rim sherds (body sherd not included in the frequency percentage).
*ILLUSTRATION:* Figure 4.8.
*PRINCIPAL IDENTIFYING ATTRIBUTES:* Slip color and texture same as Machaca Black; decoration by postslip fineline incising; occasional secondary decoration by modeling.

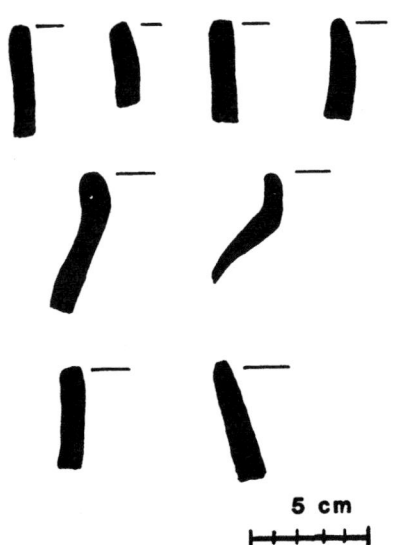

Figure 4.7. Machaca Black: Wamil Variety

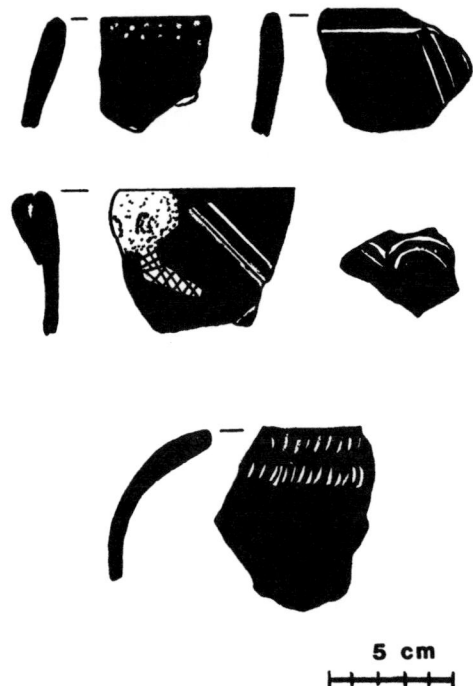

Figure 4.8. Chacalte Incised: Yo Creek Variety.

*PASTE, TEMPER, AND FIRING:* Same as Machaca Black: Machaca Variety in the Swasey Ceramic Complex (Chapter Three).

*SURFACE FINISH AND DECORATION:* For general discussion, see Chacalte Incised: Chacalte Variety in the Swasey Ceramic Complex. In addition to horizontal fine-line incisions horizontally around the exterior of vessels, there are incised diagonal parallel lines and more elaborate geometric cross-hatching that occurs on a few sherds. In some instances, modeling is a secondary decoration to create stylized "faces."

*FORMS*

1. Incurved-recurved sided bowl or dish with direct or exteriorly folded rim and round lip (33.3%). Rim diameter, 16–32 cm; wall thickness, 0.5–0.8 cm.
2. Slightly outcurving sided bowl or dish with direct or exteriorly folded rim and round lip (33.3%). Rim diameter, 20–36 cm; wall thickness, 0.5–0.8 cm.
3. Vertical to slightly flaring sided bowl or dish with direct or slightly interiorly thickened rim and round lip (16.7%). Rim diameter, 15–22 cm; wall thickness, 0.5–0.6 cm.
4. Incurving sided bowl with restricted orifice, direct or interiorly thickened rim, and round (or slightly pointed) lip (16.7%). Rim diameter, 12–20 cm; wall thickness, 0.5–0.7 cm.

*APPENDAGES:* None noted.

*INTRASITE DISTRIBUTION:* The type is defined on the basis of sealed levels of the Bladen phase material (late Early Preclassic) in the South Square excavations (grid squares 20/30, 25/30, 25/35, 20/35). Yo Creek Variety continues throughout the Bladen Ceramic Complex without any apparent changes.

*INTERSITE DISTRIBUTION:* See Chacalte Incised: Chacalte Variety in the Swasey Ceramic Complex (Chapter Three) for general discussion. The Bladen Yo Creek Variety is modally similar to the incised black types of the Real Ceramic Complex at Seibal (Sabloff 1975) and the Xe Ceramic Complex at Altar de Sacrificios (Adams 1971).

*TYPE:* Quamina Cream.
*VARIETY:* Quamina.
*ESTABLISHED AS A TYPE OR VARIETY:* Pring (1977). Pring's description was based on 35 sherds, 6 of them rims. This description is based on 3 additional rim sherds.
*GROUP:* Quamina.
*WARE:* Rio Nuevo Glossy.
*COMPLEX:* Bladen.
*SPHERE AFFILIATION:* Xe?
*FREQUENCY:* 0.2 percent of the Bladen Ceramic Complex rim sherds.
*ILLUSTRATION:* Figure 4.9.
*PRINCIPAL IDENTIFYING ATTRIBUTES:* Very pale, thin gray slip over white to cream underslip; an exceptionally high gloss to the slip.

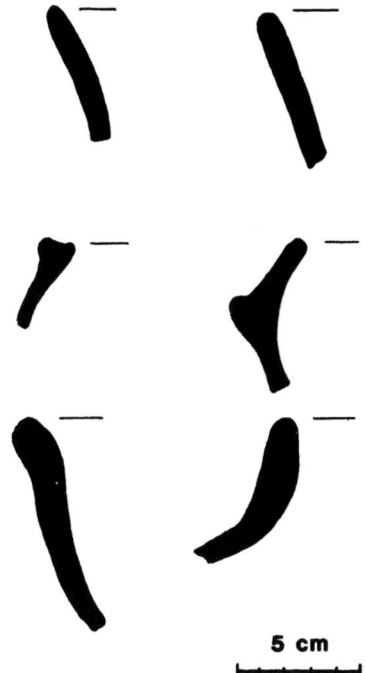

Figure 4.9 Quamina Cream: Quamina Variety (lower four sherds from Pring collections).

*PASTE, TEMPER, AND FIRING:* Paste color ranges from tan or buff to gray. It is fine to medium textured, and all sherds have carbonate inclusions. Incomplete oxidation occurred in only one sherd, leaving a darker core.

*SURFACE FINISH AND DECORATION:* The surfaces of the vessels are well-smoothed and covered with a white to cream slip over which is a secondary thin grayish slip. The gray is very pale and darkens the cream or white underslip. The colors range from 5YR 8/1 white, and 8/2 pinkish white, to 7.5YR 8/2 pinkish white, 10YR 8/2 white, and 10YR 7/2 light gray. The slip has an exceptionally high gloss and rootlet markings are common, exposing the cream underneath the faint hint of gray. Fire clouding or crackling are rare. Pring (1977) suggests that this type is typologically similar to Consejo Red in that Quamina possesses a gray overslip and Consejo possesses a red overslip.

*FORMS*

1. Incurved-recurved sided bowl or dish with direct rim and round lip (33.3%). Rim diameter, 24 cm; wall thickness, 0.5 cm.
2. Incurving sided bowl with interiorly thickened rim and round lip (33.3%). Rim diameter, 18 cm; wall thickness, 0.5 cm. Pring (1977) notes the presence of an incurving sided bowl with a short vertical neck or collar.
3. Slightly flaring sided bowl or dish with direct rim and round lip (33.3%). Rim diameter, 22 cm; wall thickness, 0.5 cm.

*APPENDAGES:* None noted.
*INTRASITE DISTRIBUTION:* The type is defined on the

basis of sealed levels of the Bladen phase material (late Early Preclassic) in the South Square excavations (grid squares 20/30, 25/30, 25/35, 20/35). Quamina Cream continues throughout the Bladen Ceramic Complex without any apparent changes. Pring (1977) originally identified Quamina Cream as part of the Swasey Ceramic Complex; however, with a larger sample it is evident that Quamina Cream begins in the later Early Preclassic levels and belongs more appropriately in the Bladen Ceramic Complex.

*INTERSITE DISTRIBUTION:* Pring (1977) has identified the presence of Quamina Cream at the site of El Pozito in northern Belize. There is a white type, Huetche White, at Seibal (Sabloff 1975), Altar de Sacrificios (Adams 1971), Yaxha-Sacnab (Rice 1979), and Colha (Adams and Valdez 1980) that is similar in color but has a dull slip. However, there are no specific comparisons.

*TYPE:* Tower Hill Red-on-cream.
*VARIETY:* Tower Hill.
*ESTABLISHED AS A TYPE OR VARIETY:* Pring (1977). Pring's description was based on 8 sherds, mostly rims. This description is based on 8 rim sherds and 5 additional body sherds.
*GROUP:* Quamina.
*WARE:* Rio Nuevo Glossy.
*COMPLEX:* Bladen.
*SPHERE AFFILIATION:* Xe?
*FREQUENCY:* 0.6 percent of the Bladen Ceramic Complex rim sherds (body sherds are not included in the frequency percentage).
*ILLUSTRATION:* Figure 4.10.
*PRINCIPAL IDENTIFYING ATTRIBUTES:* Pale cream or white underslip, with a thin secondary gray slip and a bright red overslip; decoration consists of rectangular areas of cream left exposed by application of the red slip; recurving to outcurving sided bowls or dishes.
*PASTE, TEMPER, AND FIRING:* Similar to Quamina Cream: Quamina Variety.
*SURFACE FINISH AND DECORATION:* There is a white to cream underslip over both surfaces that is secondarily covered by a thin gray slip similar to Quamina Cream: Quamina Variety. On this base is applied a red slip that is glossy and similar in color to Consejo Red. The cream slip is the same color as Quamina Cream: Quamina Variety. The red slip centers on 10R 4/8 red (85%), although the color range includes 10R 4/6 red, 2.5YR 4/8 red, 2.5YR 6/8 light red, and 5YR 5/4 reddish brown. All decoration occurs on the vessel exterior with the red slip applied in large rectangular areas, leaving the cream underslip showing in-between. The exterior of the rim is usually slipped a short way down the side, and occasionally the slip extends over the rim down into the vessel interior about 5 cm; otherwise, the interior is cream. It is difficult to tell what design was intended because the material is fragmentary, but it appears that broad strips

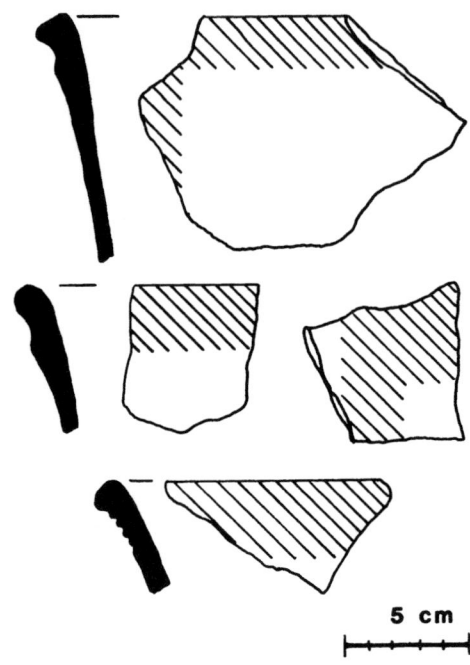

Figure 4.10. Tower Hill Red-on-cream: Tower Hill Variety.

of red run vertically from the horizontal red rim band, leaving reserve areas cream.

*FORMS*
1. Slightly recurving to outcurving sided bowl or dish with exteriorly folded rim and round lip (62.5%). Occasionally there is a molded ridge around the exterior of the vessel below the rim. Rim diameter, 22–40 cm; wall thickness, 0.6–0.9 cm.
2. Incurving sided bowl with direct or folded rim (both interiorly and exteriorly), and round or pointed lip (25%). Rim diameter, 18–24 cm; wall thickness, 0.5–0.7 cm.
3. Vertical to slightly flaring sided bowl or dish with exteriorly folded rim and round lip (12.5%). Rim diameter, 36 cm; wall thickness, 0.6 cm.

*APPENDAGES:* None noted.
*INTRASITE DISTRIBUTION:* The type is defined on the basis of sealed levels of the Bladen phase material (late Early Preclassic) in the South Square excavations (grid squares 20/30, 25/30, 25/35, 20/35). Tower Hill Red-on-cream continues throughout the Bladen Ceramic Complex without any apparent changes. Pring (1977) originally identified Tower Hill Red-on-cream as part of the Swasey Ceramic Complex; however, with a larger sample it is evident that Tower Hill Red-on-cream begins in the later Early Preclassic levels and belongs more appropriately in the Bladen Ceramic Complex. Pring (1977) does note that Tower Hill Red-on-cream gains in popularity toward the middle of the Early Preclassic and that it does not occur in the earliest levels.

*INTERSITE DISTRIBUTION:* Pring (1977) has identified the presence of Tower Hill Red-on-cream at Nohmul and San Estevan. Coe and Flannery (1967) describe a red-on-white type, Tilapa, from coastal Guatemala, Cuadros phase, that is similar in decoration. Also similar in decoration is a red-and-white bichrome from Chiapa de Corzo (Dixon 1959). There is only a broad similarity to Aac Red-on-buff at Tikal and at Yaxha-Sacnab (Rice 1979), and to Toribio Red-on-cream at Altar de Sacrificios (Adams 1971), all of which apparently postdate the Cuello type.

*TYPE:* Tower Hill Red-on-cream.
*VARIETY:* Unnamed (resist).
*ESTABLISHED AS A TYPE OR VARIETY:* Type established by Pring (1977); variety, present work. This description is based on 2 body sherds.
*GROUP:* Quamina.
*WARE:* Rio Nuevo Glossy.
*COMPLEX:* Bladen.
*SPHERE AFFILIATION:* Xe?
*FREQUENCY:* These 2 body sherds are not included in the frequency percentages of rim sherds.
*ILLUSTRATION:* Figure 4.11.
*PRINCIPAL IDENTIFYING ATTRIBUTES:* Pale cream or white underslip, with a thin secondary gray slip and a bright red overslip; decoration consists of rectangular areas of cream left exposed by application of the red slip; secondary decoration by organic resist painting.
*PASTE, TEMPER, AND FIRING:* See Tower Hill Red-on-cream: Tower Hill Variety.
*SURFACE FINISH AND DECORATION:* Same as Tower Hill Red-on-cream: Tower Hill Variety, but in addition the cream areas that are left exposed are decorated by organic resist painting, usually in geometric designs of lines or bands (Kosakowsky 1982). One sherd was elaborately decorated with an animallike figure resting upon geometric wavy lines. This sherd (22 cm in diameter) was the interior base of a flat-bottomed dish or plate and, apart from this instance, the decoration occurs on the exterior of vessels.
*FORMS:* Unknown.
*APPENDAGES:* None noted.
*INTRASITE DISTRIBUTION:* The type is defined on the basis of sealed levels of the Bladen phase material in the South Square excavations (grid squares 20/30, 25/30, 25/35, 20/35). This resist form of Tower Hill first appears in the later Bladen levels and may be an Early to Middle Preclassic transitional type. If more of this resist material is found, it should receive a separate type name in the Quamina Ceramic Group.
*INTERSITE DISTRIBUTION:* The resist technique is similar to the Canquin Black-on-red type that Pring (1977, Fig. 31) identified at the site of Cuello. There are no known specific comparisons. See Tower Hill Red-on-cream: Tower Hill Variety for general comments. Sharer (1978) illustrates a vessel from Chalchuapa of Juaya Resist: Juaya Variety that occurs in the Tok Ceramic Complex (1200–900 B.C.), and until the Cuello find it was the only other known use of the resist technique at this early date.

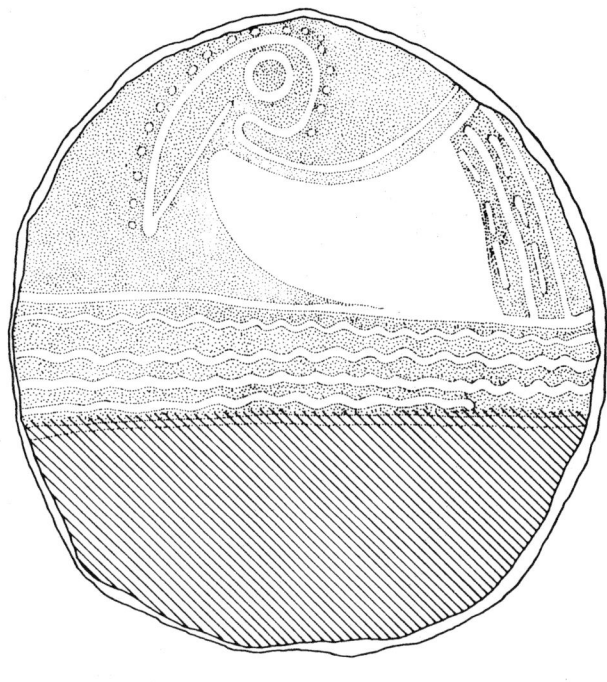

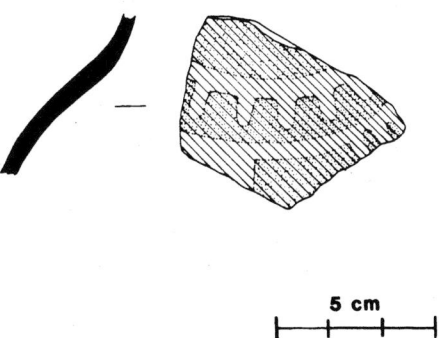

Figure 4.11. Tower Hill Red-on-cream: Unnamed variety (resist).

*OTHER QUAMINA CERAMIC GROUP POTTERY:* Unspecified.
*WARE:* Rio Nuevo Glossy.
*COMPLEX:* Bladen.
*SPHERE AFFILIATION:* Xe?
*FREQUENCY:* 0.5 percent of the Bladen Ceramic Complex rim sherds; this description is based on 1 whole vessel, 5 rim sherds, and 1 body sherd not included in the frequency percentage.
*ILLUSTRATIONS:* Figures 4.12, 4.18*e*.
*PASTE, TEMPER, AND FIRING:* Same as Quamina Cream: Quamina Variety.
*SURFACE FINISH AND DECORATION:* For general discussion, see Quamina Cream: Quamina Variety.
*FORMS*
1. Two sherds belong to incurving sided bowls with direct

34  Chapter 4

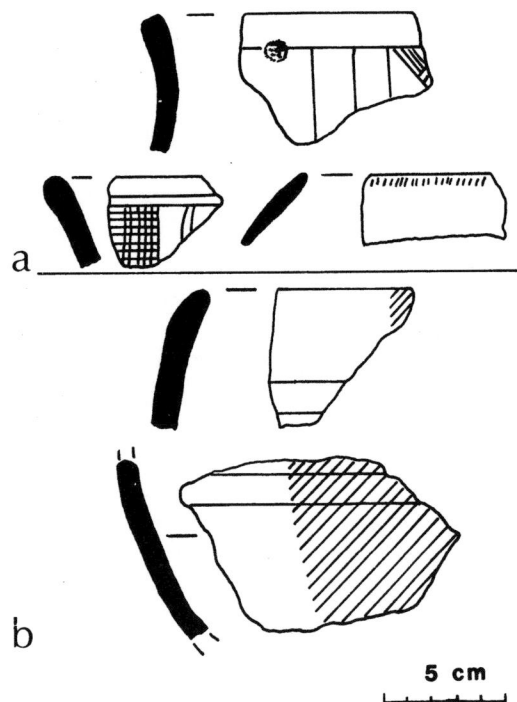

Figure 4.12. Quamina Ceramic Group pottery, unspecified: *a*, with postslip fine-line incising; *b*, with orange overslip and groove incisions.

rims and round lips. In both cases the cream slip is additionally decorated with an orange overslip on the exterior of the vessel, leaving other portions of the cream slip reserved, and with horizontal groove incisions (Fig. 4.12*b*). One whole vessel is gadrooned and gives the appearance of a squash (see Fig. 4.18*e*). This vessel comes from a late Bladen burial and measures 14.5 cm in rim diameter and 10 cm in height, with a vessel wall thickness of 0.6 cm.

2. Three sherds are additionally decorated by postslip fine-line incising in a variety of geometric patterns. This kind of decoration occurs on both slightly recurving and slightly outcurving sided bowls or dishes with direct or exteriorly folded rims and round lips (Fig. 4.12*a*). Rim diameter, 16–24 cm; wall thickness, 0.5–0.8 cm. Pring (1977) notes a sherd of this type and includes it in Quamina Cream: Quamina Variety. I have chosen to leave it Unspecified in the Quamina Ceramic Group because I suspect that with a larger sample it may be elevated to a separate incised variety of Quamina Cream, in keeping with the incised variety of the monochrome red group. It bears a faint resemblance to Comistun Incised: Unspecified Variety in the white Huetche Ceramic Group at Seibal (Sabloff 1975).

*TYPE:* Chicago Orange.
*VARIETY:* Nago Bank.
*ESTABLISHED AS A TYPE OR VARIETY:* Established as a type by Pring (1977); established as a variety, present work. This description is based on 294 rim sherds and 4 whole vessels.
  *GROUP:* Chicago.
  *WARE:* Fort George Orange.
  *COMPLEX:* Bladen.
  *SPHERE AFFILIATION:* Xe?
  *FREQUENCY:* 22.6 percent of the Bladen Ceramic Complex rim sherds.
  *ILLUSTRATIONS:* Figures 4.13, 4.17*c, d,* 4.18*a*.
  *PRINCIPAL IDENTIFYING ATTRIBUTES:* Thin, nonlustrous slip of a pale orange color, often incompletely oxidized to buff-orange; flaring or outcurving necked jars with direct rims and round or square lips; loop handles comprised of cylinders or incised deeply to give the appearance of cylinders.
  *PASTE, TEMPER, AND FIRING:* Paste color is similar to Chicago Orange: Chicago Variety in the Swasey Ceramic

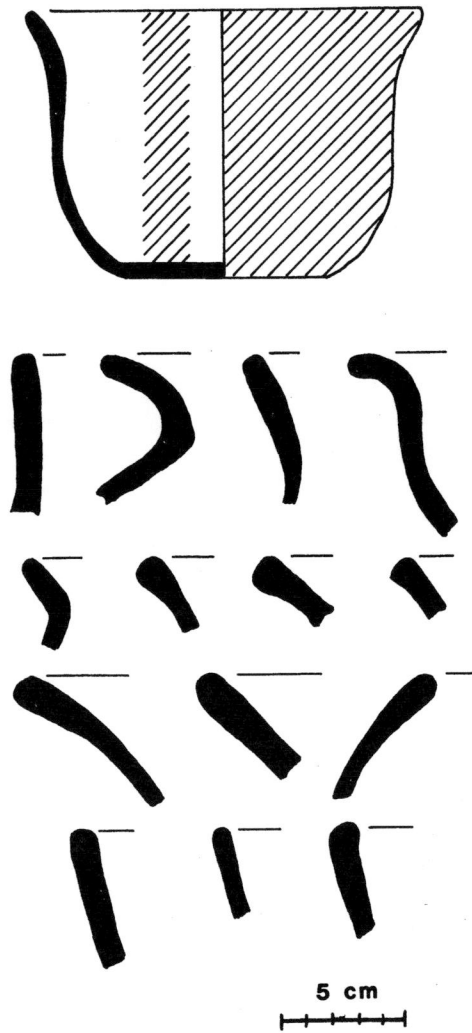

Figure 4.13. Chicago Orange: Nago Bank Variety.

Complex (Chapter Three) and ranges from pale buff to light brown and orange or pinkish orange. Paste color is normally reflected in the surface finish. The paste is fine, medium, and coarse textured with carbonate inclusions in about 85 percent of all sherds examined. Differential firing is common, with a dark core and lighter edge.

*SURFACE FINISH AND DECORATION:* Surface color is similar to Chicago Orange: Chicago Variety in the Swasey Ceramic Complex. The color centers on 5YR 7/4 pink, but includes sherds that are: 5YR 7/1–7/6 (light gray, pinkish gray, pink, and reddish yellow) and 7.5YR 7/2–7/4 (pinkish gray and gray). The surface color normally reflects the paste color and is achieved through the application of a thin slip or wash. The slip is usually nonlustrous and weathers easily. Fire clouding does occur on a number of sherds (about 25 percent of those examined). The Bladen Nago Bank Variety is often difficult to separate from the Chicago Variety in the Swasey Ceramic Complex; however, the Nago Bank Variety tends to have forms with round lips and the Chicago Variety has square lips. It is possible that the sample size of this type has been inflated somewhat by the inclusion of redeposited Swasey sherds.

*FORMS*

1. Short outcurving necked jar with direct rim, more commonly a round lip, and occasionally a square lip (32.1%). Rim diameter, 18–28 cm; wall thickness, 0.5–0.9 cm; neck height, 1.5–2.2 cm.
2. Short flaring necked jar with direct rim, more commonly a round lip, and occasionally a square lip (13.3%). Rim diameter, 18–32 cm; wall thickness, 0.5–0.9 cm; neck height, 1.2–2.4 cm.
3. Incurving bowl with direct or interiorly thickened rim and rounded lip (10.4%). Rim diameter, 16–25 cm; wall thickness, 0.5–0.8 cm.
4. Incurved-recurved sided bowl or dish with direct rim and round or square lip (8.7%). Rim diameter, 16–34 cm; wall thickness, 0.5–0.8 cm.
5. Short vertical necked jar with direct rim and round or square lip (8.1%). Rim diameter, 16–26 cm; wall thickness, 0.5–0.9 cm; neck height, 1.0–2.2 cm.
6. Long outcurving necked jar with direct rim and round or square lip (5.2%). Rim diameter, 18–28 cm; wall thickness, 0.6–0.9 cm; neck height, 3.0–5.2 cm.
7. Long flaring necked jar with direct rim and round or square lip (4.5%). Rim diameter, 22–34 cm; wall thickness, 0.6–0.9 cm; neck height, 2.5–5.0 cm.
8. Vertical to slightly flaring sided bowl or dish with direct or interiorly thickened rim and round lip (4.5%). Rim diameter, 16–28 cm; wall thickness, 0.5–0.8 cm.
9. Markedly flaring sided bowl or dish with direct rim and round lip (4.5%). Rim diameter, 18–32 cm; wall thickness, 0.5–0.8 cm.
10. Vertical or slightly tapered bottle with exteriorly folded rim and rounded or beveled out lip (4.2%). Rim diameter, 2.5–3.0 cm; wall thickness, 0.8–1.2 cm.
11. Long vertical necked jar with direct rim and round or square lip (2.9%). Rim diameter, 20–36 cm; wall thickness, 0.6–1.2 cm; neck height, 2.8–4.5 cm.
12. Outcurving sided bowl or dish with direct or exteriorly folded rim and round lip (1.6%). Rim diameter, 16–26 cm; wall thickness, 0.5–0.8 cm.

*APPENDAGES: Handles.* There are four loop handles associated with jar forms. Two of these are deeply gouged incised to give the appearance that the handle is composed of separate rolled cylinders. There are four double cylinder strap handles, but instead of being attached as a straight handle as in the Swasey Ceramic Complex, they are attached as loops.

*Spouts.* There are two spouts, one fragmentary and the other part of a small, crudely fashioned jar. Both are circular in section and about 5.0 cm long.

*Feet.* There are five hollow rounded feet and one solid rounded foot. They are all about 4.0 cm in diameter. It is not clear to what vessel form they belong, but the monopod bottle form has been identified in other late Early Preclassic deposits (see Brainerd 1958, for example), and these foot supports may belong to a similar form.

*INTRASITE DISTRIBUTION:* The type has been defined on the basis of sealed levels of the Bladen phase material (late Early Preclassic) in the South Square excavations (grid squares 20/30, 25/30, 25/35, 20/35). Nago Bank Variety continues throughout the Bladen Ceramic Complex with an increased emphasis on round lips and direct or folded rims.

*INTERSITE DISTRIBUTION:* Pring (1977) has identified the presence of the Swasey Chicago Variety of this type at El Pozito, and it is probable that the Bladen variety, Nago Bank, is also present at that site. The type has been identified at Colha in the Bolay Ceramic Complex (Kosakowsky and Valdez 1982). There are no other known comparisons. For general discussion, see Chicago Orange: Chicago Variety.

*TYPE:* Cotton Tree Incised.
*VARIETY:* Cotton Tree.
*ESTABLISHED AS A TYPE OR VARIETY:* Present work. This description is based on 16 rim sherds and 4 whole vessels.
*GROUP:* Chicago.
*WARE:* Fort George Orange.
*COMPLEX:* Bladen.
*SPHERE AFFILIATION:* Xe?
*FREQUENCY:* 1.5 percent of the Bladen Ceramic Complex rim sherds.
*ILLUSTRATIONS:* Figures 4.14; 4.17*a, b*; 4.18*b, c*.
*PRINCIPAL IDENTIFYING ATTRIBUTES:* Thin nonlustrous slip of a pale orange color similar to Chicago Orange;

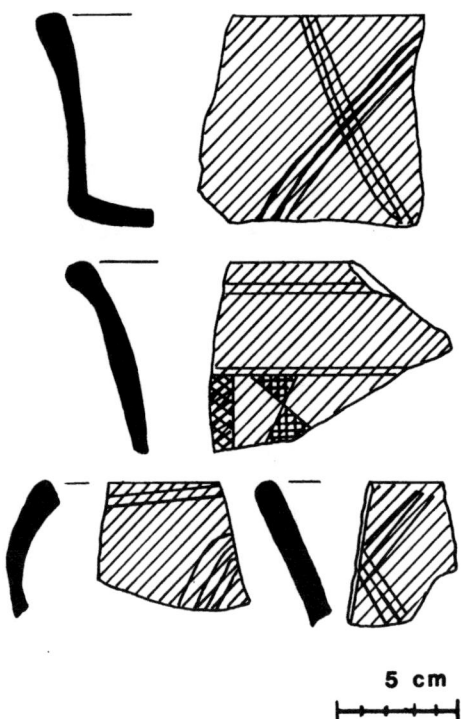

Figure 4.14. Cotton Tree Incised: Cotton Tree Variety.

secondary decoration by postslip fine-line incising in geometric patterns; incurved-recurved sided dishes or bowls.

*PASTE, TEMPER, AND FIRING:* Same as Chicago Orange: Nago Bank Variety.

*SURFACE FINISH AND DECORATION:* For general comments, see Chicago Orange: Nago Bank Variety. Secondary decoration is by postslip fine-line incision, usually in horizontal bands below the rim exteriorly and diagonal parallel or cross-hatched areas. Occasionally the design is more elaborate and includes some modeling.

*FORMS*
1. Incurved-recurved sided bowl or dish with direct rim and round lip (75%). Rim diameter, 16–28 cm; wall thickness, 0.5–0.8 cm.
2. Incurving sided bowl with direct or interiorly thickened rim and round lip (12.5%). Rim diameter, 16–22 cm; wall thickness, 0.5–0.7 cm.
3. Incurving sided bowl with short vertical neck or collar, interiorly thickened rim, and round lip (12.5%). Rim diameter, 18–20 cm; wall thickness, 0.6–0.8 cm.

*APPENDAGES:* None noted.

*INTRASITE DISTRIBUTION:* The type is defined on the basis of sealed levels of the Bladen phase material (late Early Preclassic) in the South Square excavations (grid squares 20/30, 25/30, 25/35, 20/35). Cotton Tree Incised continues throughout the Bladen Ceramic Complex without any apparent changes. Pring (1977) identified a similar buff type, Cowpen Incised: Cowpen Variety, in the Swasey Ceramic Complex at Cuello. As mentioned in the description of Chicago Orange: Chicago Variety, I include buff sherds in the orange group because they form a continuum from completely oxidized sherds (orange) to incompletely oxidized (buff-orange). It is likely that Pring's Cowpen Incised: Cowpen Variety is the same as Cotton Tree Incised: Cotton Tree Variety.

*INTERSITE DISTRIBUTION:* No specific comparisons are known. For general comments, see Chicago Orange: Nago Bank Variety. The decoration on Cotton Tree Incised is similar to the decoration on the monochrome black types Chompipi Incised: Chompipi Variety at Altar de Sacrificios (Adams 1971) and Chompipi Incised: Unspecified Variety at Seibal (Sabloff 1975).

*TYPE:* Honey Camp Orange-brown.
*VARIETY:* Honey Camp.
*ESTABLISHED AS A TYPE OR VARIETY:* Present work. This description is based on 189 rim sherds.
*GROUP:* Honey Camp.
*WARE:* Unspecified.
*COMPLEX:* Bladen.
*SPHERE AFFILIATION:* Xe?
*FREQUENCY:* 14.4 percent of the Bladen Ceramic Complex rim sherds.
*ILLUSTRATION:* Figure 4.15.
*PRINCIPAL IDENTIFYING ATTRIBUTES:* Dark orange wash over paste of a similar color; secondary decoration by dark brown smudging; incurving sided bowls; flaring sided bowls or dishes.

*PASTE, TEMPER, AND FIRING:* Paste is a dark orange or pale brown color and generally reflects surface color. The paste is fine or medium textured and all sherds examined have carbonate inclusions. Differential firing occurs, though it is not common.

*SURFACE FINISH AND DECORATION:* Surface color is highly variable. The color centers on 2.5YR 5/6 and 5/8 (red), 2.5YR 6/4 (light reddish brown), and 2.5YR 6/6 and 6/8 (light red), with 85 percent of the type comprising those colors. In addition, the color range includes: 5YR 6/3 (light reddish brown), 5YR 6/4 (light reddish brown), 5YR 6/6 (reddish yellow), 5YR 7/4 (pink), and 5YR 7/6 (reddish yellow). These colors are achieved through the application of a thin wash over a well-smoothed surface. In fact, in some cases the appearance of a wash or slip may be due to smoothing that brings fine clay particles to the surface, rather than the actual application of a wash or thin slip. Even microscopically, it is difficult to distinguish between the two processes. Secondarily, both the interior and exterior surfaces of the vessel are modified by dark brown smudging or a thin wash of dark brown, probably using some organic material. The color of the dark brown surface ranges from 4YR 4/1 (dark gray) to 5YR 5/1–5/3 (gray, reddish gray, and red brown), 5YR 6/1 (gray-light gray), 7.5YR 7/2, 7/4 (pinkish gray and pink), and 10YR 6/1, 6/2 (gray, light brown gray) and 7/1, 7/2 (light gray). Fire clouding does occur on a number of sherds. The wash is nonlustrous but does not erode easily.

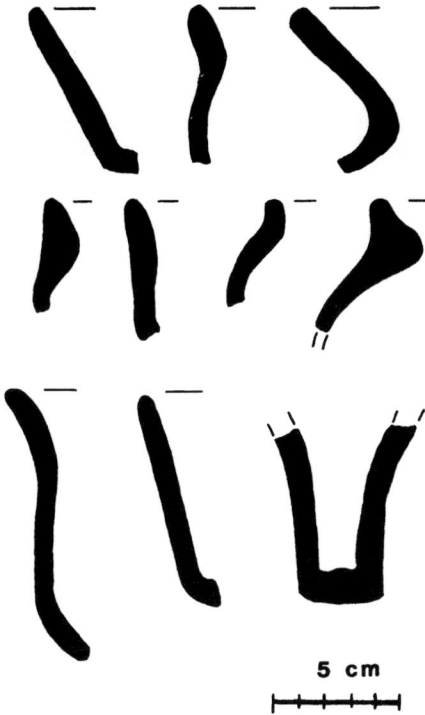

Figure 4.15. Honey Camp Orange-brown: Honey Camp Variety.

Although there may be some overlap with Chicago Orange: Nago Bank Variety, in general Honey Camp Orange-brown is much darker and has a dark orange or orange-brown paste that is easily identifiable.
*FORMS*
1. Incurving sided bowl with direct or interiorly thickened rim and round or pointed lip (31.8%). Rim diameter, 14–30 cm; wall thickness, 0.5–0.9 cm.
2. Flaring sided bowl or dish with direct or interiorly thickened rim and round lip (18.2%). Rim diameter, 18–36 cm; wall thickness, 0.5–0.8 cm.
3. Short outcurving necked jar with direct rim and round lip (13.5%). Rim diameter, 14–28 cm; wall thickness, 0.5–0.8 cm; neck height, 1.5–2.8 cm.
4. Incurved-recurved sided bowl or dish with direct or exteriorly folded rim and round lip (9.4%). Rim diameter, 16–32 cm; wall thickness, 0.5–0.8 cm.
5. Incurving sided bowl with short vertical neck or collar, interiorly thickened rim, and round or slightly pointed lip (7.6%). Rim diameter, 12–26 cm; wall thickness, 0.5–0.8 cm.
6. Long flaring necked jar with direct or slightly thickened rim and round or square lip (7.1%). Rim diameter, 18–40 cm; wall thickness, 0.5–0.8 cm; neck height, 2.5–6.6 cm.
7. Vertical to slightly flaring sided bowl or dish with direct or interiorly thickened rim and round lip (6.5%). Rim diameter, 14–25 cm; wall thickness, 0.5–0.8 cm.
8. Slightly outcurving sided bowl or dish with direct or exteriorly folded rim and round lip (5.9%). Rim diameter, 16–35 cm; wall thickness, 0.4–0.8 cm.

*APPENDAGES: Handles.* There are two loop handles associated with jar forms as well as one double cylinder handle that is attached in a loop, also on a jar form.
  *Spout.* There is one short spout, round in cross-section and crudely fashioned. Length, 3.2 cm.
  *Foot.* There is one flat bottomed foot (round in cross section), possibly from a monopod bottle or jar form; diameter, 3.6 cm.
*INTRASITE DISTRIBUTION:* The type is defined on the basis of sealed levels of the Bladen phase material (late Early Preclassic) in the South Square excavations (grid squares 20/30, 20/35, 25/35, 25/30). Honey Camp Orange-brown continues throughout the Bladen Ceramic Complex without any apparent changes.
*INTERSITE DISTRIBUTION:* The Cuello orange-brown group is apparently different from the orange-brown Jocote Ceramic Group at Barton Ramie (Gifford 1976) and at Chalchuapa (Sharer 1978); the Cuello Honey Camp pottery is decorated by a thin wash, but the Jocote pottery is unslipped. No specific comparisons are known.

*TYPE:* Copper Bank Incised.
*VARIETY:* Copper Bank.
*ESTABLISHED AS A TYPE OR VARIETY:* Present work. This description is based on 10 rim sherds and 1 body sherd.
*GROUP:* Honey Camp.
*WARE:* Unspecified.
*COMPLEX:* Bladen.
*SPHERE AFFILIATION:* Xe?
*FREQUENCY:* 0.8 percent of the Bladen Ceramic Complex rim sherds (body sherd not included in the frequency percentage).
*ILLUSTRATION:* Figure 4.16.
*PRINCIPAL IDENTIFYING ATTRIBUTES:* Slip color and dark brown smudging similar to Honey Camp Orange-brown; postslip fine-line incision as secondary decoration.
*PASTE, TEMPER, AND FIRING:* Same as Honey Camp Orange-brown: Honey Camp Variety.
*SURFACE FINISH AND DECORATION:* In general, slip characteristics are the same as Honey Camp Orange-brown: Honey Camp Variety. Secondary decoration is by fine-line postslip incision, usually in the form of cross-hatched parallel diagonal lines, along with horizontal bands around the exterior of vessels. In decoration it is similar to Cotton Tree Incised in the Chicago Ceramic Group and Chacalte Incised in the Machaca Ceramic Group.
*FORMS*
1. Incurved-recurved sided dishes with direct or exteriorly folded rim and round lip (50%). Rim diameter, 14–32 cm; wall thickness, 0.5–0.8 cm.
2. Outcurving sided bowl or dish with direct or exteriorly folded rim and round lip (30%). Rim diameter, 16–34 cm; wall thickness, 0.5–0.9 cm.
3. Vertical to slightly flaring sided bowl or dish with direct or interiorly thickened rim and round lip (20%). Rim diameter, 18–24 cm; wall thickness, 0.5–0.6 cm.

38   Chapter 4

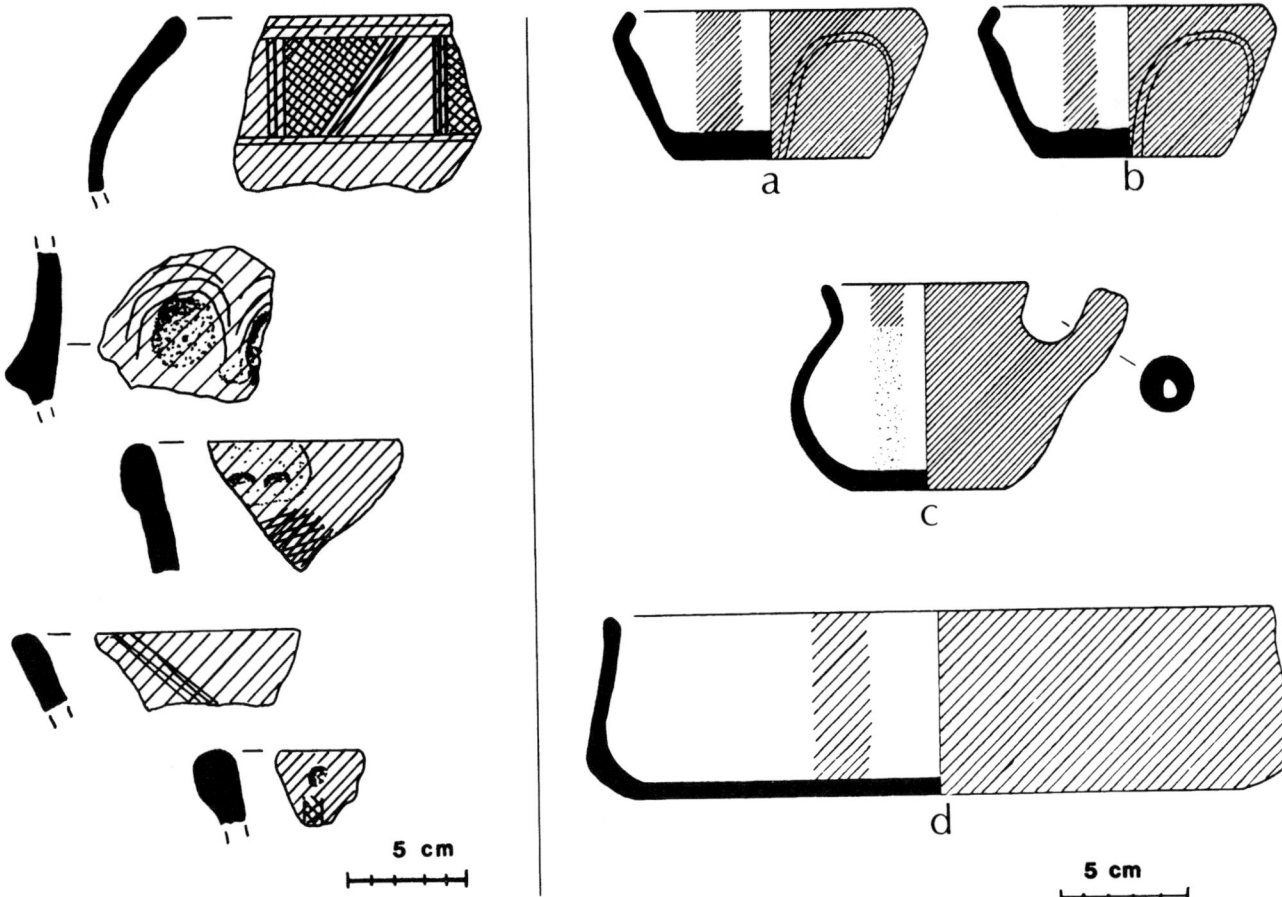

Figure 4.16. Copper Bank Incised: Copper Bank Variety.

Figure 4.17 Whole vessels from Burial Feature 219: *a, b,* Cotton Tree Incised: Cotton Tree Variety; *c, d,* Chicago Orange: Nago Bank Variety.

*APPENDAGES:* None noted.

*INTRASITE DISTRIBUTION:* The type is defined on the basis of sealed levels of the Bladen phase material (late Early Preclassic) in the South Square excavations (grid squares 20/30, 20/35, 25/35, 25/30). Copper Bank Incised continues throughout the Bladen Ceramic Complex without any apparent changes.

*INTERSITE DISTRIBUTION:* See Honey Camp Orange-brown: Honey Camp Variety for a general discussion. The decoration on Copper Bank Incised is dissimilar to the decoration commonly found on the orange-brown groups from Chalchuapa and Barton Ramie (see Sharer 1978 and Gifford 1976), which consists of punctated or impressed fillets on outcurving necked jars. Copper Bank decoration is more in keeping with the monochrome black Chompipi Incised from Altar de Sacrificios (Adams 1971) and Seibal (Sabloff 1975). No specific comparisons are known.

## MORTUARY VESSELS

### Burial Feature 219

Two vessels of Cotton Tree Incised: Cotton Tree Variety from Burial Feature 219 are nearly identical (Fig. 4.17*a, b*). They are both small, flaring sided bowls with interiorly everted rims and round lips. Each is about 12 cm in diameter and 6.5 cm in height. Vessel wall thickness is variable, from 0.5 cm at the rim to 1.2 cm at the base. In both cases decoration consists of parallel fine-line incisions that trace arches around the exterior of the vessels.

The two remaining vessels from this burial are Chicago Orange: Nago Bank Variety. One is a miniature spouted jar with short outcurving neck, direct rim, and round lip (Fig. 4.17*c*). The spout is circular in section and about 4 cm long. The jar measures 9 cm in rim diameter, 9 cm in height, and vessel wall thickness is 0.6 cm. The jar is differentially fired and fire clouding is present. The second vessel of this type (Fig. 4.17*d*) is a slightly recurving sided bowl or dish with direct rim and round lip. The vessel measures 29 cm in rim diameter, 8 cm in height, and vessel wall thickness is 0.8 cm.

All the vessels in this burial are incompletely oxidized and tend to be buff-orange in color. The burial is that of a child, age two to four years, sex indeterminate, and grave goods included a ceramic bird whistle, a drilled shell, and a jade bead along with the four vessels.

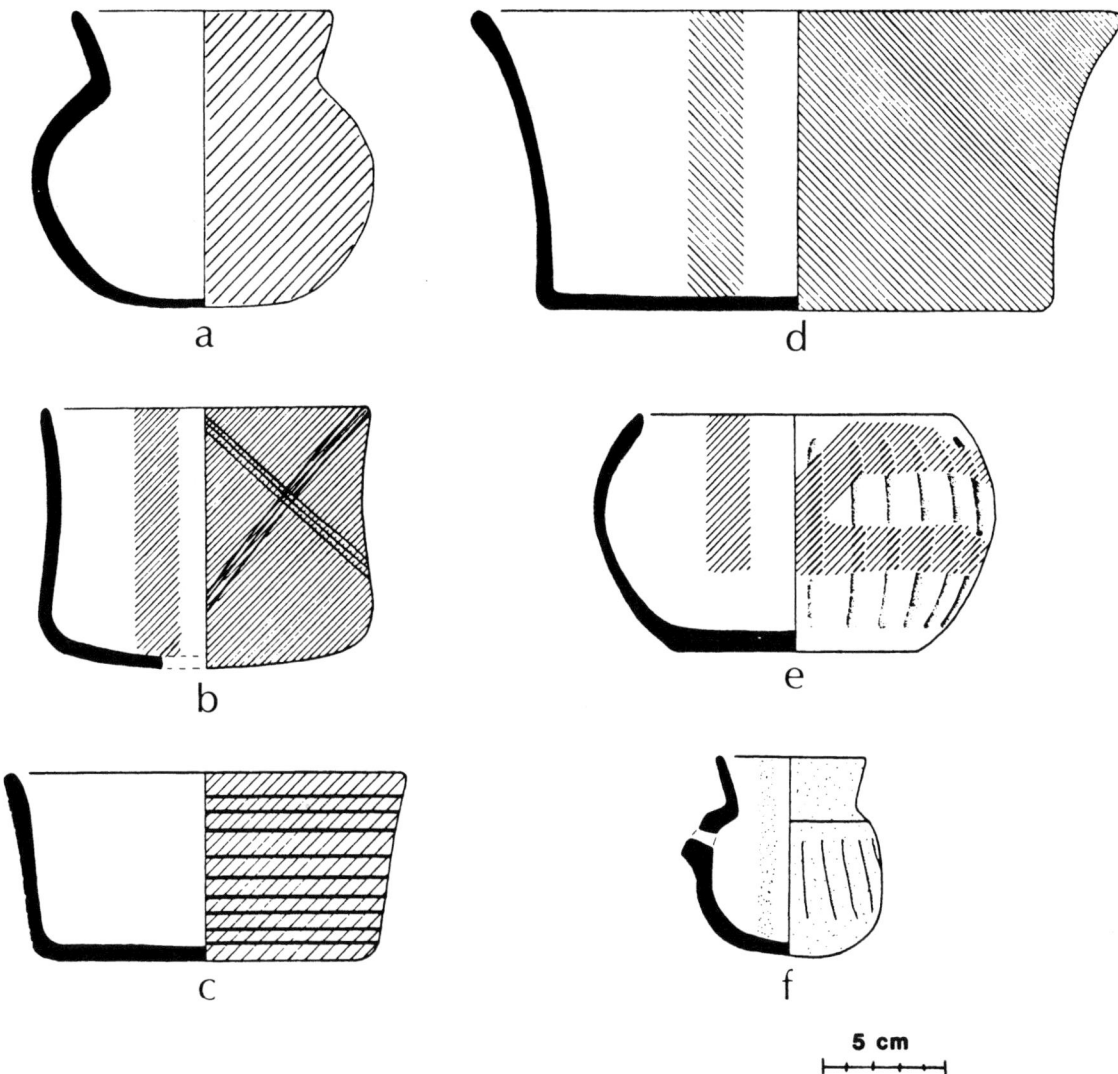

Figure 4.18. Whole vessels from Burial Feature 251: *a*, Chicago Orange: Nago Bank Variety; *b, c*, Cotton Tree Incised: Cotton Tree Variety; *d*, Consejo Red: Estrella Variety; *e*, Quamina Ceramic Group, unspecified; *f*, Copetilla Unslipped: Gallon Jug Variety.

### Burial Feature 251

Six vessels were found in Burial Feature 251. One jar of Chicago Orange: Nago Bank Variety has a short, slightly outcurving neck (Fig. 4.18*a*). The jar is 12.4 cm high and 11 cm in rim diameter; vessel wall thickness is 0.8 cm. Two vessels are Cotton Tree Incised: Cotton Tree Variety. One of them is a vertical to slightly recurving sided bowl with direct rim and pointed lip (Fig. 4.18*b*). The rim diameter of the vessel is 14.5 cm, the height is 11 cm, and vessel wall thickness is 0.7 cm. Decoration consists of cross-hatched diagonal fine-line incisions. The second Cotton Tree Incised vessel (Fig. 4.18*c*) is a bit unusual. It is a slightly flaring sided bowl with direct rim and round lip. The vessel is 18 cm in rim diameter, 8 cm in height, and vessel wall thickness is 0.6 cm. Decoration consists of thick incisions in horizontal parallel bands around the exterior of the vessel, giving the appearance of grooved incising. A vessel of Consejo Red: Estrella Variety (Fig. 4.18*d*) is an outcurving sided dish or bowl with slightly exteriorly thickened rim and round lip. Rim diameter of the vessel is 23 cm, height is 12.5 cm, and vessel wall thickness is 0.6 cm. An Unspecified vessel of the cream Quamina Ceramic Group (Fig. 4.18*e*) was described at the end of the Quamina Ceramic Group section. A miniature jar of Copetilla Unslipped: Gallon Jug Variety has a short flaring neck, direct rim, and round lip; the spout is missing (Fig. 4.18*f*). It is 7 cm in rim diameter and 8.5 cm in height, with a vessel wall thickness of 0.8 cm. It is decorated in an unusual fashion with irregular incisions placed vertically around the exterior of the vessel.

**Table 4.2. Major Discriminating Features of Pottery Varieties in the Swasey and Bladen Ceramic Complexes**

| Swasey Ceramic Complex | Bladen Ceramic Complex |
|---|---|
| *Copetilla Unslipped* | |
| Copetilla Variety<br>  Well-smoothed surfaces<br>  Double cylinder strap handle<br>  Square lips on thickened rims | Gallon Jug Variety<br>  Unsmoothed surfaces<br>  Incised loop handles<br>  Round lips on thickened rims |
| *Consejo Red* | |
| Consejo Variety<br>  Wide range of surface color for the red slip<br>  Round bases<br>  Square lips | Estrella Variety<br>  Surface color centered on 10R 4/8 (red)<br>  Flat bases<br>  Round lips |
| Backlanding Incised<br>  Decoration restricted to horizontal parallel lines | Barquedier Incised<br>  Decoration with diagonal parallel lines and horizontal lines |
| Pettville Red-and-cream<br>  Wide range of surface color for the red slip<br>  Round bases<br>  Square lips | Fireburn Red-and-cream<br>  Surface color centered on 10R 4/8 (red)<br>  Flat bases<br>  Round lips |
| *Machaca Black* | |
| Machaca Variety<br>  Surface finish difficult to differentiate<br>  Vertical sided bowls<br>  Square lips | Wamil Variety<br>  Surface finish difficult to differentiate<br>  Incurved-recurved sided bowls<br>  Round lips |
| *Chacalte Incised* | |
| Chacalte Variety<br>  Decoration restricted to horizontal parallel lines | Yo Creek Variety<br>  Decoration with cross-hatching and elaborate incising |
| *Chicago Orange* | |
| Chicago Variety<br>  Double cylinder strap handles<br>  Square lips on thickened rims | Nago Bank Variety<br>  Incised loop handles<br>  Round lips on direct rims |

The burial is of a young to mature male adult. Grave goods included two hook-ended implements manufactured from deer metapodials, a fragment of a metate, and the six vessels.

## DIFFERENTIATING FEATURES BETWEEN THE SWASEY AND BLADEN CERAMIC COMPLEXES

The pottery of the Swasey and Bladen ceramic complexes is similar and presents some sorting problems to the ceramicist. The Bladen ceramics are clearly identifiable in temporally mixed deposits by the presence of such markers as Tower Hill Red-on-cream, Quamina Cream, Honey Camp Orange-brown, and incised decoration on the orange ceramic group (Cotton Tree Incised). However, in temporally mixed deposits differentiation among the other ceramic types is often difficult based on surface finish and decoration alone. Table 4.2 lists the major discriminating features of the Swasey and Bladen varieties of each type. It is important to remember that while surface finish and decoration may not change, vessel form and rim and lip treatment in the Swasey complex are different from those in the Bladen complex. For all types in the Bladen complex, vessel forms tend to have rounder lips and folded rims instead of square lips and direct rims.

Although one may argue (with reason) that the same varietal names should have been used for both the Swasey and Bladen types, I used new varietal names for the Bladen complex in keeping with other ceramic research in northern Belize. The Bladen Ceramic Complex is clearly separable on stratigraphic grounds and on vessel form changes, and when taken in conjunction with minute surface finish characteristics and the appearance of a new ceramic group (Quamina), the pottery attributes bring a strong integrity to the definition of the complex.

CHAPTER FIVE

# Lopez Ceramic Complex

The Lopez Ceramic Complex spans the period from about 1000 or 900 B.C. to about 400 B.C. The selected sample intensively analyzed from Lopez phase levels consists of 2 whole vessels, 10 body sherds, and 273 rim sherds, supplemented by an additional 547 redeposited Lopez rim sherds in Cocos phase levels that brings the total sample to 820 rim sherds (total number excavated). The complex is composed of 6 major ceramic groups and 10 types and varieties, and the relative frequencies of the groups are given in Table 5.1. As indicated, 96.2 percent of Lopez Ceramic Complex pottery is slipped; Richardson Peak is the only unslipped type. Of the slipped pottery, approximately 44.0 percent is decorated in some fashion by incising (23.6%), dichrome slips (19.3%), chamfering (0.6%), or modeling (0.5%).

The Lopez Ceramic Complex was defined by Pring (1977), and this study redefines it as stratigraphically positioned between the Bladen Ceramic Complex and the succeeding Cocos Ceramic Complex in the South Square excavations of Platform 34 (grid sqaures 20/30, 25/30, 25/35, and 20/35). It thus comprises the Middle Preclassic period and belongs securely within the Mamom Ceramic Sphere. Many varieties of typical Mamom sphere pottery types are found at Cuello that are also present at other Middle Preclassic sites in the Maya Lowlands.

**TYPE DESCRIPTIONS**
**(Mamom Ceramic Sphere)**

*TYPE:* Richardson Peak Unslipped.
*VARIETY:* Richardson Peak (Lopez).
*ESTABLISHED AS A TYPE OR VARIETY:* Pring (1977); this variety was left Unspecified by Pring, but because he first recognized and named it, it is actually the established variety. Pring's description was based on 40 rim sherds. This description is based on a total of 31 rim sherds, 24 from Lopez levels and 7 from Cocos levels.
*GROUP:* Richardson Peak(?)
*WARE:* Uaxactun Unslipped.
*COMPLEX:* Lopez.
*SPHERE AFFILIATION:* Mamom.
*FREQUENCY:* 3.8 percent of the Lopez Ceramic Complex rim sherds.
*ILLUSTRATION:* Figure 5.1.
*PRINCIPAL IDENTIFYING ATTRIBUTES:* Rough, unslipped, tan, gray, or orange surfaces; short vertical or outcurving necked jars; many forms have rims that are exteriorly folded or thickened.
*PASTE, TEMPER, AND FIRING:* The paste color ranges from 5YR 5/1 (gray) through 5YR 6/1–6/6 (gray to reddish yellow), 10YR 5/1–6/3 (gray to pale brown), and 2.5 YR 5/2

Table 5.1. Classification of Pottery in the Lopez Ceramic Complex
(Group frequency based on 820 rim sherds)

| Ware | Group | Type | Variety |
|---|---|---|---|
| Uaxactun Unslipped | Richardson Peak* (3.8%) | Richardson Peak Unslipped | Richardson Peak Variety (Lopez) |
| Flores Waxy | Joventud (39.9%) | Joventud Red | Palmasito Variety |
| | | Guitara Incised | Grooved-incised Variety |
| | | Desvario Chamfered | Desvario Variety |
| | | Other Joventud Ceramic Group | Unspecified (3 punctated, 4 modeled) |
| | Chunhinta (2.0%) | Chunhinta Black | Chunhinta Variety |
| | | Deprecio Incised | Grooved-incised Variety |
| | Pital (1.7%) | Pital Cream | Variety Unspecified |
| | | Paso Danto Incised | Variety Unspecified |
| | Muxanal (19.3%) | Muxanal Red-on-cream | San Lazaro Variety |
| | | Other Muxanal Ceramic Group | Unspecified (3 composite) |
| Fort George Orange | Chicago (33.3%) | Chicago Orange | Warrie Camp Variety |

*Pending comparisons with other unslipped groups of Uaxactun Unslipped Ware.

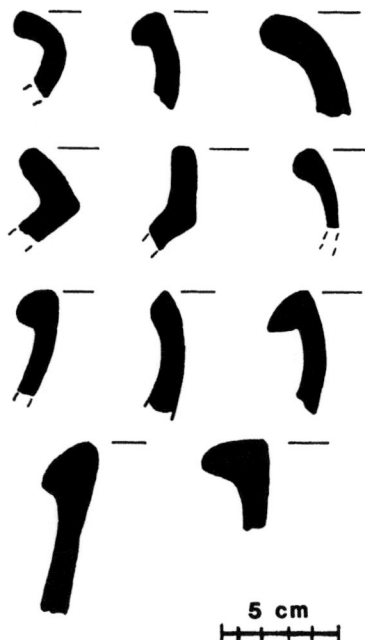

Figure 5.1. Richardson Peak Unslipped: Richardson Peak Variety (Lopez).

(grayish brown). The color is highly variable with no one color comprising a major percentage of the sample. Paste texture is medium to coarse grained. Differential firing is common, leaving either a darker core or one side of the vessel a darker color than the other. Carbonate inclusions are present in all sherds.

*SURFACE FINISH AND DECORATION:* The surface is usually unsmoothed with a color range the same as the paste color. Fire clouding is also common.

*FORMS*
1. Short vertical necked jar with direct, exteriorly folded or everted rim, and round lip (32.3%). Rim diameter, 15–26 cm; wall thickness, 0.6–1.0 cm; neck height, 1.2–3.0 cm.
2. Short outcurving necked jar with direct or exteriorly folded rim and round lip (29%). Rim diameter, 16–24 cm; wall thickness, 0.6–0.9 cm; neck height, 1.5–3.0 cm.
3. Long outcurving necked jar with direct, exteriorly folded, or everted rim and round lip (9.3%). Rim diameter, 16–28 cm; wall thickness, 0.6–1.0 cm; neck height, 3.2–5.4 cm.
4. Medium to high flaring necked jar with direct or exteriorly folded rim and round lip (6.5%). Rim diameter, 18–30 cm; wall thickness, 0.6–1.0 cm; neck height, 2.5–5.5 cm.
5. Incurved-recurved sided bowl or dish with direct or exteriorly folded rim and round lip (6.5%). Rim diameter, 18–28 cm; wall thickness, 0.5–0.9 cm.
6. Flaring sided bowl or dish with direct or exteriorly folded or everted rim and round lip (3.2%). Rim diameter, 24 cm; wall thickness, 0.5 cm.
7. Vertical or slightly tapered bottle with exteriorly folded rim and round or beveled out lip (3.2%). Rim diameter, 2.9 cm; wall thickness, 0.6 cm.

*APPENDAGES: Handles.* All handles are associated with jar forms. One is a simple loop handle, circular to ovoid in cross section. A second is a strap handle that is almost flat in cross section. Two loop handles have deep gouge incisions on them to give the appearance of being composed of three separate cylinders.

*INTRASITE DISTRIBUTION:* This variety is defined on the basis of sealed levels of the Lopez phase material (Middle Preclassic) in the South Square excavations (grid sqaures 20/30, 25/30, 25/35, 20/35). Richardson Peak Variety continues throughout the Lopez Ceramic Complex without any apparent changes. In fact, it is difficult to distinguish the Lopez variety of Richardson Peak Unslipped from the succeeding Cocos variety of the same type solely on the basis of surface color or texture. There are some differences in vessel form distribution and lip and rim treatment, but it is possible that the sample size of this type has been elevated by the addition of Cocos unslipped sherds. In general, it is difficult to sort the unslipped material of the Middle Preclassic from the unslipped material of the Late Preclassic except in temporally pure deposits.

*INTERSITE DISTRIBUTION:* Pring (1977) identified the presence of the Lopez variety of Richardson Peak Unslipped in small numbers at the sites of Santa Rita, San Estevan, and Colha in northern Belize. The Middle Preclassic unslipped type at Cuello is modally similar to most other Middle Preclassic unslipped types from sites in the Maya Lowlands. For a complete description, see Pring (1977).

*TYPE:* Joventud Red.
*VARIETY:* Palmasito.
*ESTABLISHED AS A TYPE OR VARIETY:* Type, Smith and Gifford (1966). Variety, Pring (1977). Pring's description was based on 150 rim sherds and 1 whole vessel. This description is based on 135 rim sherds, 56 from Mamom levels and 79 from Cocos levels.
*GROUP:* Joventud.
*WARE:* Flores Waxy.
*COMPLEX:* Lopez.
*SPHERE AFFILIATION:* Mamom.
*FREQUENCY:* 16.4 percent of the Lopez Ceramic Complex rim sherds.
*ILLUSTRATION:* Figure 5.2.
*PRINCIPAL IDENTIFYING ATTRIBUTES:* Thick, soft, dark red slip with a pronounced waxy feel; extensive fire-crackling of the slip; outcurving sided dishes or plates with flat bases; incurving sided bowls with restricted orifices (tecomates).
*PASTE, TEMPER, AND FIRING:* Paste color varies from tan to buff or light brown. Paste tends to be uniform in color with little differential firing. Paste is medium textured and tempering includes carbonate particles, often fairly large in size, in all sherds, and crushed sherds in about 15 to 25 percent of the sample. The paste tends to crumble easily.
*SURFACE FINISH AND DECORATION:* Slip color is fairly homogeneous centering on 10R 4/6, 4/8, 5/6, 5/8 (red, 90 percent of all sherds), with a number of sherds of 2.5YR

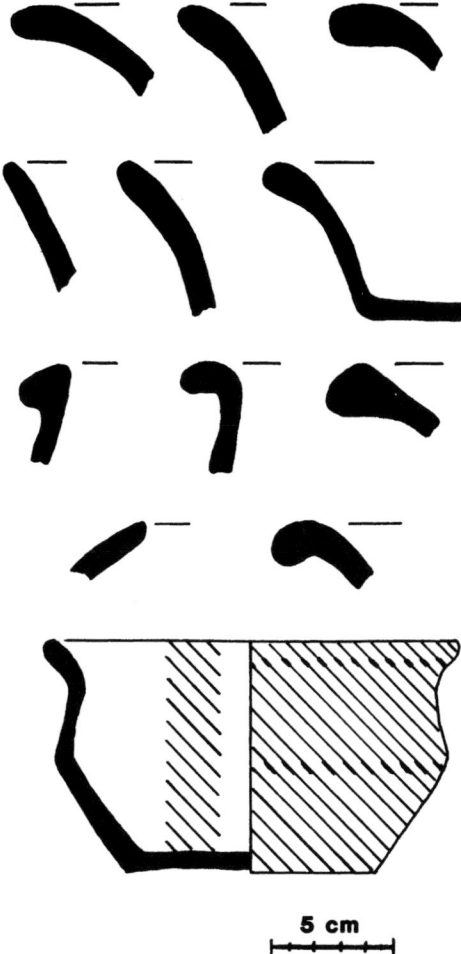

Figure 5.2. Joventud Red: Palmasito Variety (whole vessel from Pring collections).

4/8 and 4/6 (red). The slip is very soft and scratches easily or erodes in a characteristic fashion, flaking off in small patches. The slip tends to be thick and dull, with a pronouncedly waxy feel. Fire crackling or crazing is extremely common and is present on almost all sherds. The slip is often mottled with black specks, perhaps caused by the presence of organic material in the slip clay. The Joventud Red at Cuello is apparently easier to identify than the Joventud Red varieties at other sites in the Maya Lowlands. It is readily distinguishable from the later Sierra Red because the slip is darker red, not as glossy, and much waxier and softer, which is an unusual distinction.

*FORMS*
1. Outcurving sided dish or plate with direct, exteriorly folded, or everted rim, round lip, and flat base (53.5%). Rim diameter, 16–46 cm; wall thickness, 0.4–0.9 cm.
2. Incurving sided bowl with markedly restricted orifice (tecomate), direct or interiorly folded rim, and round or pointed lip (14.7%). Rim diameter, 8–20 cm; wall thickness, 0.3–0.5 cm.
3. Vertical or slightly tapered bottle with exteriorly folded rim and round or beveled out lip (8.1%). Rim diameter, 3.5–5.0 cm; wall thickness, 0.4–0.7 cm.
4. Incurved-recurved sided bowl or dish with exteriorly folded or everted rim and round lip (5.9%). Rim diameter, 18–32 cm; wall thickness, 0.5–0.8 cm.
5. Medium to long vertical to slightly outcurving necked jar with direct, exteriorly folded, or slightly everted rim, and round lip (5.9%). Rim diameter, 14–24 cm; wall thickness, 0.4–0.8 cm; neck height, 2.8–5.2 cm.
6. Flaring sided bowl or dish with exteriorly folded or everted rim and round lip (5.3%). Rim diameter, 22–36 cm; wall thickness, 0.4–0.8 cm.
7. Incurving sided bowl with unrestricted orifice, direct or interiorly folded rim, and round lip (4.4%). Rim diameter, 20–36 cm; wall thickness, 0.5–0.9 cm.
8. Vertical sided bowl or dish with direct rim and round lip (2.2%). Rim diameter, 18–24 cm; wall thickness, 0.4–0.5 cm.

*APPENDAGES: Spouts.* There are two spouts that are ovate in cross section and roughly 2.0 cm in diameter. The height of each, though incomplete, is about 6.0 cm. Ovate spouts are considered diagnostic markers of Mamom Ceramic Sphere pottery (Willey, Culbert, and Adams 1967).

*Foot:* There is one hollow, round foot about 5 cm in diameter where it is broken. It is possible that the foot belongs to a monopod bottle as described by Brainerd (1958) at Mani. A similar complete monopod bottle in the Joventud Ceramic Group was found in the 1979 excavations at Cuello (Kosakowsky 1982).

*INTRASITE DISTRIBUTION:* The type is defined on the basis of sealed levels of the Lopez phase material (Middle Preclassic) in the South Square excavations (grid squares 20/30, 25/30, 25/35, 20/35). Palmasito Variety continues throughout the Lopez Ceramic Complex without any apparent changes.

*INTERSITE DISTRIBUTION:* Pring (1977) identified the presence of Joventud Red at San Estevan, Chowacol, Nohmul, Colha, Santa Rita, Caledonia, and El Pozito in northern Belize. Joventud Red: Palmasito Variety is similar to the Joventud Variety at Uaxactun (Smith 1955; Smith and Gifford 1966), the Mocho Variety at Altar de Sacrificios (Adams 1971), the Unspecified Variety at Seibal (Sabloff 1975), Black Rock Red at Barton Ramie (Gifford 1976), the Joventud Variety at Yaxha-Sacnab (Rice 1979) and at Tikal, and the Jolote Variety at Becan (Ball 1977a). Though there are similarities among all these types and varieties such as the waxiness of the slip with a tendency to fire crackling, oval section spouts, and outcurving sided dishes, it is important to note that there is still a great deal of diversity at the varietal level. The Cuello variety is perhaps closest to the Jolote Variety at Becan in surface color and slip texture, as well as in the distribution of vessel forms.

*TYPE:* Guitara Incised.
*VARIETY:* Grooved-incised.

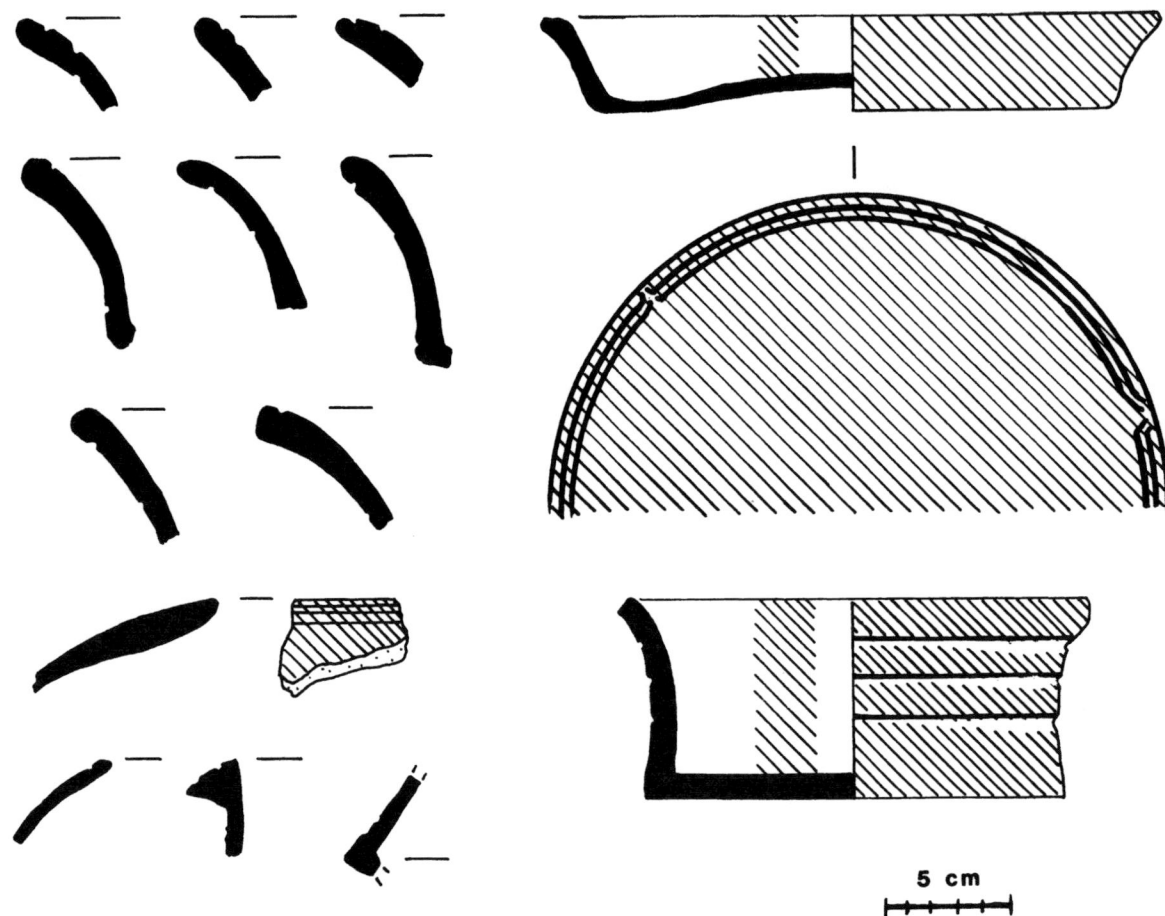

Figure 5.3. Guitara Incised: Grooved-incised Variety (bottom right whole vessel from Pring collections).

*ESTABLISHED AS A TYPE OR VARIETY:* Type, Smith and Gifford (1966). Variety, Pring (1977). Pring's description was based on 150 rim sherds and a whole vessel. This description is based on 1 whole vessel, 1 body sherd, and 183 rim sherds, 67 from Lopez levels and 116 from Cocos levels.
*GROUP:* Joventud.
*WARE:* Flores Waxy.
*COMPLEX:* Lopez.
*SPHERE AFFILIATION:* Mamom.
*FREQUENCY:* 22.4 percent of the Lopez Ceramic Complex rim sherds (body sherd not included in the frequency percentage).
*ILLUSTRATIONS:* Figures 5.3, 5.4.
*PRINCIPAL IDENTIFYING ATTRIBUTES:* Slip color and texture same as Joventud Red: Palmasito Variety; decoration by preslip groove-incising on rim interior and on vessel exterior at the rim or occasionally at the base; "double-line break" motif; outcurving sided dishes or plates with flat bases.
*PASTE, TEMPER, AND FIRING:* Same as Joventud Red: Palmasito Variety.
*SURFACE FINISH AND DECORATION:* For general comments, see Joventud Red: Palmasito Variety. Slip color and texture of Guitara Incised are the same as the Palmasito Variety of Joventud Red. Decoration is by shallow preslip groove-incising extending in horizontal bands around the exterior of vessels. Most vessels are outcurving sided dishes or plates with everted rims, on the interior of which is the groove-incising, usually in parallel concentric bands or with the "double-line break" motif. The incisions are shallow and about 0.1 to 0.2 cm wide. Additional decoration occurs occasionally in the form of a vertical appliqué ridge starting at the base of the rim and extending over about a third or a half of the vessel exterior.
*FORMS*
1. Outcurving sided dish or plate with direct, exteriorly folded, or exteriorly everted rim, and round lip, (89.1%). Rim diameter, 16–48 cm (mostly 26–44 cm); wall thickness, 0.5–0.8 cm.
2. Incurving sided bowl with restricted orifice (tecomate), direct or interiorly folded rim, and round or pointed lip (4.9%). Rim diameter, 10–16 cm; wall thickness, 0.3–0.5 cm.
3. Incurved-recurved sided bowl with medial angle, direct or exteriorly thickened rim, and round lip (2.2%). Rim diameter, 16–28 cm; wall thickness, 0.5–0.8 cm.
4. Flaring sided dish or bowl with direct or exteriorly thickened rim and round lip (1.6%). Rim diameter, 16–24 cm;

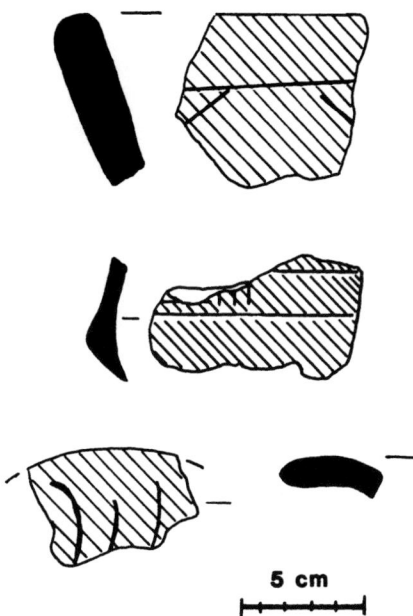

Figure 5.4. Guitara Incised: Grooved-incised Variety (similar to the Guitara Variety, see text).

wall thickness, 0.4–0.8 cm.
5. Vertical sided bowl or dish with direct or exteriorly folded rim and round lip (1.1%). Rim diameter, 18–20 cm; wall thickness, 0.5 cm.
6. Incurved-recurved bowl or dish with direct or exteriorly folded rim and round lip (1.1%). Rim diameter, 16–20 cm; wall thickness, 0.5–0.6 cm.
   *APPENDAGES:* None noted.
   *INTRASITE DISTRIBUTION:* The type is defined on the basis of sealed levels of the Lopez phase material (Middle Preclassic) in the South Square excavations (grid squares 20/30, 25/30, 25/35, 20/35). Guitara Incised continues throughout the Lopez Ceramic Complex without any apparent changes.
   *INTERSITE DISTRIBUTION:* For a general discussion, see Joventud Red: Palmasito Variety. Guitara Incised: Grooved-incised Variety is similar to grooved-incised varieties from Uaxactun (Smith 1955; Smith and Gifford 1966), Seibal (Sabloff 1975), Altar de Sacrificios (Adams 1971), Barton Ramie (Gifford 1976), Yaxha-Sacnab (Rice 1979), Tikal, and Becan (Ball 1977a). The "double-line break" motif has been found on ceramics as far away as the Olmec Heartlands on the Gulf Coast. For a more complete discussion, see Pring (1977).

In addition, Pring (1977) identified a Guitara Variety of this type at Cuello that is characterized by preslip fine-line and postslip incisions in geometric patterns other than horizontal lines. He identified four sherds of this type. Three sherds were found in the 1980 excavations that had more elaborate incising, two preslip and one postslip (Fig. 5.4). The sample is too small to warrant a separate variety. Because no whole vessels were found, it is often difficult to discern whether a single vessel combines both forms of incising. All the incised material should be included in a single type and, until a larger sample is available, a single variety as well.

*TYPE:* Desvario Chamfered.
*VARIETY:* Desvario.
*ESTABLISHED AS A TYPE OR VARIETY:* Smith and Gifford (1966). This description is based on 5 rim sherds.
*GROUP:* Joventud.
*WARE:* Flores Waxy.
*COMPLEX:* Lopez.
*SPHERE AFFILIATION:* Mamom.
*FREQUENCY:* 0.6 percent of the Lopez Ceramic Complex rim sherds.
*ILLUSTRATION:* Figure 5.5a.
*PRINCIPAL IDENTIFYING ATTRIBUTES:* Slip color and texture the same as Joventud Red: Palmasito Variety; chamfering on vessel wall exteriors.
*PASTE, TEMPER, AND FIRING:* The same as Joventud Red: Palmasito Variety.
*SURFACE FINISH AND DECORATION:* Slip texture and color the same as Joventud Red: Palmasito Variety. Decoration is by horizontal chamfers around the exterior of vessels.

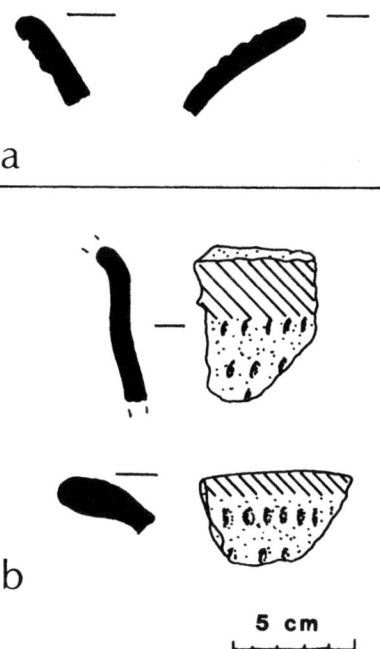

Figure 5.5. Joventud Ceramic Group pottery: *a*, Desvario Chamfered: Desvario Variety; *b*, with fingernail impressions.

In keeping with Pring (1977), I have called this the Desvario Variety. Considering the small sample from Cuello and Pring's equally small sample of ten sherds, however, I would have preferred to label this an Unspecified Variety until more material from Cuello is excavated.

## 46  Chapter 5

*FORMS*
1. Round to slightly incurving sided bowl or dish with direct or slightly exteriorly thickened rim and round lip (60%). Rim diameter, 20–24 cm; wall thickness, 0.6–0.7 cm.
2. Outcurving sided dish or plate with direct, or slightly exteriorly everted rim and round lip (40%). Rim diameter, 20–22 cm; wall thickness, 0.6 cm.

*APPENDAGES:* None noted.

*INTRASITE DISTRIBUTION:* The type is defined on the basis of sealed levels of the Lopez phase material (Middle Preclassic) in the South Square excavations (grid squares 20/30, 25/30, 25/35, 20/35). Desvario Chamfered continues throughout the Lopez Ceramic Complex without any apparent changes, though it seems to first appear in the later Middle Preclassic levels.

*INTERSITE DISTRIBUTION:* Chamfering is considered a diagnostic marker of the Mamom Ceramic Sphere (Willey, Culbert, and Adams 1967). The Cuello variety is the same as that found at Uaxactun (Smith 1955; Smith and Gifford 1966), at Tikal, and at Altar de Sacrificios (Adams 1971), and is similar to chamfered varieties at Seibal (Sabloff 1975) and at Becan (Ball 1977a).

*OTHER JOVENTUD CERAMIC GROUP POTTERY:* Unspecified.
*WARE:* Flores Waxy.
*COMPLEX:* Lopez.
*SPHERE AFFILIATION:* Mamom.
*FREQUENCY:* 0.5 percent of the Lopez Ceramic Complex rim sherds. This description is based on 4 rim sherds, and 3 body sherds not included in the frequency percentage.
*ILLUSTRATIONS:* Figures 5.5b, 5.6.
*PASTE, TEMPER, AND FIRING:* Same as Joventud Red: Palmasito Variety.
*SURFACE FINISH AND DECORATION:* See *Forms*.
*FORMS*
1. Three sherds are similar to Bobo Red-and-unslipped (Pring 1977). Two are body sherds and the third is an incurved-recurved sided bowl or dish. The interior and rim of the exterior are slipped red, similar to Joventud Red: Palmasito Variety. The remaining exterior surface is unslipped and irregularly punctated with fingernail impressions (Fig. 5.5b).
2. Four sherds are modeled faces with secondary incised and punctated decoration (Fig. 5.6). One sherd is a modeled human face (Fig. 5.6a, slip color not shown). Pring (1977) described a modeled effigy jar from Kichpanha that is similar, although he identified it as belonging to the red Sierra Ceramic Group. I have examined the vessel currently in the vault of the Department of Archaeology of the Government of Belize in Belmopan and feel that it belongs more appropriately in the Joventud Ceramic Group. Two sherds (Fig. 5.6b, c) are incurving sided bowls with modeled faces on either a labial flange or labial eversion. The fourth modeled sherd (Fig. 5.6d) is a small adorno, from an unknown vessel

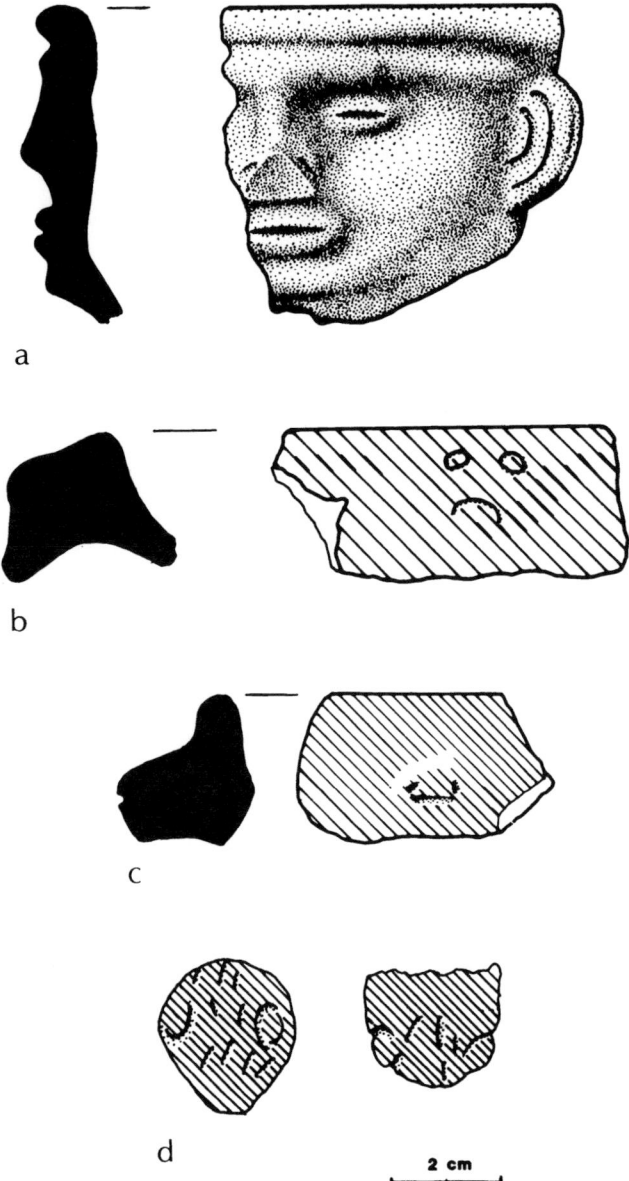

Figure 5.6. Joventud Ceramic Group pottery, modeled and incised.

form, that is in the shape of an unidentifiable animal head. Pring (1977) noted the presence of modeled faces in the Lopez Ceramic Complex.

*APPENDAGES:* None noted.
*INTRASITE DISTRIBUTION:* See Joventud Red: Palmasito Variety.
*INTERSITE DISTRIBUTION:* A red, unslipped, and impressed variety has been identified in the Joventud Ceramic Group at Uaxactun (Smith 1955; Smith and Gifford 1966). Modeling has been identified in the Joventud group at San Estevan (Pring 1977), at Uaxactun (Smith 1955), and at Altar de Sacrificios (Adams 1971). Pring (1977) identified a punctated (Melinda) type, an impressed (Resaca) type, an

appliquéd (Patos) type, and a black-on-red (Pinol) type in the Joventud group. I did not encounter sherds of these types in my sample, although they may occur at Cuello.

*TYPE:* Chunhinta Black.
*VARIETY:* Chunhinta.
*ESTABLISHED AS A TYPE OR VARIETY:* Smith and Gifford (1966). This description is based on 7 rim sherds.
*GROUP:* Chunhinta.
*WARE:* Flores Waxy.
*COMPLEX:* Lopez.
*SPHERE AFFILIATION:* Mamom.
*FREQUENCY:* 0.9 percent of the Lopez Ceramic Complex rim sherds.
*ILLUSTRATION:* Figure 5.7a.
*PRINCIPAL IDENTIFYING ATTRIBUTES:* Thick, soft, and dull black slip with a pronounced waxy feel; extensive fire crackling of the slip; outcurving sided dishes or plates with flat bases.
*PASTE, TEMPER, AND FIRING:* Paste color ranges from pale orange or brown to tan, buff, and as the dominant color a pale gray or brownish gray. Differential firing is common, leaving one side of the vessel darker than the other. Paste texture is medium grained, and all sherds have carbonate inclusions.
*SURFACE FINISH AND DECORATION:* All sherds are covered with a thick, soft, dull black slip that has a pronounced waxy feel. The slip scratches easily and erodes in a characteristic fashion, flaking off in patches. The color of the slip centers on 2.5YR N2.5/0 (black) and 2.5Y N2/0 (black), 2.5Y N3/0 (very dark gray). Occasionally the slip has a slight reddish cast to it (10R 2/1 reddish black, or 2.5YR 2/2 very dusky red). Fire clouding is common on all sherds, as is fire crackling.
*FORMS*
1. Outcurving sided dish or plate with direct or exteriorly thickened rim and round lip (57.1%). Rim diameter, 16–28 cm; wall thickness, 0.5–0.8 cm.
2. Incurving sided bowl with generally unrestricted orifice, interiorly thickened rim, and round lip (28.6%). Rim diameter, no measurement; wall thickness, 0.5–0.7 cm.
3. Flaring sided dish or bowl with everted rim and round lip (14.3%). Rim diameter, no measurement; wall thickness, 0.6 cm.
*APPENDAGES:* None noted in this collection. Pring (1977) identified a hollow foot and two spouts.
*INTRASITE DISTRIBUTION:* The type is defined on the basis of sealed levels of the Lopez phase material (Middle Preclassic) in the South Square excavations (grid squares 20/30, 25/30, 25/35, 20/35). Chunhinta Black continues throughout the Lopez Ceramic Complex without any apparent changes.
*INTERSITE DISTRIBUTION:* Pring (1977) identified small amounts of this type at almost all sites in northern

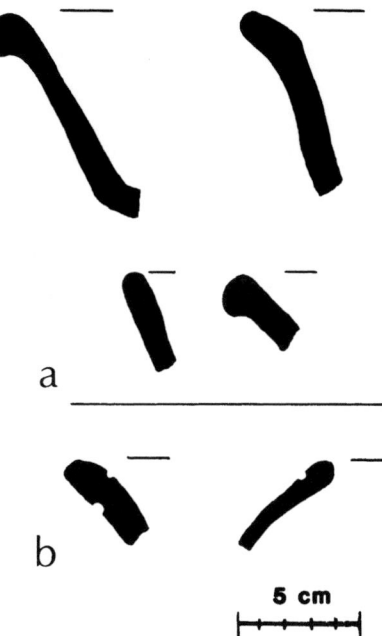

Figure 5.7. Chunhinta Ceramic Group pottery: *a*, Chunhinta Black: Chunhinta Variety; *b*, Deprecio Incised: Grooved-incised Variety.

Belize. The Cuello type is similar to Chunhinta Black from Uaxactun (Smith 1955; Smith and Gifford 1966), Altar de Sacrificios (Adams 1971), Barton Ramie (Gifford 1976), Seibal (Sabloff 1975), Yaxha-Sacnab (Rice 1979), Tikal, and the Capaz Variety of Chunhinta Black at Becan (Ball 1977a).

*TYPE:* Deprecio Incised.
*VARIETY:* Grooved-incised.
*ESTABLISHED AS A TYPE OR VARIETY:* Type, Smith and Gifford (1966). Variety, present work. Pring (1977) described a similar Unspecified Variety based on 12 sherds. This description is based on 9 rim sherds.
*GROUP:* Chunhinta.
*WARE:* Flores Waxy.
*COMPLEX:* Lopez.
*SPHERE AFFILIATION:* Mamom.
*FREQUENCY:* 1.1 percent of the Lopez Ceramic Complex rim sherds.
*ILLUSTRATION:* Figure 5.7b.
*PRINCIPAL IDENTIFYING ATTRIBUTES:* Slip color and texture the same as Chunhinta Black: Chunhinta Variety; secondary decoration of preslip groove-incising.
*PASTE, TEMPER, AND FIRING:* Same as Chunhinta Black: Chunhinta Variety.
*SURFACE FINISH AND DECORATION:* Slip color and texture the same as Chunhinta Black: Chunhinta Variety. Secondary decoration of preslip horizontal groove-incising is placed around the exterior of vessels and on the interior just below the rim.

48  Chapter 5

*FORMS*
1. Outcurving sided dish or plate with direct or exteriorly folded or everted rim and round lip (55.6%). Rim diameter, 24–38 cm; wall thickness, 0.5–0.8 cm.
2. Incurving sided bowl with generally unrestricted orifice, interiorly folded rim, and round lip (44.4%). Rim diameter, 16–24 cm; wall thickness, 0.4–0.8 cm.

*APPENDAGES:* None noted.

*INTRASITE DISTRIBUTION:* The type is defined on the basis of sealed levels of the Lopez phase material (Middle Preclassic) in the South Square excavations (grid squares 20/30, 25/30, 25/35, 20/35). Deprecio Incised continues throughout the Lopez Ceramic Complex without any apparent changes. Pring (1977) suggested the possibility that the Cuello type may be composed of two varieties, one with plain horizontal groove-incising and the other with more elaborate incised designs. Similar material at Tikal was divided into simple incised and design incised varieties by Culbert, but the sample from Cuello is too small to make such distinctions at this time.

*INTERSITE DISTRIBUTION:* For general discussion, see Chunhinta Black: Chunhinta Variety. The Cuello type is similar to Deprecio Incised at Uaxactun (Smith 1955; Smith and Gifford 1966), Altar de Sacrificios (Adams 1971), Barton Ramie (Gifford 1976), Seibal (Sabloff 1975), Yaxha-Sacnab (Rice 1979), Tikal, and Becan (Ball 1977a).


*TYPE:* Pital Cream.
*VARIETY:* Unspecified.
*ESTABLISHED AS A TYPE OR VARIETY:* Type, Smith and Gifford (1966). Variety, Pring (1977). Pring's description was based on 14 sherds. This description is based on 13 rim sherds.
*GROUP:* Pital.
*WARE:* Flores Waxy.
*COMPLEX:* Lopez.
*SPHERE AFFILIATION:* Mamom.
*FREQUENCY:* 1.6 percent of the Lopez Ceramic Complex rim sherds.
*ILLUSTRATION:* Figure 5.8a.
*PRINCIPAL IDENTIFYING ATTRIBUTES:* Thick, soft cream slip with a pronounced waxy feel; fire crackling, smudging, and clouding are extensive; outcurving sided dishes or plates with flat bases.
*PASTE, TEMPER, AND FIRING:* Paste color is tan, buff, or light brown in most cases, though differential firing occasionally causes the paste to turn a light or dark gray. Paste is medium textured with carbonate inclusions in all sherds.
*SURFACE FINISH AND DECORATION:* The color of the slip tends to be 7.5YR 7/2–7/4, 8/2–8/4 (pinkish gray, pink, and white) or 5YR 7/2, 8/2 (pinkish gray and pinkish white). However, the surfaces of all sherds are highly variable in color because of extensive fire clouding that causes patches of pink, red, black, or different shades of cream. The slip is soft, thick, and waxy. The slip tends to be extensively fire crackled and smudged, in addition to fire-clouded.

One sherd (Fig. 5.8b) in the Pital Ceramic Group is an unusual form. Irregular modeling creates the impression of chamfering on the exterior of an outcurving sided dish. Another sherd (Fig. 5.8c) may be Barranco Red-on-cream (Pring 1977). The sherd possesses a Pital Cream slip that is covered on the interior by a red slip. Perhaps intentionally, though probably due to firing and organic material in the slip clay, there is a dark black band around the exterior just below the rim. Although Barranco Red-on-cream is similar in form and decoration to Muxanal Red-on-cream, the cream slip on Barranco is very different from the cream of Muxanal and tends to be heavily fire clouded into black, red, orange, and pink colors. This sherd possesses that sort of cream slip.

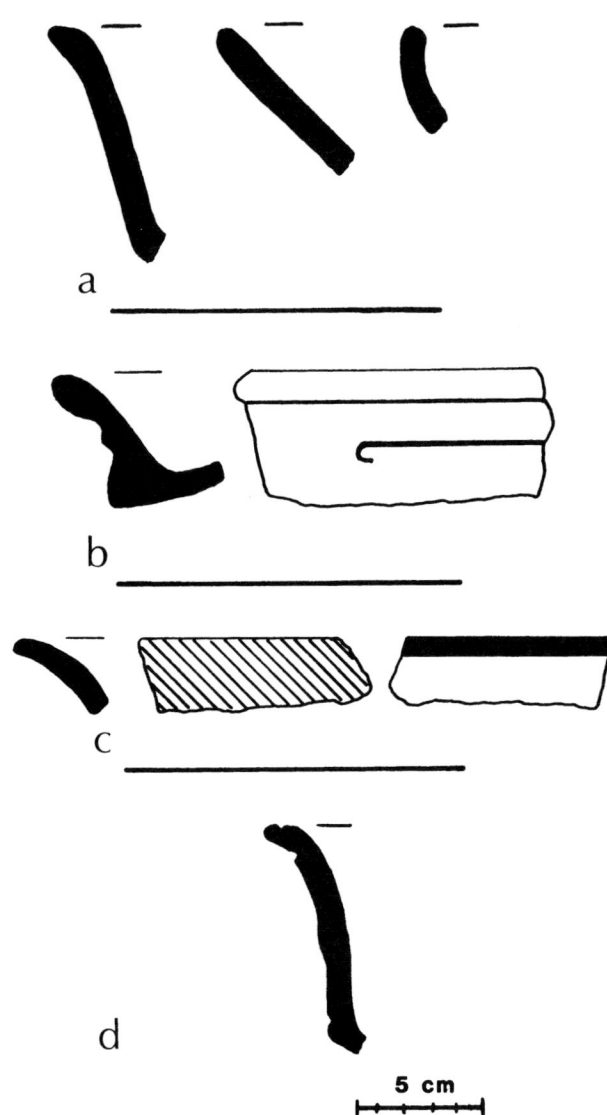

Figure 5.8. Pital Ceramic Group pottery: *a,* Pital Cream: Variety Unspecified; *b,* with modeling; *c,* with red-slipped interior and black rim band; *d,* Paso Danto Incised: Variety Unspecified.

*FORMS*
1. Outcurving sided dish or plate with direct, exteriorly folded, or everted rim, and round lip (46.1%). Rim diameter, 22–42 cm; wall thickness, 0.5–0.8 cm.
2. Incurving sided bowl with generally unrestricted orifice, slightly interiorly folded rim, and round lip (38.5%). Rim diameter, 16–34 cm; wall thickness, 0.5–0.7 cm.
3. Incurved-recurved sided bowl or dish with direct rim and round lip (15.4%). Rim diameter, 18–20 cm; wall thickness, 0.5 cm.
*APPENDAGES: Foot.* There is one solid foot, oval in cross section and about 5.5 cm in length to where it is broken. It is not known to what vessel form it belongs.
*INTRASITE DISTRIBUTION:* The type is defined on the basis of sealed levels of the Lopez phase material (Middle Preclassic) in the South Square excavations (grid squares 20/30, 25/30, 25/35, 20/35). Pital Cream continues throughout the Lopez Ceramic Complex without any apparent changes.
*INTERSITE DISTRIBUTION:* Pring (1977) identified the presence of this type at the site of San Estevan in northern Belize. Pring also suggested that with a larger sample it is probable that the Cuello variety of Pital Cream can be subsumed in the Pital Variety, although with the small sample size it seemed more appropriate to identify the variety as Unspecified. I am in accordance with Pring on this matter. Almost all Maya Lowland sites with Middle Preclassic ceramics possess sherds of Pital Cream. It is rare at Uaxactun (Smith 1955; Smith and Gifford 1966), at Altar de Sacrificios (Adams 1971), and at Yaxha-Sacnab (Rice 1979). It is present in larger numbers at Barton Ramie (Gifford 1976), at Seibal (Sabloff 1975), and at Becan (Ball 1977a). I follow both Pring (1977) and Sabloff (1975) in subsuming blotchy slipped material in the same variety with the purer cream slipped sherds, but at Altar de Sacrificios (Adams 1971) and Becan (Ball 1977a), a separate variety was created.

*TYPE:* Paso Danto Incised.
*VARIETY:* Unspecified.
*ESTABLISHED AS A TYPE OR VARIETY:* Type, Smith and Gifford (1966). Variety, Pring (1977). Pring's description was based on 3 rim sherds. This description is based on 1 rim sherd.
*GROUP:* Pital.
*WARE:* Flores Waxy.
*COMPLEX:* Lopez.
*SPHERE AFFILIATION:* Mamom.
*FREQUENCY:* 0.1 percent of the Lopez Ceramic Complex rim sherds.
*ILLUSTRATION:* Figure 5.8d.
*PRINCIPAL IDENTIFYING ATTRIBUTES:* Slip color and texture the same as Pital Cream; secondary decoration by preslip groove incising.
*PASTE, TEMPER, AND FIRING:* Same as Pital Cream: Unspecified Variety.
*SURFACE FINISH AND DECORATION:* For general description, see Pital Cream: Unspecified Variety. Secondary decoration is by horizontal, preslip groove-incising placed on the exterior near the rim and the base and on the interior just below the rim.
*FORMS:* Outcurving sided dish with exteriorly everted rim and round lip (1 example). Rim diameter, 35 cm; wall thickness, 0.5 cm.
*APPENDAGES:* None noted.
*INTRASITE DISTRIBUTION:* The type is defined on the basis of sealed levels of the Lopez phase material (Middle Preclassic) in the South Square excavations (grid squares 20/30, 25/30, 25/35, 20/35).
*INTERSITE DISTRIBUTION:* Pring (1977) identified one sherd of this type at San Estevan in northern Belize. The Cuello type is similar to Paso Danto Incised at Uaxactun (Smith 1955), at Seibal (Sabloff 1975), at Yaxha-Sacnab (Rice 1979), at Barton Ramie (Gifford 1976), and at Becan (Ball 1977a).

*TYPE:* Muxanal Red-on-cream.
*VARIETY:* San Lazaro.
*ESTABLISHED AS A TYPE OR VARIETY:* Type, Smith and Gifford (1966). Originally established as Lazaro Variety, (Pring 1977, Kosakowsky 1983). However, the name "Lazaro" has been used previously for an unrelated Late Classic red type at Lubaantun (Norman Hammond, 1975, Lubaantun: A Classic Maya Realm, *Monographs of the Peabody Museum* 2, Harvard University, Cambridge, Massachusetts). Thus the Cuello variety of Muxanal Red-on-cream has been renamed and it is established as San Lazaro Variety herein. Pring's description was based on 38 sherds and 1 whole vessel. This description is based on 4 body sherds and a total of 158 rim sherds, 23 from Lopez levels and 135 from Cocos levels.
*GROUP:* Muxanal.
*WARE:* Flores Waxy.
*COMPLEX:* Lopez.
*SPHERE AFFILIATION:* Mamom.
*FREQUENCY:* 19.2 percent of the Lopez Ceramic Complex rim sherds (body sherds not included in the frequency percentage).
*ILLUSTRATION:* Figure 5.9.
*PRINCIPAL IDENTIFYING ATTRIBUTES:* Primary slip that is thin and cream colored; secondary red slip on the interior of vessels and on the exterior in bands, dots, or other geometric designs; secondary decoration by preslip groove-incising in horizontal bands on the exterior of vessels; outcurving sided dishes or plates with flat bases.
*PASTE, TEMPER, AND FIRING:* Paste is buff, tan, light brown, or pinkish gray color. Differential firing occurs, leaving a darker core, though it is not common. Paste is medium textured and all sherds examined have carbonate inclusions.

50    Chapter 5

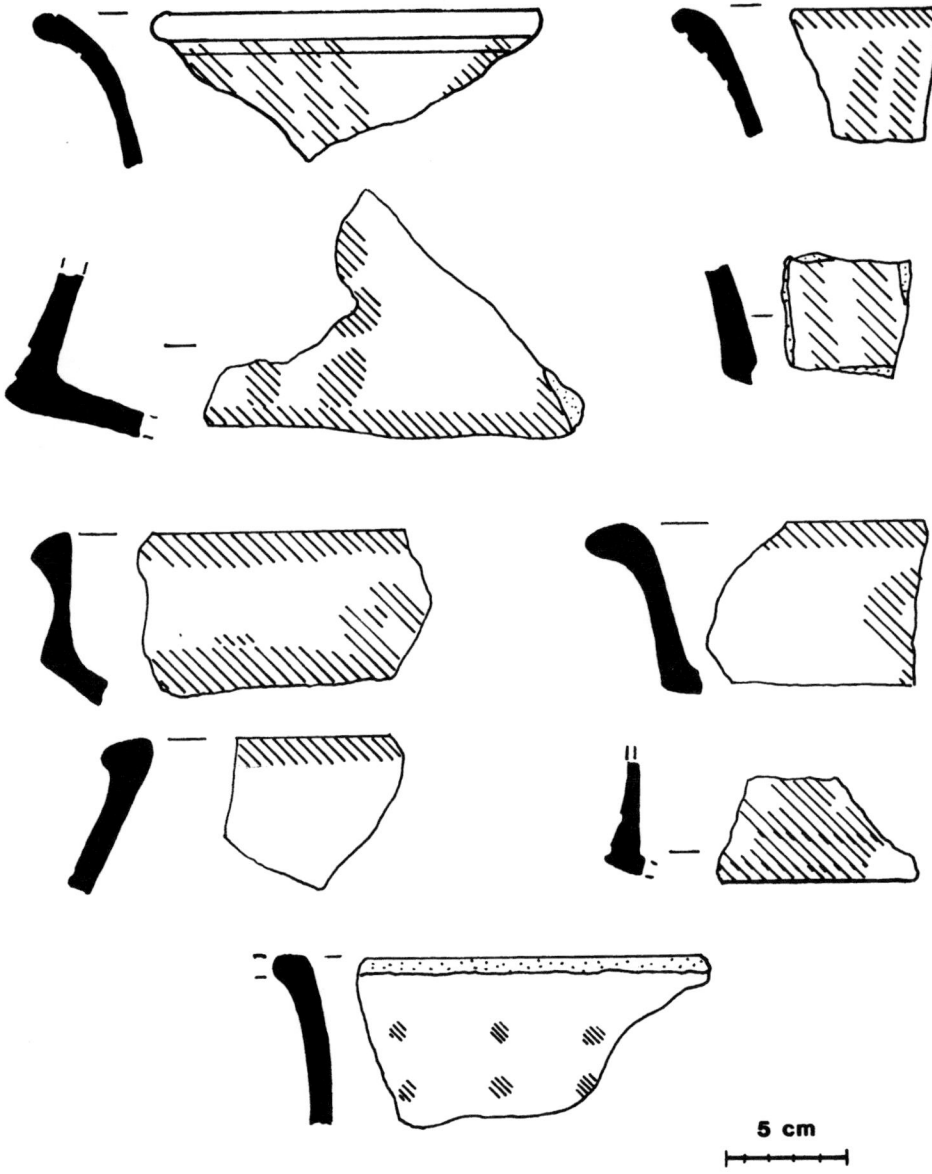

Figure 5.9. Muxanal Red-on-cream: San Lazaro Variety.

*SURFACE FINISH AND DECORATION:* A thin primary cream slip is applied over the interior and exterior of the vessel. The color of the slip is 10YR 8/2 (white), 7.5YR 8/2 (pinkish white), and 5YR 8/2, 8/4, 7/2, 7/3 (pinkish white, pinkish gray, and pink). A red, secondary slip is placed over the cream slip on vessel interiors, just over the rim on the exterior of outcurving sided dishes or plates, and on the basal portion of medial angle vessels. In addition, the red slip is applied in parallel diagonal bands or stripes, dots, or circles on the exterior of vessels. The color of this slip is the same as Joventud Red: Palmasito Variety (10R 4/6, 4/8, 5/6, 5/8 red). Often the exterior of outcurving sided dishes or plates is secondarily decorated with preslip horizontal groove-incisions placed around the base and just below the rim. Occasionally a vertical appliqué ridge divides design areas on the exterior of the vessel.

*FORMS*
1. Outcurving sided dish or plate with direct or exteriorly everted rim and round lip (90.5%). Rim diameter, 26–48 cm; wall thickness, 0.4–0.9 cm.
2. Incurved-recurved sided bowl with sharp medial angle or break, direct or exteriorly folded rim, and round lip (6.9%). The bottom half of the exterior of this vessel form is slipped red, with decoration restricted to the upper portion. Rim diameter, 16–32 cm; wall thickness 0.5–0.8 cm.
3. Incurved-recurved sided bowl or dish with direct or exteriorly folded rim and round lip (1.3%). Rim diameter, 16–28 cm; wall thickness, 0.5–0.8 cm.
4. Flaring sided bowl or dish with direct or slightly exteriorly thickened rim and round lip (1.3%). Rim diameter, 22–34 cm; wall thickness 0.5–0.7 cm.

*APPENDAGES:* None noted.

*INTRASITE DISTRIBUTION:* The variety is defined on the basis of sealed levels of the Lopez phase material (Middle Preclassic) in the South Square excavations (grid squares 20/30, 25/30, 25/35, 20/35). San Lazaro Variety continues throughout the Lopez Ceramic Complex without any apparent changes.

*INTERSITE DISTRIBUTION:* Pring (1977) identified the presence of this type at San Estevan, Nohmul, Colha, Santa Rita, and Caledonia in northern Belize. The Cuello type is broadly similar to Muxanal Red-on-cream at Uaxactun (Smith 1955; Smith and Gifford 1966) and to the small amounts at Altar de Sacrificios (Adams 1971). It is similar to the Muxanal Red-on-cream at Yaxha-Sacnab (Rice 1979), although I am in disagreement with Rice's placement of this type in the Pital Ceramic Group. It is most similar to the Comprimido Variety of Muxanal Red-on-cream at Becan (Ball 1977a). I am in agreement with both Ball and Pring (1977) in the creation of a ceramic group separate from Pital for this material, because the cream slip on Muxanal Red-on-cream is dissimilar to the cream slip of the Pital Ceramic Group.

*OTHER MUXANAL CERAMIC GROUP POTTERY:* Unspecified.
    *WARE:* Flores Waxy.
    *COMPLEX:* Lopez.
    *SPHERE AFFILIATION:* Mamom.
    *FREQUENCY:* 0.1 percent of the Lopez Ceramic Complex rim sherds. This description is based on 1 rim sherd and 2 body sherds not included in the frequency percentage.
    *ILLUSTRATION:* Figure 5.10.
    *PRINCIPAL IDENTIFYING ATTRIBUTES:* Primary slip that is thin and cream colored, same as the San Lazaro Variety; secondary red slip in various designs; decoration with modeling, incising, punctating, and impressing.
    *PASTE, TEMPER, AND FIRING:* Same as Muxanal Red-on-cream: San Lazaro Variety.
    *SURFACE FINISH AND DECORATION:* For general discussion, see Muxanal Red-on-cream: San Lazaro Variety. Additional decoration is primarily in the form of modeling to create human and animal faces, with the use of punctating, incising, and impressing to create the features of the faces.
    *FORMS:* It is uncertain to what forms these sherds belong. Only one is a rim; it appears to belong to a vessel that is outcurving at the rim, but in fact may be recurving below. This sherd is modeled in the appearance of a human face (Fig. 5.10a). Another sherd appears to be an effigy of a monkeylike animal (Fig. 5.10c). The third sherd is a small adorno in the shape of an unknown animal. From the curvature of the vessel wall, it would appear to belong to an incurving sided bowl or dish (Fig. 5.10b).
    *APPENDAGES:* None noted.
    *INTRASITE DISTRIBUTION:* These sherds came from sealed levels of the Lopez phase material (Middle Preclassic) in the South Square excavations (grid squares 20/30, 25/30,

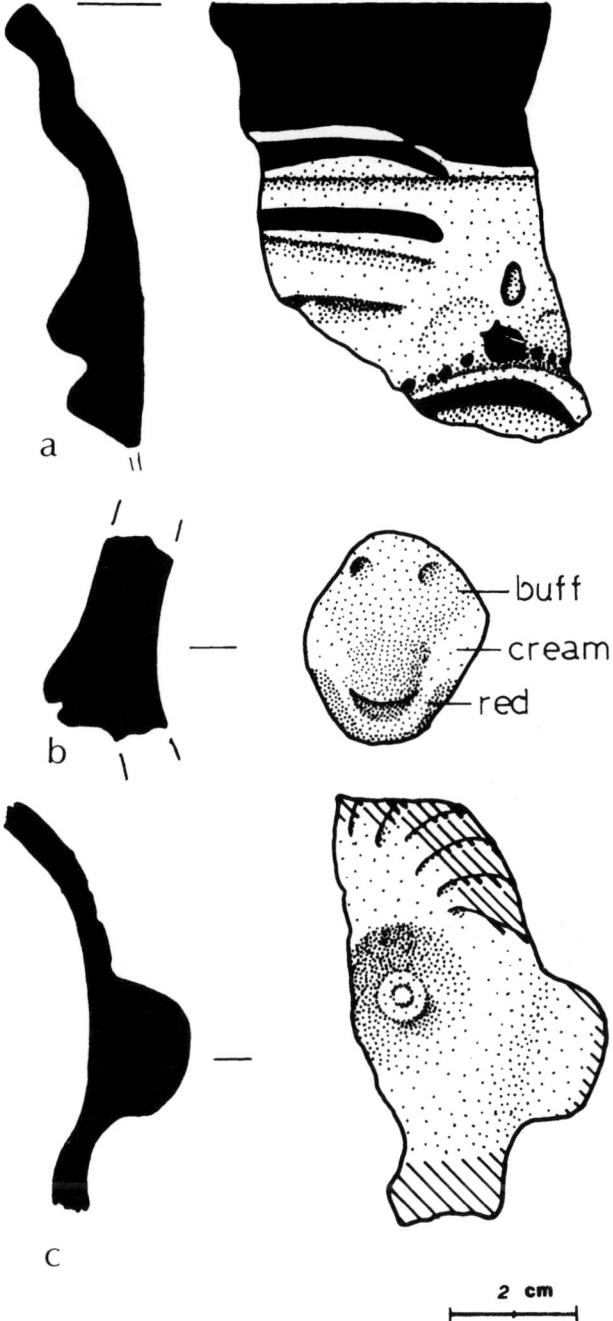

Figure 5.10. Muxanal Ceramic Group pottery, unspecified, with modeling.

25/35, 20/35). Muxanal modeled pieces may first appear only in the later Lopez phase levels, although the sample size is too small to be certain.
    *INTERSITE DISTRIBUTION:* Pring (1977) tentatively identified Muxanal modeling at El Pozito in northern Belize. In addition, it is similar to modeled vessels from the Mamom horizon at Uaxactun (Smith 1955). Modeling is present in the Acachen Ceramic Complex at Becan (Ball 1977a) and at Altar de Sacrificios (Adams 1971).

*TYPE:* Chicago Orange.
*VARIETY:* Warrie Camp.
*ESTABLISHED AS A TYPE OR VARIETY:* Pring (1977). Pring's description was based on 6 rim sherds. This description is based on 1 whole vessel and 273 rim sherds, 63 from Lopez levels and 210 from Cocos levels.
*GROUP:* Chicago.
*WARE:* Fort George Orange.
*COMPLEX:* Lopez.
*SPHERE AFFILIATION:* Mamom.
*FREQUENCY:* 33.3 percent of the Lopez Ceramic Complex rim sherds.
*ILLUSTRATION:* Figure 5.11.
*PRINCIPAL IDENTIFYING ATTRIBUTES:* Thin nonlustrous slip or wash of a pale orange color, often incompletely oxidized to buff-orange; short to long outcurving necked jars with round lips.
*PASTE, TEMPER, AND FIRING:* Paste color is broadly similar to the Chicago and Nago Bank varieties of Chicago Orange. It is usually a pale orange color but tends to be a pale buff, light brown, or pinkish orange. Paste color is normally reflected in surface color and finish. The paste is fine, medium, and coarse textured, and almost all sherds have carbonate inclusions. Differential firing is common, leaving a darker core.
*SURFACE FINISH AND DECORATION:* Surface color is similar to the Chicago and Nago Bank varieties of Chicago Orange. The color centers on 5YR 7/4 (pink), but includes sherds that are 5YR 7/1–7/6 (light gray, pinkish gray, pink, and reddish yellow), and 7.5YR 7/2–7/4 (pinkish gray and gray). The surface color reflects the paste color and is achieved through the application of a thin slip or wash. The slip is usually nonlustrous and weathers easily. Fire clouding occurs occasionally, although more frequently incomplete oxidation produces a buff-orange color. The Lopez Warrie Camp Variety of Chicago Orange is difficult to separate from the earlier Chicago Variety in the Swasey Ceramic Complex and the Nago Bank Variety in the Bladen Ceramic Complex. It is probable that the sample size of this type has been elevated by the inclusion of redeposited Early Preclassic varieties of Chicago Orange. This is a difficult sorting problem that as yet is unresolved.

Two sherds from the same vessel, a short outcurving necked jar with direct rim and round lip have fingernail impressions in two rows around the neck body juncture (Fig. 5.11, bottom). Otherwise, there are no decorations on the Lopez variety of Chicago Orange.

Pring (1977) originally identified a buff group, Machiquila, in the Lopez Ceramic Complex at Cuello. As indicated previously, it is my opinion that the buff and orange sherds form a continuum, with the incompletely oxidized material tending to buff-orange and the completely oxidized pottery to a purer orange color. It is probable, therefore, that the range of variation in my definition of Chicago Orange in-

Figure 5.11. Chicago Orange: Warrie Camp Variety.

cludes Pring's Machiquila Buff. The whole vessel Pring (1977, Fig. 44) identified as part of the Machiquila Ceramic Group is more appropriately placed in the Pital Ceramic Group, although it is unusually heavily mottled and fire clouded, even for Pital Cream.

*FORMS*

1. Short outcurving necked jar with direct rim and round lip (21.2%). Rim diameter, 16–28 cm; wall thickness, 0.5–0.7 cm; neck height, 1.5–2.8 cm.

2. Medium to long outcurving necked jar with direct rim and round lip (17.2%). Rim diameter, 18–32 cm; wall thickness, 0.5–0.7 cm; neck height, 3.0–5.0 cm.

3. Outcurving sided dish or plate with direct or exteriorly folded or everted rim and round lip (16.5%). Rim diameter, 16–36 cm; wall thickness, 0.5–0.8 cm.

4. Incurving sided bowl with unrestricted orifice, direct or interiorly folded rim, and round lip (10.6%). Rim diameter, 18–30 cm; wall thickness, 0.5–0.8 cm.

5. Incurved-recurved sided bowl or dish with direct or exteriorly folded rim and round lip (8.1%). Rim diameter, 16–24 cm; wall thickness, 0.5–0.8 cm.

6. Short vertical necked jar with direct rim and round lip (8.1%). Rim diameter, 12–25 cm; wall thickness, 0.5–0.8 cm; neck height, 1.2–2.0 cm.

7. Short flaring necked jar with direct rim and round lip (4.0%). Rim diameter, 16–30 cm; wall thickness, 0.5–0.8 cm; neck height, 1.5–2.8 cm.

8. Vertical sided bowl or dish with direct or exteriorly thickened rim and round lip (4.0%). Rim diameter, 14–28 cm; wall thickness, 0.4–0.7 cm.

9. Long flaring necked jar with direct rim and round lip (3.3%). Rim diameter, 22–36 cm; wall thickness, 0.5–0.8 cm; neck height, 2.8–4.6 cm.

10. Long vertical necked jar with direct rim and round lip (2.2%). Rim diameter, 24–38 cm; wall thickness, 0.5–0.8 cm; neck height, 2.5–4.2 cm.

11. Incurving sided bowl with restricted orifice (tecomate), interiorly folded rim, and round lip (2.2%). Rim diameter, 10–18 cm; wall thickness, 0.4–0.7 cm.

12. Flaring sided bowl or dish with direct or exteriorly thickened rim and round lip (1.5%). Rim diameter, 18–32 cm; wall thickness, 0.5–0.7 cm.

13. Vertical to slightly tapered bottle neck with exteriorly folded rim and round or beveled out lip (1.1%). It is possible that this form is actually an Early Preclassic shape, but the difficulty of differentiating between the Early and Middle Preclassic varieties of Chicago Orange makes the placement of the bottle form in doubt. The fact that the bottle form occurs in the red Joventud Ceramic Group suggests that it may be appropriate to place the bottle form in the Lopez variety of Chicago Orange as well. Rim diameter, 4.5 cm; wall thickness, 0.5–0.7 cm.

*APPENDAGES: Handles.* One nubbin handle is about 1.0 cm high, a second handle is a simple loop, and a third is a loop handle that is deeply gouged-incised to give the appearance of three attached cylinders.

*Spout.* There is one unsupported spout, oval in section, and about 5.5 cm long to where it is broken.

*Feet.* There are two hollow rounded feet, perhaps belonging to the monopod bottle form (Brainerd 1958). The feet are round to slightly oval in cross section and are about 6.0 cm long to where they are broken.

*INTRASITE DISTRIBUTION:* The type is defined on the basis of sealed levels of the Lopez phase material (Middle Preclassic) in the South Square excavations (grid squares 20/30, 25/30, 25/35, 20/35). Warrie Camp Variety continues throughout the Lopez Ceramic Complex without any apparent changes.

*INTERSITE DISTRIBUTION:* Pring (1977) identified the presence of this type at San Estevan, Nohmul, and Colha in northern Belize. There are no other known comparisons for the Middle Preclassic at other sites. Chicago Orange: Warrie Camp Variety does not seem to be related to Mars Orange, the major Middle Preclassic orange ware at other Lowland Maya sites.

CHAPTER SIX

# Cocos Ceramic Complex

The Cocos Ceramic Complex spans a period from about 400 B.C. to A.D. 250. The selected sample intensively analyzed from Cocos levels consists of 2,437 rim sherds, 65 diagnostic body sherds, and 77 whole vessels. The complex is composed of 8 ceramic groups and 23 types and varieties, and the relative frequencies of the groups are given in Table 6.1. As indicated, 95.9 percent of the Cocos Ceramic Complex is slipped, as Richardson Peak (?) and Sapote are the only unslipped groups. Of the slipped pottery, 22.7 percent is decorated in some fashion by incising (2.7%), punctating (0.5%), impressing (0.1%), appliqué (only body sherds), modeling (0.1%), with dichrome slips (13.4%), or with composite decoration (5.9%).

The Cocos Ceramic Complex is defined on the basis of work by Pring (1977) and by this research. The Cocos material is stratigraphically later than that of the preceding Lopez complex, and is identified in the South Square excavations on Platform 34 (in grid squares 20/30, 25/30, 25/35, 20/35) and in the North Square excavations (in grid squares 40/30, 45/30, 45/35, 40/35). It thus comprises the Late Preclassic occupation of the site of Cuello and the ceramics belong securely within the Chicanel Ceramic Sphere.

Table 6.1. Classification of Pottery in the Cocos Ceramic Complex
(Group frequency based on 2437 rim sherds)

| Ware | Group | Type | Variety |
|---|---|---|---|
| Uaxactun Unslipped | Richardson Peak* (3.4%) | Richardson Peak Unslipped | Richardson Peak Variety (Cocos) |
| | Sapote (0.7%) | Sapote Striated | Variety Unspecified |
| Paso Caballo Waxy | Sierra (72.9%) | Sierra Red | Ahuacan Variety |
| | | Ahchab Red-and-buff | Variety Unspecified |
| | | Sierra Red | Sierra Variety |
| | | Sierra Red | Big Pond Variety |
| | | Society Hall Red | Society Hall Variety |
| | | Society Hall Red | Bound to Shine Variety |
| | | Society Hall Red | Unnamed Variety (dichrome) |
| | | Laguna Verde Incised | Grooved-incised Variety |
| | | Launga Verde Incised | Laguna Verde Variety |
| | | Lagartos Punctated | Lagartos Variety |
| | | Repollo Impressed | Variety Unspecified |
| | | Union Appliquéd | Variety Unspecified |
| | | Puletan Red-and-unslipped | Puletan Variety |
| | | Puletan Red-and-unslipped | Unnamed Variety |
| | | Other Sierra Ceramic Group | Unspecified (18 modeled) |
| | Polvero (2.4%) | Polvero Black | Polvero Variety |
| | | Lechugal Incised | Grooved-incised Variety |
| | Flor (1.0%) | Flor Cream | Variety Unspecified |
| | Matamore (3.2%) | Matamore Dichrome | Matamore Variety |
| | Escobal (0.6%) | Escobal Red-on-buff | Variety Unspecified |
| Fort George Orange | Chicago (15.8%) | Chicago Orange | Chucun Variety |
| | | Chicago Orange | Chucun Variety (Black-rimmed) |

*Pending comparisons with other unslipped groups of Uaxactun Unslipped Ware.

[54]

## TYPE DESCRIPTIONS
### (Chicanel Ceramic Sphere)

*TYPE:* Richardson Peak Unslipped.
*VARIETY:* Richardson Peak (Cocos).
*ESTABLISHED AS A TYPE OR VARIETY:* Pring (1977). Pring's description was based on 370 sherds, of which 70 were rims. This description is based on 84 rim sherds, 1 body sherd, and 2 whole vessels.
*GROUP:* Richardson Peak (?).
*WARE:* Uaxactun Unslipped.
*COMPLEX:* Cocos.
*SPHERE AFFILIATION:* Chicanel.
*FREQUENCY:* 3.4 percent of the Cocos Ceramic Complex rim sherds (body sherd not included in the frequency percentage).
*ILLUSTRATION:* Figure 6.1.
*PRINCIPAL IDENTIFYING ATTRIBUTES:* Rough surfaces that are gray, tan, or buff; jar forms with medium to high outcurving necks.
*PASTE, TEMPER, AND FIRING:* Paste color is variable and ranges from gray to brown, tan, and buff. Differential firing is common, leaving one side of the vessel darker than the other. Paste texture is medium to coarse grained, and all sherds possess carbonate inclusions that are large in size and angular in shape. About two percent of all sherds have mica inclusions that give off a reflected glitter.
*SURFACE FINISH AND DECORATION:* Paste color reflects surface color and is variable. The color ranges from 5YR 6/4 (light reddish brown), 5YR 6/6 (reddish yellow), 10YR 6/1–6/4 (gray to light yellowish brown), to 2.5Y 5/2–6/2 (grayish brown to light brownish gray). The darker range of colors usually occurs on the interiors of the vessels as a result of differential firing. Neither surface is well-smoothed, and texture is rough to the touch as a result of both the lack of smoothing and the carbonate inclusions that often extrude through the surface. Fire clouding is common.
*FORMS:* Two fragmentary ring bases of this type were noted.
1. Wide mouthed jar with long outcurving neck, direct exteriorly folded or thickened rim, and round lip (29.8%). Rim diameter, 18–42 cm; wall thickness, 0.9–1.4 cm; neck height, 2.0–4.5 cm.
2. Short vertical necked jar with direct, folded, or thickened rim and round lip (21.4%). Rim diameter, 14–26 cm; wall thickness, 0.7–0.9 cm; neck height, 1.2–3.2 cm.
3. Wide mouthed jar with short outcurving neck, direct or exteriorly folded rim, and round lip (13.1%). Rim diameter, 15–32 cm; wall thickness, 0.7–1.2 cm; neck height, 1.0–2.2 cm.
4. Long vertical or insloping necked jar with direct or exteriorly folded rim and round lip (9.5%). Rim diameter, 18–35 cm; wall thickness, 0.8–1.2 cm; neck height, 1.8–4.6 cm.
5. Wide mouthed jar with medium to high flaring neck, direct or exteriorly folded rim, and round lip (8.3%). Rim diameter, 18–34 cm; wall thickness, 0.8–1.2 cm; neck height, 1.8–4.0 cm.
6. Outcurving sided bowl or dish with direct or exteriorly folded rim and round lip (8.3%). Rim diameter, 15–36 cm; wall thickness, 0.6–0.9 cm.
7. Flaring sided dish or plate with interiorly thickened rim and round or square lip (6.0%). Rim diameter, 18–22 cm; wall thickness, 0.6–1.0 cm.
8. Incurving sided bowl with slightly restricted orifice, direct or interiorly thickened rim, and round lip (3.6%). Rim diameter, 16–35 cm; wall thickness, 0.7–0.9 cm.
*APPENDAGES:* None noted.
*INTRASITE DISTRIBUTION:* This variety of Richardson Peak Unslipped is defined on the basis of sealed levels of the Cocos phase material (Late Preclassic) in the South Square excavations (grid squares 20/30, 25/30, 25/35, 20/35) and in the North Square excavations (grid squares 40/30, 45/30, 45/35, 40/35). This variety continues throughout the Cocos Ceramic Complex without any apparent changes. In fact,

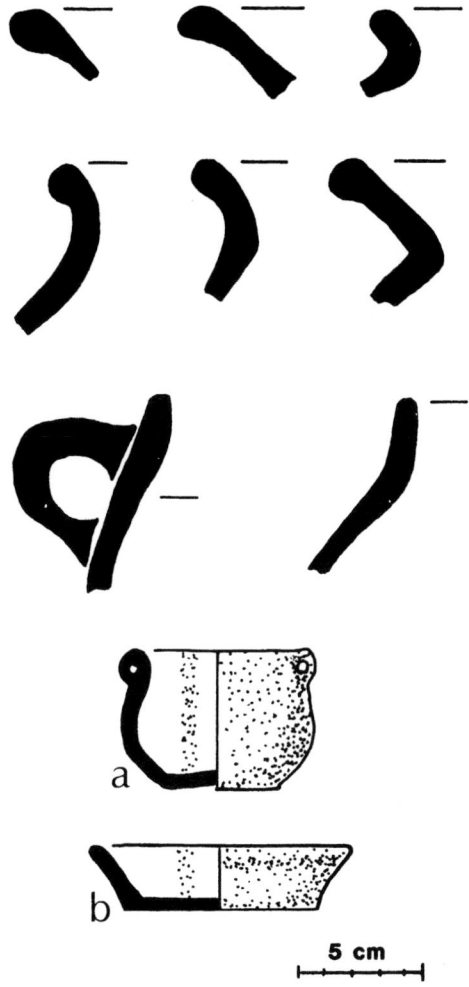

Figure 6.1. Richardson Peak Unslipped: Richardson Peak Variety (Cocos).

as indicated previously, the unslipped variety of the preceding Lopez Ceramic Complex is difficult to differentiate from the Cocos unslipped variety. This presents a difficult sorting problem when examining the paste and surface characteristics of the Middle and Late Preclassic unslipped types. There are vessel form differences, as described above, that aid with classification.

*INTERSITE DISTRIBUTION:* Pring (1977) identified this type at Santa Rita, Nohmul, San Estevan, Chowacol, and Colha in northern Belize and the unslipped type from Cuello is similar to unslipped material from most other sites in the Maya Lowlands. Until more detailed comparisons are made, the Cuello unslipped type is placed in its own ceramic group, Richardson Peak.


*TYPE:* Sapote Striated.
*VARIETY:* Unspecified.
*ESTABLISHED AS A TYPE OR VARIETY:* Smith and Gifford (1966). This description is based on 17 rim sherds and 24 body sherds.
*GROUP:* Sapote.
*WARE:* Uaxactun Unslipped.
*COMPLEX:* Cocos.
*SPHERE AFFILIATION:* Chicanel.
*FREQUENCY:* 0.7 percent of the Cocos Ceramic Complex rim sherds (body sherds not included in the frequency percentage).
*ILLUSTRATION:* Figure 6.2.
*PRINCIPAL IDENTIFYING ATTRIBUTES:* Unslipped surfaces with irregular striations on body and neck; jar forms with medium to high outcurving or flaring neck; rims that are exteriorly thickened or folded.
*PASTE, TEMPER, AND FIRING:* Paste color is variable, ranging from brown to tan and buff, and less commonly gray. Differential firing is present in half of all sherds, producing one side of the vessel that is darker than the other and occasionally a darker core. Paste texture is medium to coarse grained and crumbles when broken. Carbonate inclusions are present in all sherds, and mica is in about 45 percent of the sherds.
*SURFACE FINISH AND DECORATION:* Paste color reflects surface color and ranges from 5YR 6/1–6/2 (gray to pinkish gray), 5YR 7/1–7/2 (light gray to pinkish gray), to 5YR 6/3 (light reddish brown). The surfaces of the vessels are only minimally smoothed. Striations are generally vertical and occur on the neck and body of the exterior of vessels, but there appears to be no regularity in their application. Vessels of Sapote Striated usually are thinner walled than those of Richardson Peak Unslipped, so in cases where the striations are eroded, Sapote Striated is still easily identifiable.
*FORMS*
1. Medium to high outcurving necked jar with exteriorly thickened or folded rim and round or beveled out lip (70.5%). Rim diameter, 16–34 cm; wall thickness, 0.5–1.1 cm; neck height, 1.8–5.2 cm.
2. Short outcurving necked jar with exteriorly thickened or folded rim and round or beveled out lip (11.8%). Rim diameter, 15–28 cm; wall thickness, 0.5–0.9 cm; neck height, 0.8–1.5 cm.
3. Short flaring necked jar with direct or exteriorly thickened rim and round lip (11.8%). Rim diameter, 14–30 cm; wall thickness, 0.7–0.9 cm; neck height, 0.7–1.2 cm.
4. Flaring sided bowl or dish with exteriorly folded rim and beveled out lip (5.9%). Rim diameter, 17 cm; wall thickness, 0.8 cm.
*APPENDAGES:* None noted.
*INTRASITE DISTRIBUTION:* The type is defined on the basis of sealed levels of the Cocos phase material (Late Preclassic) in the South Square excavations (grid squares 20/30, 25/30, 25/35, 20/35) and in the North Square excavations (grid squares 40/30, 45/30, 45/35, 40/35). The type makes its appearance in the later Cocos levels.
*INTERSITE DISTRIBUTION:* The type is present at Nohmul, San Estevan, and Cerros in late Chicanel deposits (Pring 1977; Robertson-Freidel 1980). Sapote Striated is found at most Lowland Maya sites, although many of the Late Preclassic striated types at other sites do not have striations on the neck.

Figure 6.2. Sapote Striated: Variety Unspecified.

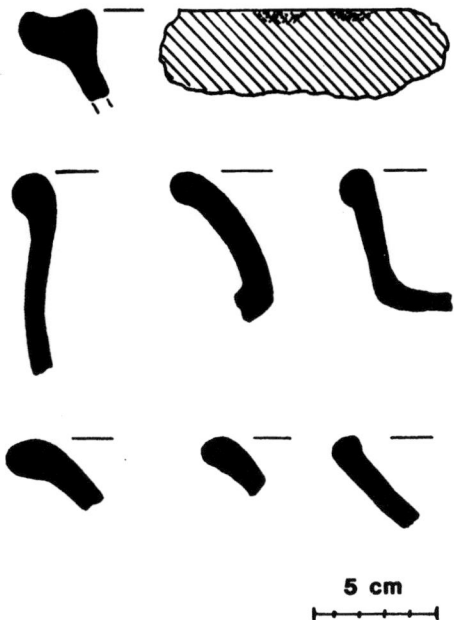

Figure 6.3. Sierra Red: Ahuacan Variety.

*TYPE:* Sierra Red.
*VARIETY:* Ahuacan.
*ESTABLISHED AS A TYPE OR VARIETY:* Variety established by Culbert in the Tikal ceramic analysis. This description is based on 111 rim sherds and 2 whole vessels.
*GROUP:* Sierra.
*WARE:* Paso Caballo Waxy.
*COMPLEX:* Cocos.
*SPHERE AFFILIATION:* Chicanel (Early).
*FREQUENCY:* 4.5 percent of the Cocos Ceramic Complex rim sherds.
*ILLUSTRATIONS:* Figures 6.3, 6.29c, d.
*PRINCIPAL IDENTIFYING ATTRIBUTES:* Soft, red, and faintly waxy slip that scratches easily; fire clouding to orange and yellow is common; outcurving sided vessels.
*PASTE, TEMPER, AND FIRING:* Paste color is variable, ranging from tan or buff to light orange or pink. The paste is medium textured and tends to crumble. All sherds possess carbonate inclusions and about 20 percent also have crushed sherd temper. Dark cores are uncommon.
*SURFACE FINISH AND DECORATION:* The surfaces of the vessels are well-smoothed. A red slip is applied over the interior and exterior of vessels. The color of the slip centers on 2.5YR 5/8 (red), but tends to be patchy and have lighter orange and yellow areas due to firing. These areas are usually 5YR 6/8 (reddish yellow). Fire clouding, crackling, and crazing occur on most sherds. The slip is soft, thick, and weathers easily. Ahuacan appears to be a transitional variety between Joventud Red and the Sierra Variety of Sierra Red at Cuello. At this site it presents a sorting problem because it tends to have surface characteristics similar to Joventud Red, with vessel forms and rim and lip treatments similar to Sierra Red: Sierra Variety, emphasizing its early placement in the complex.
*FORMS*
1. Outcurving sided bowl or dish with exteriorly folded rim and round lip (49.6%). Rim diameter, 16–24 cm; wall thickness, 0.5–0.8 cm.
2. Outcurving sided bucket with exteriorly folded or everted rim and round lip (20.7%). Rim diameter, 20–32 cm; wall thickness, 0.6–0.8 cm.
3. Incurving sided bowl with unrestricted orifice, interiorly folded rim, and round lip (9.8%). One piece has a labial flange. Rim diameter, 16–25 cm; wall thickness, 0.6–0.8 cm.
4. Flaring sided bowl or dish with exteriorly folded rim and round lip (9.8%). Rim diameter, 16–28 cm; wall thickness, 0.5–0.8 cm.
5. Medium to long outcurving necked jar or "chocolate pot" with exteriorly folded rim and round lip (8.1%). Rim diameter, 12–20 cm; wall thickness, 0.5–0.7 cm; neck height, 1.8–2.6 cm. The whole vessel of this form (Fig. 6.29d) is additionally decorated with punctation at the neck-body juncture.
6. Recurving sided bowl or dish with exteriorly folded rim and round lip (2%). Rim diameter, 18–26 cm; wall thickness, 0.5–0.8 cm. One whole vessel is almost a cuspidor shape but is a bit squat in height (Fig. 6.29c).
*APPENDAGES: Handle.* There is one loop handle from an unknown vessel form.
*Spouts.* There are two spouts that are circular in cross section and broken off at the end, and one of the whole vessels is a spouted "chocolate pot" (see Fig. 6.29d). The spouts are all about 5.0 cm in length and 2.0 cm in diameter.
*INTRASITE DISTRIBUTION:* Ahuacan Variety is defined on the basis of sealed levels of the lower Cocos phase material (early Late Preclassic) in the South Square excavations (grid squares 20/30, 25/30, 25/35, 20/35). Ahuacan first appears in the early Cocos levels and is used along with the Sierra Variety in the early Late Preclassic at Cuello. It apparently has a short-lived usage at Cuello, where it is replaced later entirely by the Sierra Variety.
*INTERSITE DISTRIBUTION:* The variety was originally defined by Culbert in the Tzec Ceramic Complex at Tikal, which is a transitional Mamom-Chicanel complex. In Culbert's examination of the Cuello collection, he identified the presence of the same transitional material. There are no other known comparisons.

*TYPE:* Ahchab Red-and-Buff.
*VARIETY:* Unspecified.
*ESTABLISHED AS A TYPE OR VARIETY:* Type established by Culbert in the Tikal ceramic analysis. Variety, present work. This description is based on 83 rim sherds and 1 whole vessel.

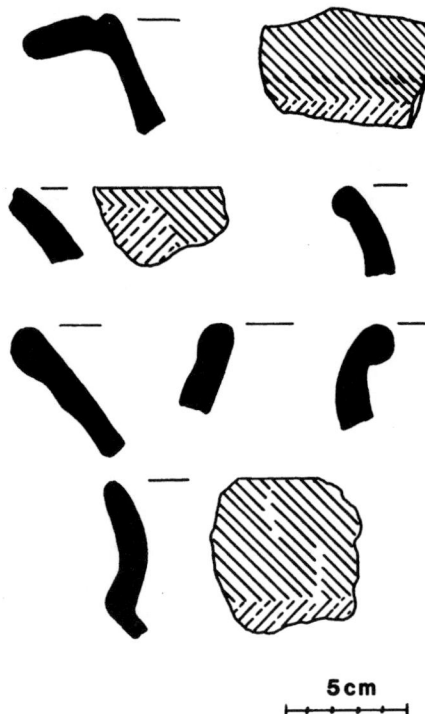

Figure 6.4. Ahchab Red-and-buff: Variety Unspecified.

*GROUP:* Sierra.
*WARE:* Paso Caballo Waxy.
*COMPLEX:* Cocos.
*SPHERE AFFILIATION:* Chicanel (Early).
*FREQUENCY:* 3.3 percent of the Cocos Ceramic Complex rim sherds.
*ILLUSTRATIONS:* Figures 6.4, 6.29f.
*PRINCIPAL IDENTIFYING ATTRIBUTES:* Application of a buff slip, over which is placed a resist agent and then a red slip; red slip similar to Sierra Red: Ahuacan Variety; outcurving sided vessels.
*PASTE, TEMPER, AND FIRING:* Slip color is variable, ranging from tan or buff to a light orange or pink. Paste texture is medium and all sherds contain carbonate inclusions. Differential firing is not common.
*SURFACE FINISH AND DECORATION:* The surfaces of vessels are well-smoothed and carry a buff slip. The buff is variable in color and ranges from 5YR 6/4 (light reddish brown), 5YR 7/4 (pink), 5YR 6/6, 7/6 (reddish yellow), to 7.5YR 6/4 (light brown), and 7.5YR 6/6, 7/6 (reddish yellow). The buff slip is covered with a resist agent and then a red slip is applied of the same color as Sierra Red: Ahuacan Variety. The boundaries between the two colors are not well defined in most cases, although one or two sherds and the whole vessel (Fig. 6.29f) have defined edges between the red and buff. Design patterns appear to be irregular, with patchy areas of red and buff occurring on the exterior of vessels and solid red on the interior of vessels. It is probable that some Ahchab Red-and-buff sherds were included in Sierra Red: Ahuacan Variety because they lacked areas that showed the two-color decoration. From the descriptions one might suppose a sorting problem exists between Matamore Dichrome and Ahchab Red-and-buff. However, Matamore is much glossier and appears later in time than Ahchab. Furthermore, Ahchab Red-and-buff clearly utilizes a resist technique; Matamore Dichrome apparently is a two-slip process that may or may not use a resist agent, causing the boundaries between slip colors on Matamore to be clearly defined.

*FORMS*

1. Outcurving sided bowl with exteriorly folded rim and round lip (65.2%). Rim diameter, 18–34 cm; wall thickness, 0.5–0.8 cm. One whole vessel is a cuspidor shape (Fig. 6.29f) with a double ridge on the exterior below the rim.
2. Flaring sided bowl with exteriorly folded rim and round lip (10.8%). Rim diameter, 18–28 cm; wall thickness, 0.5–0.9 cm. One example has a labial flange.
3. Incurving sided bowl with interiorly folded rim and round lip (9.6%). Rim diameter, 16–22 cm; wall thickness, 0.5–0.8 cm.
4. Outcurving sided bucket with exteriorly folded rim and round lip (7.2%). Rim diameter, 25–38 cm; wall thickness, 0.6–0.9 cm.
5. Medium to long outcurving or slightly flaring necked jar with exteriorly folded rim and round lip (7.2%). Rim diameter, 16–24 cm; wall thickness, 0.5–0.8 cm; neck height, 2.0–3.6 cm.

*APPENDAGES:* None noted.
*INTRASITE DISTRIBUTION:* The type is defined on the basis of sealed levels of the early Cocos phase material (early Late Preclassic) in the South Square excavations (grid squares 20/30, 25/30, 25/35, 20/35). This pottery first appears in the early part of the Late Preclassic and then rapidly declines in usage.
*INTERSITE DISTRIBUTION:* The type is present in the Tzec and early Chuen ceramic complexes at Tikal, where decoration occurs on the interior as well as the exterior of vessels. The cuspidor and dish-lip plates found at Tikal are infrequent at Cuello. There are no other known occurrences.

*TYPE:* Sierra Red.
*VARIETY:* Sierra.
*ESTABLISHED AS A TYPE OR VARIETY:* Smith and Gifford (1966). This description is based on 721 rim sherds, 1 body sherd, and 36 whole vessels.
*GROUP:* Sierra.
*WARE:* Paso Caballo Waxy.
*COMPLEX:* Cocos.
*SPHERE AFFILIATION:* Chicanel.
*FREQUENCY:* 30.1 percent of the Cocos Ceramic Complex rim sherds (body sherd not included in the frequency percentage).
*ILLUSTRATIONS:* Figures 6.5–6.8, 6.29a, b, e; 6.30a–c, e, f; 6.31a.
*PRINCIPAL IDENTIFYING ATTRIBUTES:* Red slip that

is consistent in color; outcurving sided vessels; modifications of vessel rims and bodies that include flanges, ridging, and eversions.

*PASTE, TEMPER, AND FIRING:* Paste color is variable, ranging from tan or buff to brown, gray, and light orange. Paste texture is medium grained, with carbonate inclusions in all sherds and mica present in about half the sherds. Differential firing is common, leaving a dark core.

*SURFACE FINISH AND DECORATION:* Surfaces of vessels are generally well-smoothed, covered with a red slip that ranges from 2.5YR 4/8, 5/8, 4/6, 5/6 (red) to 7/5R 4/8 (red) and 10R 4/8, 5/8 (red). The slip has a faintly waxy feel in the earlier Cocos levels, but it reaches a fairly lustrous sheen by the later Cocos levels. With future research and a larger sample, this change in surface luster might support separation into different types. Fire clouding is common, but crackling and crazing occur only rarely (5%). Fire clouds of black, brown, or buff colors may cause some differentiation problems among Ahchab Red-and-buff, Matamore dichrome, and Sierra Red: Sierra Variety.

*FORMS*

1. Outcurving sided bowl with slightly rounded base, exteriorly folded or everted rim, and round lip (42.0%). Rim diameter, 16–32 cm; wall thickness, 0.5–0.8 cm.
2. Outcurving sided bucket with exteriorly folded or everted rim and round lip (15.3%). Rim diameter, 24–38 cm; wall thickness, 0.6–0.9 cm.
3. Incurving sided bowl with unrestricted orifice, interiorly thickened or direct rim, and round lip (13.7%); 29 examples have medial ridges, 10 have a sharp medial break with insloping upper portion, 2 have medial flanges, 6 have labial flanges, 1 has a basal flange, and 2 have basal ridges. Rim diameter, 16–48 cm; wall thickness, 0.5–0.8 cm.
4. Narrow-mouthed jar with short to medium slightly outcurving or flaring neck, exteriorly folded or direct rim, and round lip (11.8%). Rim diameter, 12–18 cm; wall thickness, 0.5–0.8 cm; neck height, 1.2–2.5 cm.
5. Flaring sided bowl with exteriorly folded or everted rim and round lip (9.1%). Rim diameter, 18–28 cm; wall thickness, 0.5–0.8 cm.
6. Recurving sided bowl, almost a "cuspidor" in shape, with exteriorly folded or everted rim and round lip (3.1%); 9 examples have medial ridges. Rim diameter, 16–26 cm; wall thickness, 0.5–0.8 cm.
7. Long outcurving or slightly outflaring necked jar with narrow mouth, exteriorly folded rim, and round lip (2.9%). Rim diameter, 16–25 cm; wall thickness, 0.5–0.8 cm; neck height, 2.6–4.2 cm.
8. Incurving sided bowl with restricted orifice (tecomate), interiorly thickened or folded rim, and round lip (2.1%). Rim diameter, 8–18 cm; wall thickness, 0.4–0.7 cm.

*APPENDAGES: Handles.* There are 17 handles associated with Sierra Red; 9 of these are flat strap handles, 6 are single loop handles, and 2 are nubbin lug handles.

*Spouts.* There are 19 spouts, all circular in section. One of these is a bridged or supported spout, and the rest are unbridged. Median spout length is 5.2 cm.

*Feet.* There are three foot supports; one is a solid conical foot and the other two are hollow. Each foot is about 5.6 cm in height.

*INTRASITE DISTRIBUTION:* The Sierra Variety is defined on the basis of sealed levels of Cocos phase material (Late Preclassic) in the South Square excavations (grid squares 20/30, 25/30, 25/35, 20/35) and in the North Square excavations (grid squares 40/30, 45/30, 45/35, 40/35). Sierra Variety pottery appears to lose some of its surface waxiness through time, and by the end of the Late Preclassic it has a glossy luster, approaching the glossiness of Classic period ceramics.

*INTERSITE DISTRIBUTION:* Sierra Red is the major component of the ceramic assemblages at most Lowland Maya sites with Late Preclassic material. It was originally

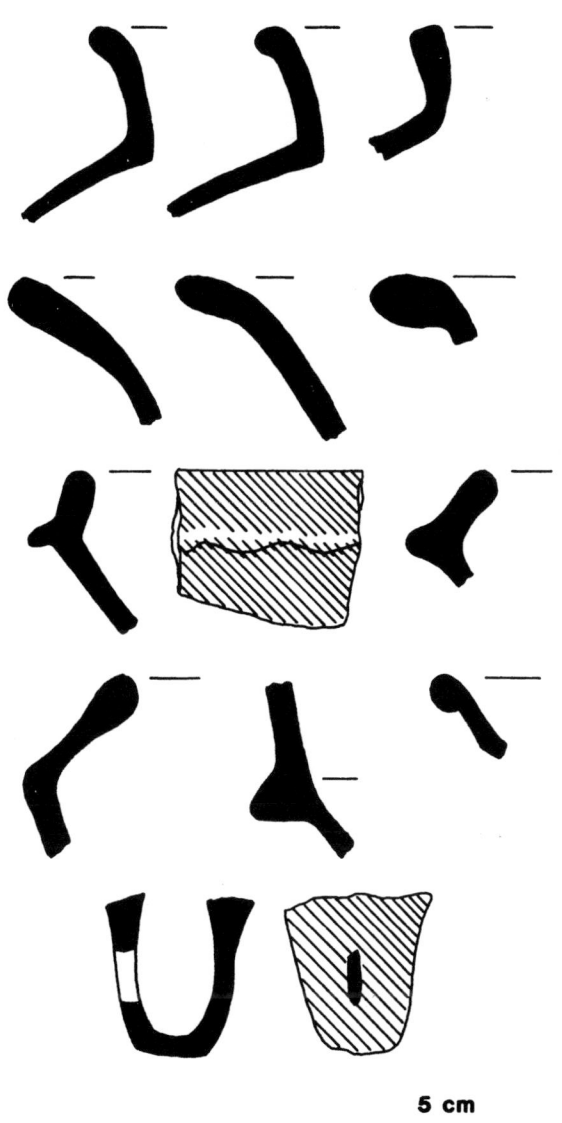

Figure 6.5. Sierra Red: Sierra Variety.

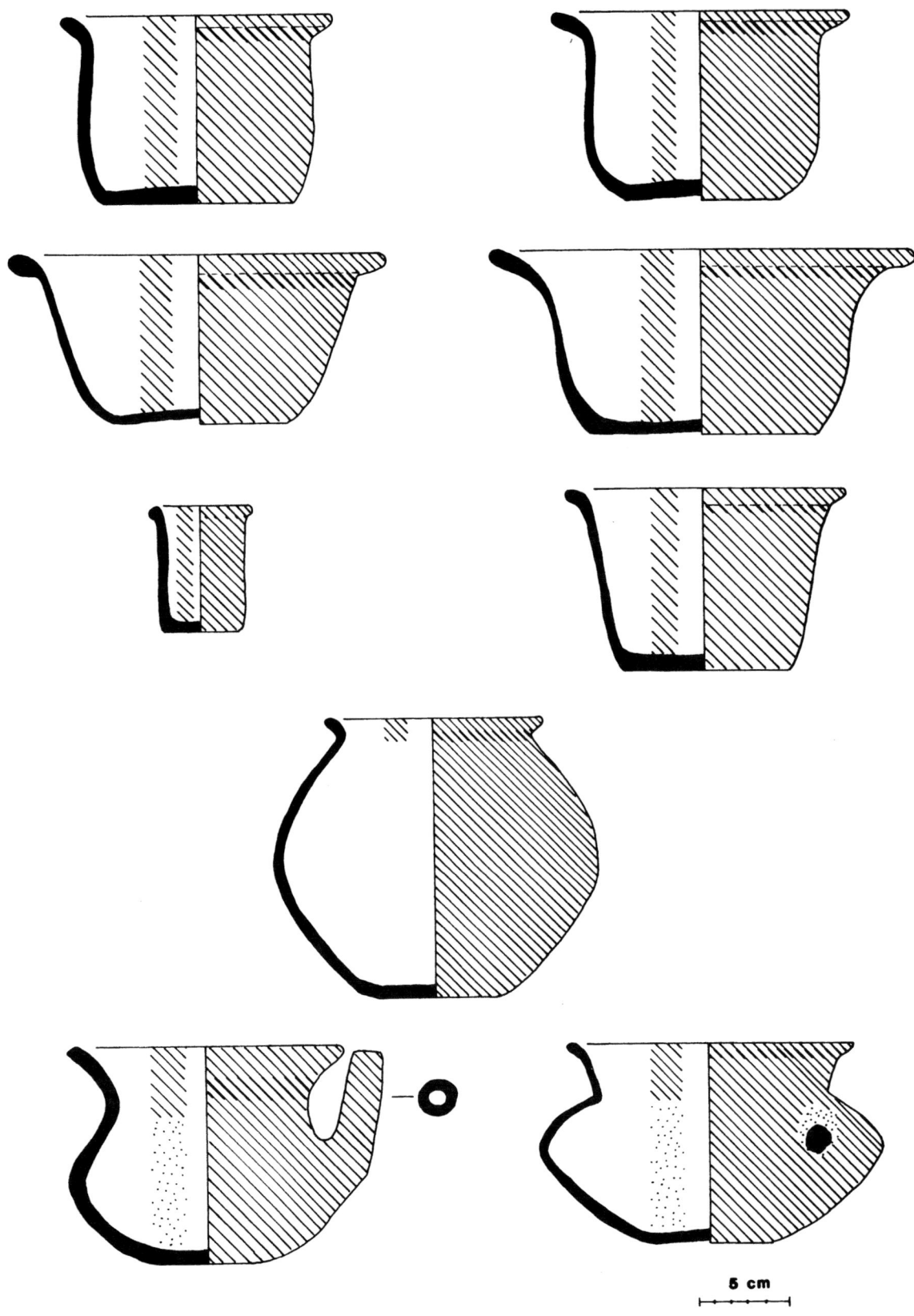

Figure 6.6. Whole vessels of Sierra Red: Sierra Variety, buckets and jars.

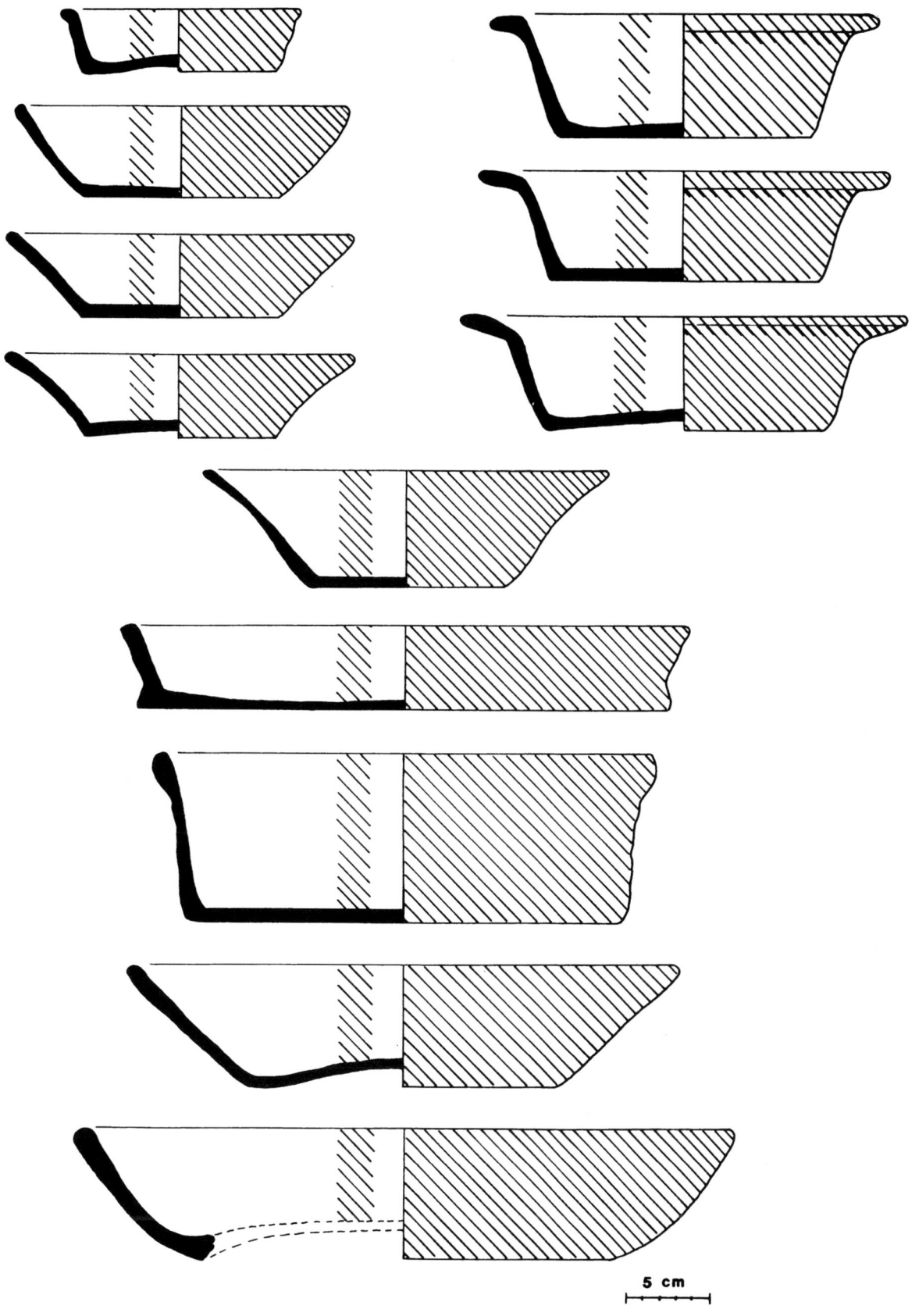

Figure 6.7. Whole vessels of Sierra Red: Sierra Variety, plates and dishes.

62   *Chapter 6*

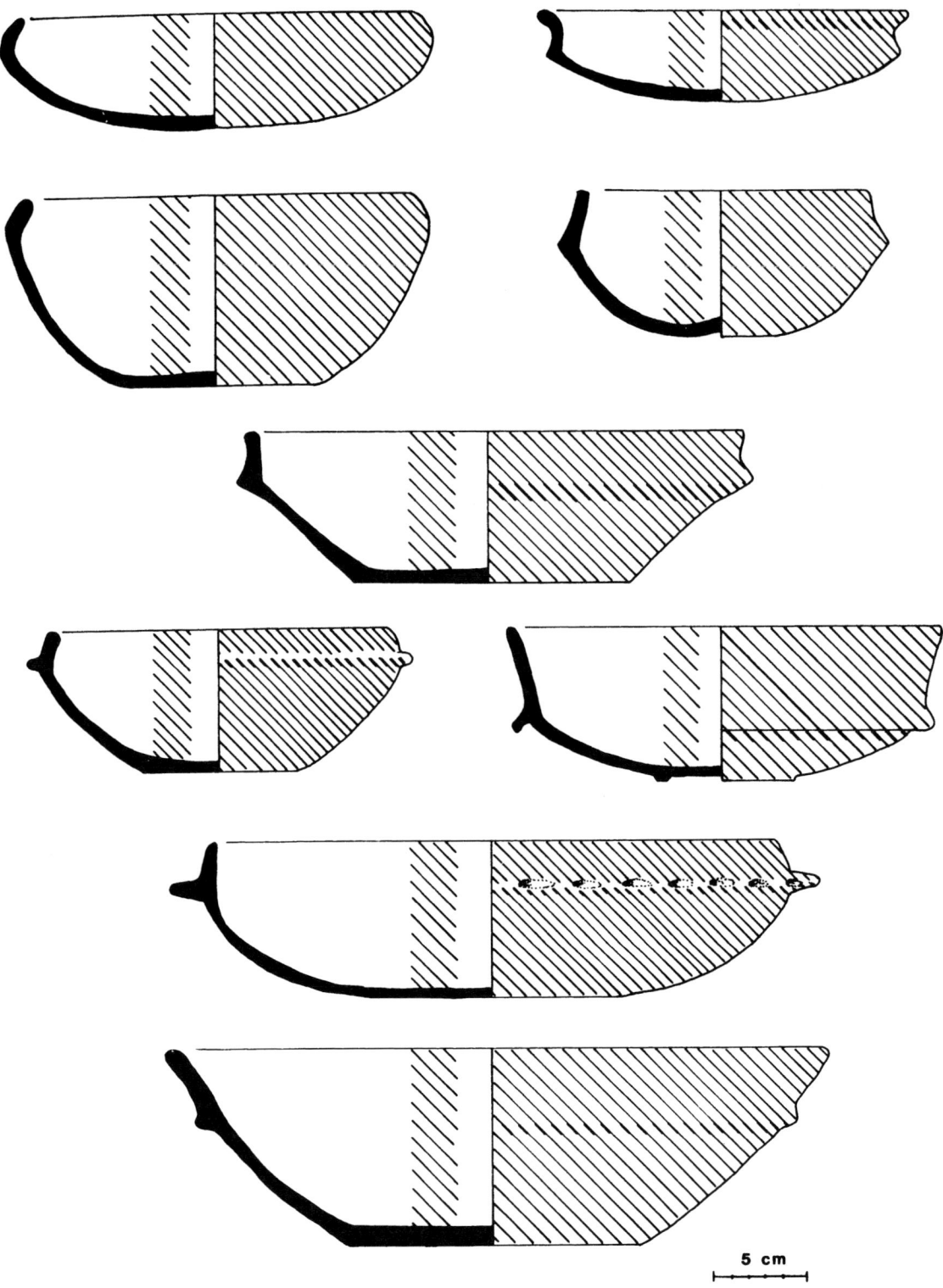

Figure 6.8.   Whole vessels of Sierra Red: Sierra Variety, bowls.

reported at Uaxactun (Smith 1955; Smith and Gifford 1966) and has been identified at Altar de Sacrificios, Seibal, Barton Ramie, Mayapan, Becan, Tikal, Cerros, Colha, Santa Rita, and Nohmul.

*TYPE:* Sierra Red.
*VARIETY:* Big Pond.
*ESTABLISHED AS A TYPE OR VARIETY:* Type, Smith and Gifford (1966). Variety, Pring (1977). Pring's description was

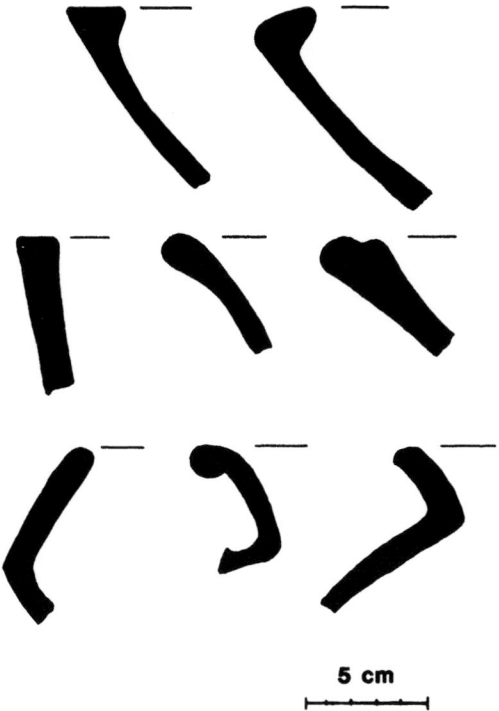

Figure 6.9 Sierra Red: Big Pond Variety.

based on 200 sherds, of which 65 were rims or large body sherds indicating form. This description is based on 69 rim sherds.

GROUP: Sierra.
WARE: Paso Caballo Waxy.
COMPLEX: Cocos.
SPHERE AFFILIATION: Chicanel.
FREQUENCY: 2.7 percent of the Cocos Ceramic Complex rim sherds.
ILLUSTRATIONS: Figure 6.9.
PRINCIPAL IDENTIFYING ATTRIBUTES: Dark red, double slip that is extremely glossy and homogeneous in color; fairly consistent paste color that is light pink or pinkish-orange; interiorly everted rims on incurving sided bowls; outcurving sided vessels.
PASTE, TEMPER, AND FIRING: The paste color is remarkably consistent and easily identifiable, centering on a light pink or pinkish-orange. Paste texture is fine to medium grained; all sherds possess mica inclusions, and about 75 percent have carbonate inclusions. Differential firing occurs only rarely, leaving the base (usually) of the vessel a dark gray.
SURFACE FINISH AND DECORATION: The surfaces of vessels are generally well-smoothed, over which is applied a double red slip. The color of the slip is remarkably consistent and centers on 10R 4/6 or 4/8 (red). This consistency is achieved by the double slip, which also intensifies the slip's glossiness. It is difficult to identify the presence of a double slip, because both slips are the same color; only in areas where the top slip has begun to erode and flake off is the bottom slip discernible. The sherds tend to be thinner than those of the Sierra Variety. The surface characteristics are reminiscent of Classic period gloss wares.

FORMS
1. Outcurving sided bowl or dish with exteriorly folded or everted rim and round lip (46.4%). Rim diameter, 16–25 cm; wall thickness, 0.5–0.6 cm.
2. Incurving sided bowl with unrestricted orifice, interiorly everted or beveled rim, and round or slightly grooved lip (18.9%). Two examples have a sharp medial break or angle with an insloping upper portion. Rim diameter, 16–28 cm; wall thickness, 0.5–0.7 cm.
3. Flaring sided bowl with exteriorly folded or everted rim and round lip (13.0%). Rim diameter, 18–26 cm; wall thickness, 0.5–0.7 cm.
4. Narrow-mouthed jar with short to medium outcurving neck, exteriorly folded or direct rim, and round lip (11.6%). Rim diameter, 12–18 cm; wall thickness, 0.4–0.6 cm; neck height, 1.8–3.2 cm.
5. Incurving sided bowl with restricted orifice (tecomate), interiorly folded rim, and round lip (10.1%). Two examples have sharp medial breaks and insloping upper portions. Rim diameter, 12–18 cm; wall thickness, 0.4–0.5 cm.

APPRENDAGES: Spout. There is one unbridged spout that is circular in section. It is slightly tapered at the end, and about 5.0 cm in length to where it is broken.
INTRASITE DISTRIBUTION: Big Pond Variety is defined on the basis of sealed levels of the Cocos phase material (Late Preclassic) in the South Square excavations (grid squares 20/30, 25/30, 25/35, 20/35) and in the North Square excavations (grid squares 40/30, 45/30, 45/35, 40/35). Big Pond pottery does not appear in the very earliest Cocos levels and seems to gain in popularity throughout the Late Preclassic. Sherds are most numerous in the later Late Preclassic levels. Pring (1977) originally identified Big Pond as a Late Facet Cocos variety. It seems from my analysis that Pring was not completely correct, and that although Big Pond is absent from the earliest Cocos levels, it does appear in the middle Cocos levels and is not strictly a late variety.
INTERSITE DISTRIBUTION: Pring (1977) identified the presence of this variety at San Estevan, Nohmul, Colha, and Chowacol in northern Belize. Although there are no specific comparisons, a trend toward glossiness in the monochrome reds in the later portion of the Late Preclassic period has been noted at Tikal, where there is also a double slipped red. In addition, there is some overlap between Big Pond and the late Chicanel type, Cabro Red, identified by Robertson-Freidel (1980) in the Tulix Ceramic Complex at Cerros. She mentions the glossiness of the slip of Cabro Red and suggests it is due to burnishing. She further notes that when the slip erodes, it leaves patches of unburnished slip that are lighter in color (Robertson-Freidel 1980). There is also some similarity to Vaquero Creek Red in the Mount Hope Ceramic Complex at Barton Ramie (Gifford 1976).

*TYPE:* Society Hall Red.
*VARIETY:* Society Hall.
*ESTABLISHED AS A TYPE OR VARIETY:* Type, present work. Originally established as a variety of Sierra Red, Smith and Gifford (1966). Society Hall was identified as a separate variety of Sierra Red mainly because of prominent concentric horizontal streaky marks on vessel surfaces. In keeping with the flexibility of type-variety analysis, the variety has been changed to a type within the Sierra Ceramic Group based on the larger sample and whole vessels recovered from Cuello, indicating that the streaky effect was intentional and not an occasional mishap in manufacturing, and on the need to keep separate the specific identifiable varieties within Society Hall for future sociocultural interpretations. This description is based on 481 rim sherds and 23 whole vessels.
*GROUP:* Sierra.
*WARE:* Paso Caballo Waxy.
*COMPLEX:* Cocos.
*SPHERE AFFILIATION:* Chicanel.
*FREQUENCY:* 20.0 percent of the Cocos Ceramic Complex rim sherds.
*ILLUSTRATIONS:* Figures 6.10–6.12.
*PRINCIPAL IDENTIFYING ATTRIBUTES:* Thin red slip with streaky horizontal marks on both interior and exterior surfaces of vessels; slip color similar to Sierra Red: Sierra Variety, but often glossier; outcurving sided bowls or buckets; a high percentage of outcurving or flaring sided dishes or bowls have concave bases.
*PASTE, TEMPER, AND FIRING:* Similar to Sierra Red: Sierra Variety. However, a higher percentage of Society Hall Red sherds are differentially fired, producing a gray or black core.
*SURFACE FINISH AND DECORATION:* Surfaces are generally not well-smoothed. A thin slip is applied over the interior and usually on the exterior, although occasionally on flaring sided bowls the exterior is left unslipped. The slip is applied using a wiping technique that produces a streaky effect, and no effort is made to even out the slip. The streakiness is an easy marker that identifies the type, and it becomes more pronounced toward the end of the Late Preclassic. In the early levels, Society Hall pottery is less streaky. In nine examples the exterior of flaring sided bowls are additionally decorated with thumbnail impressions (Fig. 6.10), and perhaps future research will suggest the establishment of an impressed type. The concentric streakiness produces variable coloration on the surface of the vessel because of the differential thickness of the slip. In general, Society Hall Red tends to be slightly more orange than Sierra Red. The color range includes 2.5YR 5/8 (red), 2.5YR 6/8 (light red), 10R 5/6, 5/8 (red), and 5YR 5/6 (yellowish red).

Originally, Pring (1977) identified a Xaibe Variety of Sierra Red at Cuello that corresponded to the Society Hall Variety of Sierra Red identified at many other sites, but according to Pring it appeared in the Cuello sequence as a late facet Cocos marker and therefore was given a new name. The current evidence suggests this interpretation is not cor-

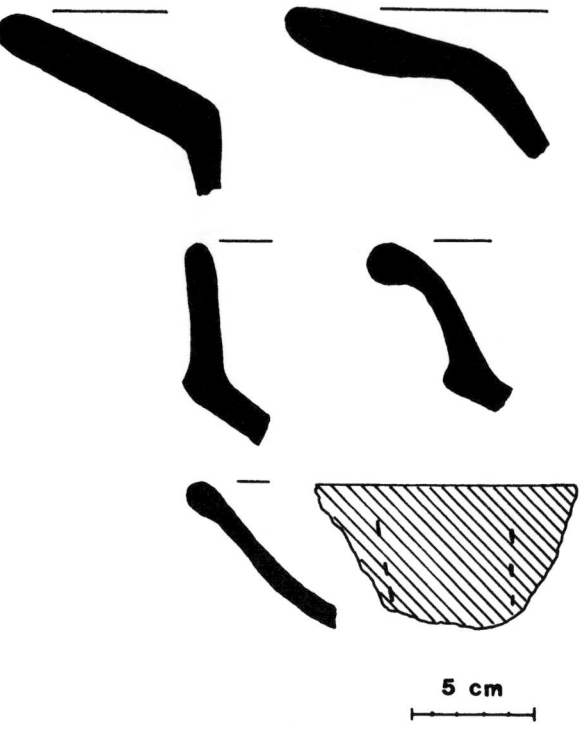

Figure 6.10   Society Hall Red: Society Hall Variety.

rect and the Cuello "streaky red" appears in the early Late Preclassic at the same time as at other sites. For this reason, the Cuello material may be included within Society Hall. (The name Xaibe has been utilized for another ceramic ware.)

At most other sites in the Maya Lowlands that have streaky red pottery in the Chicanel Ceramic Sphere, the pottery represents only a small percentage of the entire ceramic assemblage. At Barton Ramie, Society Hall is only 4 percent of the entire Sierra Ceramic Group (Gifford 1976). At Cuello, the range of variability within Society Hall is much greater, and it makes up a larger percentage of the ceramic assemblage (20 percent of the Cocos Ceramic Complex; 26.8 percent of the Sierra Ceramic Group). Because of the variability observed in the Cuello material, I have elevated Society Hall to the status of a type within the Sierra Ceramic Group. I hope this analytical refinement will provide a framework for further definition of the varieties of this unique method of slip application.

*FORMS*
1. Outcurving sided bowl or dish with slightly rounded base, exteriorly folded or everted rim, and round lip (46.6%). Rim diameter, 18–48 cm; wall thickness, 0.5–0.9 cm.
2. Incurving sided bowl with exteriorly folded, everted, or direct rim and round lip (21%). Most of these sherds have some form of modification. There are 5 examples with basal ridges, 16 with medial ridges, 3 with medial flanges, and 5 with medial angles. Rim diameter, 18–38 cm; wall thickness, 0.5–0.8 cm.

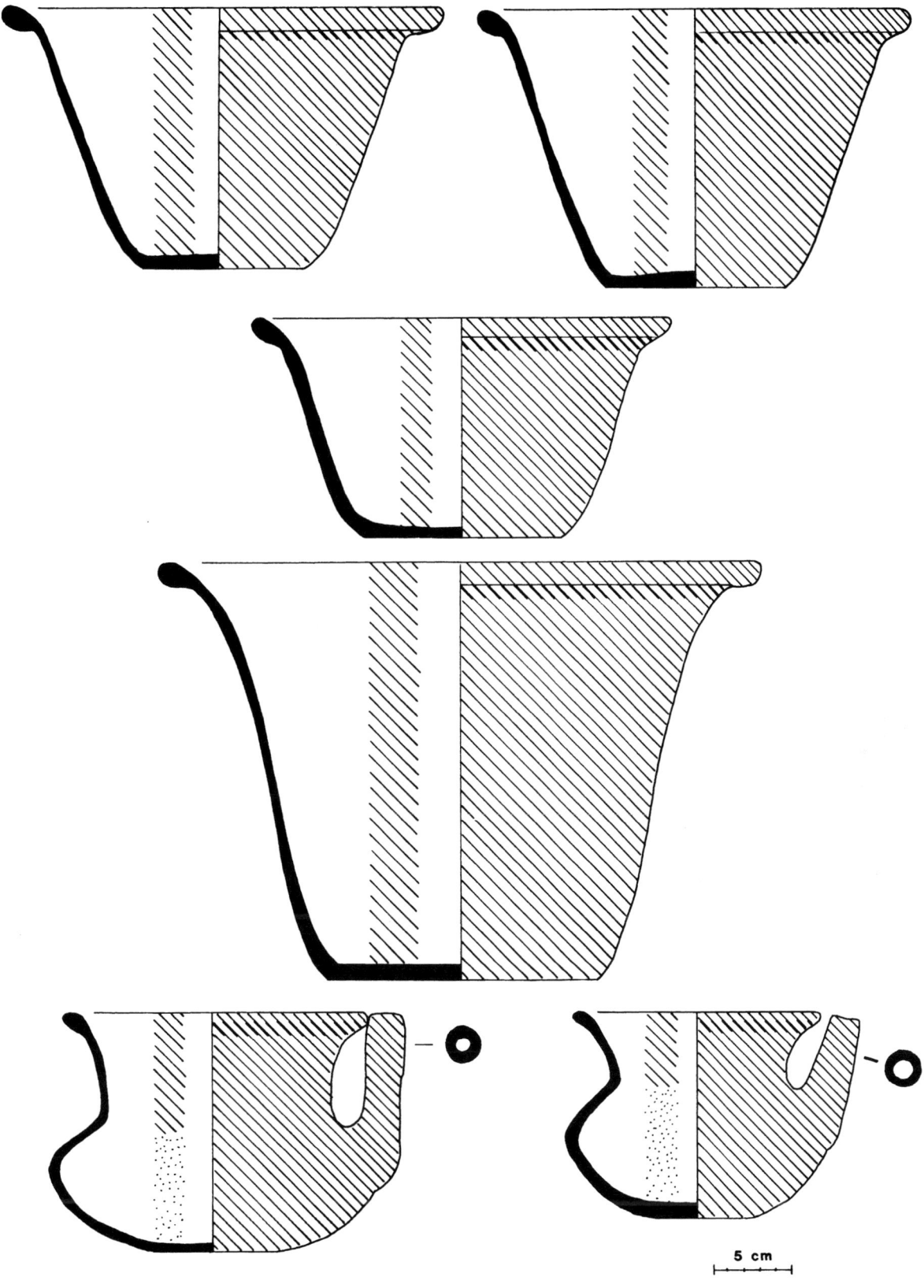

Figure 6.11　Whole vessels of Society Hall Red: Society Hall Variety, buckets and jars.

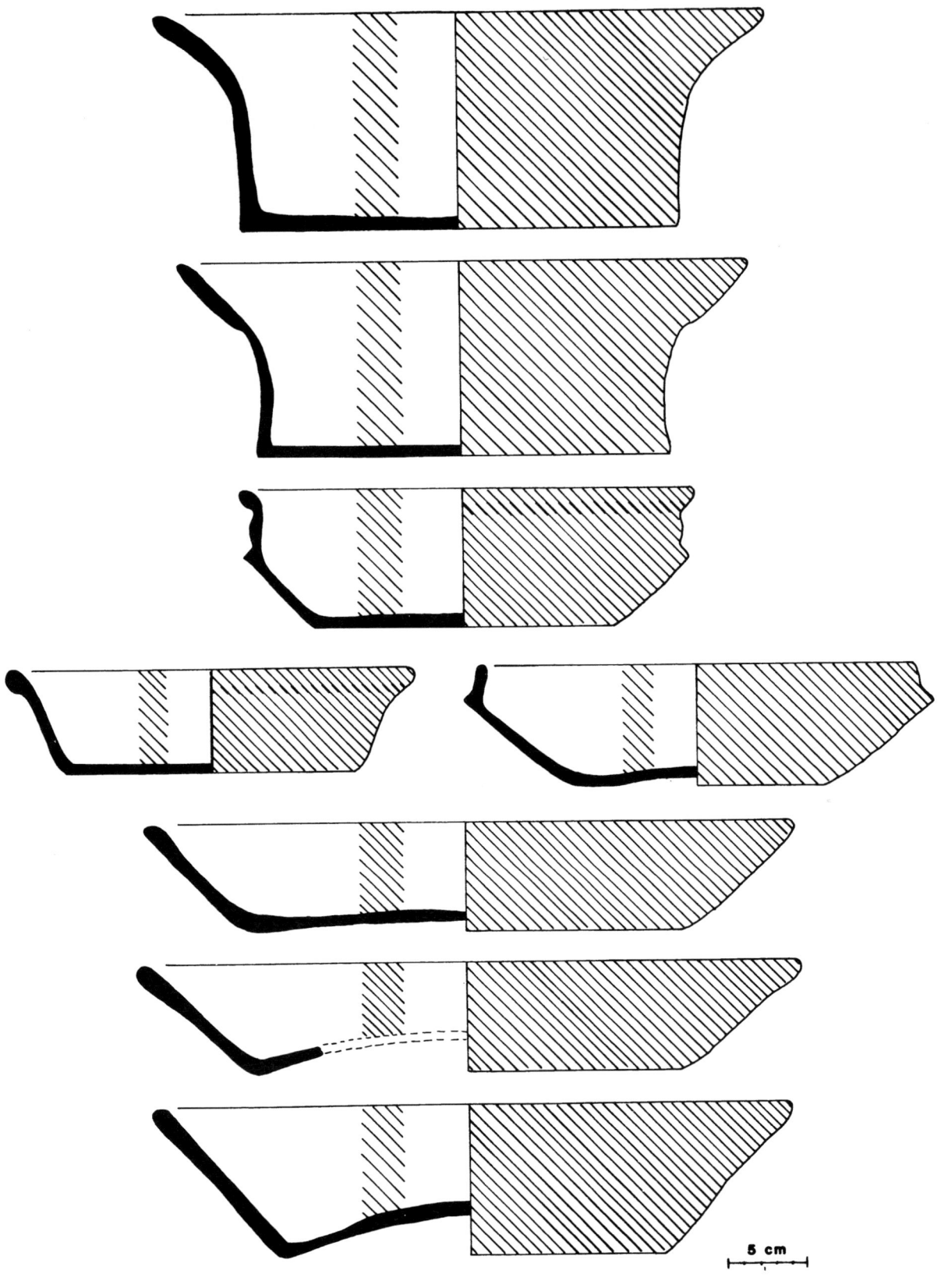

Figure 6.12  Whole vessles of Society Hall Red: Society Hall Variety, dishes and bowls.

3. Outcurving sided bucket with exteriorly folded or everted rim and round lip (13.7%). These vessels are exceptionally tall and have been dubbed "flower pots" or "champagne buckets" because of their shape. Rim diameter, 26–42 cm (one example is 62 cm in diameter); wall thickness, 0.6–1.0 cm.

4. Flaring sided bowl or dish with exteriorly folded or direct rim and round lip (12.3%); concave bases are prevalent. One sherd has a medial ridge. Rim diameter, 22–48 cm; wall thickness, 0.5–0.9 cm.

5. Recurving to outcurving sided bowl or dish with sharp medial break, exteriorly folded or direct rim, and round lip (3.7%); most examples have concave bases. Rim diameter, 24–48 cm (one example is 62 cm in diameter); wall thickness, 0.5–1.0 cm.

6. Short to medium necked jar or "chocolate pot" with exteriorly folded or direct rim and round lip (2.7%). Rim diameter, 16–22 cm; wall thickness, 0.5–0.8 cm; neck height, 1.7–2.8 cm.

*APPENDAGES: Handles.* A strap handle and a single loop handle are present.

*Spouts.* The seven spouts are unbridged and circular in section. Median length of the spouts is 5.6 cm.

*INTRASITE DISTRIBUTION:* The type is defined on the basis of sealed levels of the Cocos phase material (Late Preclassic) in the South Square excavations (grid squares 20/30, 25/30, 25/35, 20/35) and in the North Square excavations (grid squares 40/30, 45/30, 45/35, 40/35). Society Hall pottery tends to get streakier, glossier, and more abundant in the later levels of the Cocos Ceramic Complex.

*INTERSITE DISTRIBUTION:* Pring (1977) has identified the presence of "streaky red" pottery at San Estevan, Nohmul, Colha, and Chowacol in northern Belize. Although Pring (1977) originally thought the Barton Ramie variety was chronologically earlier, it now appears that the earliest levels at Cuello containing Society Hall are probably chronologically equivalent to the Barton Ramie material. The small sample at Barton Ramie does not include the same elaborate Society Hall material that appears in the later levels at Cuello. Similar varieties are present at Cerros (Robertson-Freidel 1980), Colha (Adams and Valdez, 1980), and Tikal.

*TYPE:* Society Hall Red.
*VARIETY:* Bound to Shine.
*ESTABLISHED AS A TYPE OR VARIETY:* Present work. This description is based on 53 rim sherds and 1 whole vessel.
*GROUP:* Sierra.
*WARE:* Paso Caballo Waxy.
*COMPLEX:* Cocos.
*SPHERE AFFILIATION:* Chicanel.
*FREQUENCY:* 2.1 percent of the Cocos Ceramic Complex rim sherds.
*ILLUSTRATION:* Figure 6.13.
*PRINCIPAL IDENTIFYING ATTRIBUTES:* Thin brown or yellow-orange slip with streaky horizontal markings; slip texture that is glossy; outcurving sided vessels; a high percentage of forms have concave bases.
*PASTE, TEMPER, AND FIRING:* Same as Society Hall Red: Society Hall Variety.
*SURFACE FINISH AND DECORATION:* In technique of application, the slip on Bound to Shine Variety is similar to that of Society Hall Red: Society Hall Variety. However, the surface color is not within the same range as the Society Hall Variety. Pring (1977) mentions that some of the material he analyzed was brown, brown-black, and yellowish orange. Because this color range is not the same as Sierra Red and there is a large amount of this material, I established a new variety. The color range includes 2.5YR 4/4 (reddish brown), 2.5YR 4/6 (red), 2.5YR 3/2 (dusky red), 5YR 4/4, 5/4 (reddish brown), 5YR 5/6 (yellowish red), 5YR 6/6, 6/8 (yellowish red), and 7.5YR 5/6–6/8 (strong brown-reddish yellow). All sherds that were red and followed the normal color range of Sierra Red were included in the Society Hall Variety in an attempt to restrict the definition and range of variation in Bound to Shine. In two cases, the exterior of outcurving sided bowls have fingernail impressions. It is probable that the color difference of the Bound to Shine Variety was caused by firing technique and, because of the large sample, that it was an intentional distinction rather than accidental firing. In addition, the distribution of Bound to Shine Variety suggests it first appears later than the Society Hall Variety and then gains in popularity later in the Late Preclassic. One sorting problem is with the reddish yellow end of the color range where there may be some overlap with the Society Hall Variety, although in general the color distinction is readily apparent.

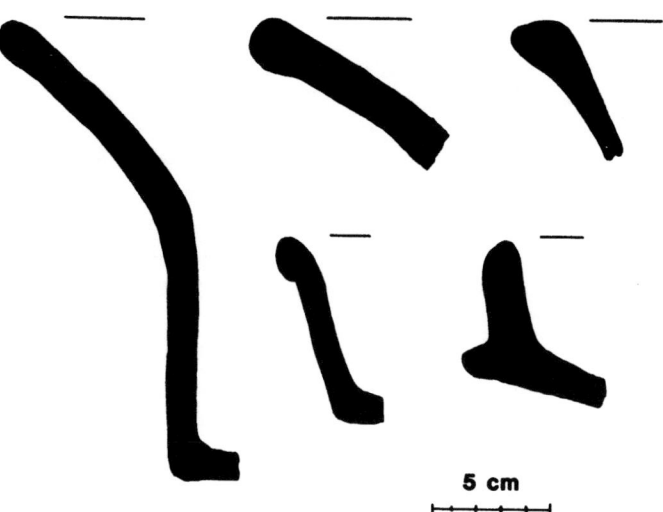

Figure 6.13. Society Hall Red: Bound to Shine Variety.

*FORMS*
1. Outcurving sided bowl or dish with direct or exteriorly folded or everted rim and round lip (43.4%). Rim diameter, 22–45 cm; wall thickness, 0.5–0.9 cm.
2. Incurving sided bowl with exteriorly or interiorly folded rim or direct rim and round lip (28.3%). Rim diameter, 22–46 cm; wall thickness, 0.6–0.9 cm; four have medial ridges.
3. Outcurving sided bucket with exteriorly folded or everted rim and round lip (9.4%). Rim diameter, 26–52 cm; wall thickness, 0.6–0.9 cm.
4. Recurving to outcurving sided bowl or dish with exteriorly folded or direct rim and round lip (9.4%). All sherds possess a medial ridge and a sharp medial break. Rim diameter, 22–36 cm; wall thickness, 0.5–0.8 cm.
5. Flaring sided bowl or dish with direct or exteriorly folded rim and round lip (5.7%); most have concave bases. Rim diameter, 24–45 cm; wall thickness, 0.5–0.9 cm.
6. Medium to high outcurving necked jar with exteriorly folded or direct rim and round lip (3.8%). Rim diameter, 12–18 cm; wall thickness, 0.5–0.8 cm; neck height, 2.2–4.0 cm.

*APPENDAGES:* None noted.

*INTRASITE DISTRIBUTION:* Bound to Shine Variety is defined on the basis of sealed levels of the Cocos phase material (Late Preclassic) in the South Square excavations (grid squares 20/30, 25/30, 25/35, 20/35) and in the North Square excavations (grid squares 40/30, 45/30, 45/35, 40/35). Bound to Shine pottery first appears in the middle levels of the Cocos Ceramic Complex and gains in popularity by the end of the Late Preclassic.

*INTERSITE DISTRIBUTION:* See Society Hall Red: Society Hall Variety for general discussion. There is a streaky effect, similar in color, on some of the San Antonio Golden-brown sherds at Altar de Sacrificios (Adams 1971) and at Colha (Kosakowsky and Valdez 1982).

*TYPE:* Society Hall Red.
*VARIETY:* Unnamed (dichrome).
*ESTABLISHED AS A TYPE OR VARIETY:* Present work. This description is based on 38 rim sherds.
*GROUP:* Sierra.
*WARE:* Paso Caballo Waxy.
*COMPLEX:* Cocos.
*SPHERE AFFILIATION:* Chicanel (Late).
*FREQUENCY:* 1.5 percent of the Cocos Ceramic Complex rim sherds.
*ILLUSTRATION:* Figure 6.14.
*PRINCIPAL IDENTIFYING ATTRIBUTES:* Thin streaky slip that is applied with horizontal wipings; dichrome effect achieved with either the interior or exterior red and the other side buff, brown, black, or yellow-orange or, alternatively, with bands of red alternating with the other colors on the vessel surfaces; outcurving sided vessels.
*PASTE, TEMPER, AND FIRING:* Same as Society Hall Red: Society Hall Variety.
*SURFACE FINISH AND DECORATION:* Slip application is the same as on Society Hall Red: Society Hall Variety, but there appears to have been an intentional effort to create dichromes. In some cases the interior or exterior of the vessel is streaky red, the same color as Society Hall Variety, and the other side is a brown, black, buff, or yellowish-orange, the same as Bound to Shine Variety. In other cases both the interior and exterior of the vessel have alternating bands or patchy areas of different colors. It is not clear from macroscopic examination how this effect was achieved.

*FORMS*
1. Outcurving sided bowl or dish with exteriorly folded or everted rim and round lip (57.8%). One example has a medial ridge. Rim diameter, 24–42 cm; wall thickness, 0.6–0.9 cm.
2. Outcurving sided bucket with exteriorly folded or everted rim and round lip (15.8%). Rim diameter, 28–48 cm; wall thickness, 0.6–0.9 cm.
3. Incurving sided bowl or dish with exteriorly or interiorly thickened rim or direct rim and round lip (13.2%). One example has a medial ridge and two have a sharp medial break. Rim diameter, 22–34 cm; wall thickness, 0.5–0.8 cm.
4. Flaring sided bowl or dish with direct or exteriorly folded rim and round lip (7.9%). Rim diameter, 22–35 cm; wall thickness, 0.5–0.9 cm.
5. Short slightly outcurving or flaring necked jar with exteriorly folded or direct rim and round lip (5.3%). Rim diameter, 14–16 cm; wall thickness, 0.6–0.7 cm; neck height, 1.5–2.8 cm.

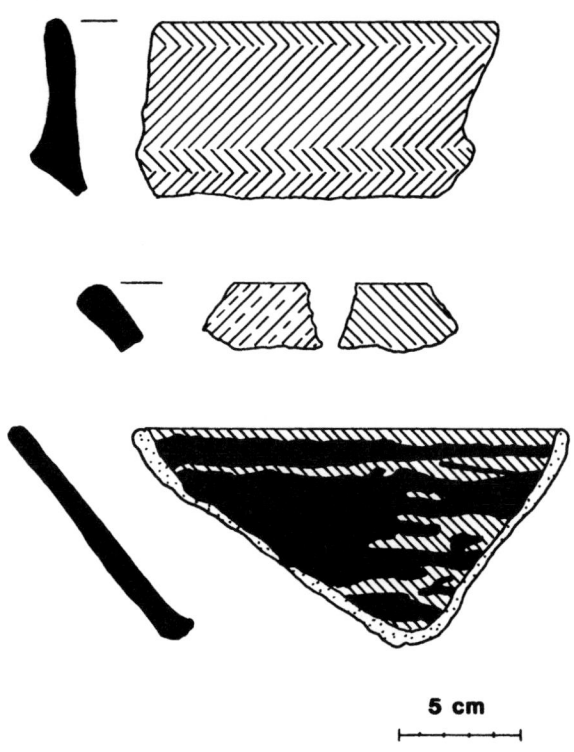

Figure 6.14. Society Hall Red: Unnamed variety (dichrome).

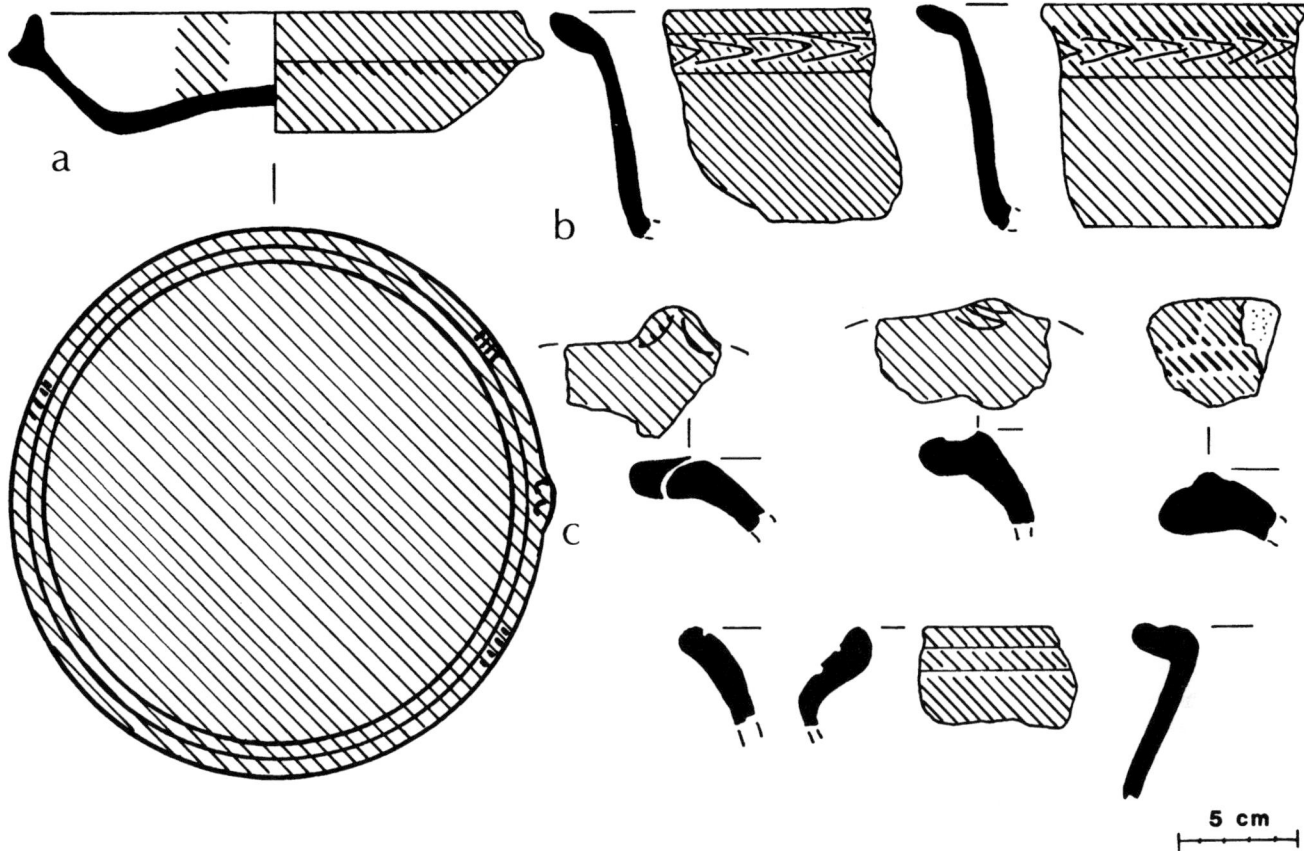

Figure 6.15. Laguna Verde Incised: Grooved-incised Variety.

*APPENDAGES:* None noted.
*INTRASITE DISTRIBUTION:* See Society Hall Red: Bound to Shine Variety. The dichrome sherds seem to appear even later in the Late Preclassic than the Bound to Shine pottery.
*INTERSITE DISTRIBUTION:* No known comparisons.

*TYPE:* Laguna Verde Incised.
*VARIETY:* Grooved-incised.
*ESTABLISHED AS A TYPE OR VARIETY:* Type, Smith and Gifford (1966). Variety, Sabloff (1975). This description is based on 46 rim sherds and 2 whole vessels.
*GROUP:* Sierra.
*WARE:* Paso Caballo Waxy.
*COMPLEX:* Cocos.
*SPHERE AFFILIATION:* Chicanel.
*FREQUENCY:* 1.9 percent of the Cocos Ceramic Complex rim sherds.
*ILLUSTRATION:* Figure 6.15.
*PRINCIPAL IDENTIFYING ATTRIBUTES:* Preslip groove-incising in horizontal, circumferential bands on the exterior of vessels or interiorly just below the rim; red slip identical to Sierra Red: Sierra Variety; outcurving sided bowls or dishes with modified rims.
*PASTE, TEMPER, AND FIRING:* Same as Sierra Red: Sierra Variety.

*SURFACE FINISH AND DECORATION:* Color and texture of the slip are identical to Sierra Red: Sierra Variety. Decoration consists of horizontal bands around the exterior of vessels or interiorly just below the rim. These bands are always preslip grooved-incised. On vessels that have rims with tabs, the tabs are often incised with slightly more elaborate decorations consisting of parallel lines at right angles to the rim.
*FORMS*
1. Outcurving sided bowl or dish with thickened or exteriorly everted rim and round lip (78.2%). Eight examples have rims modified by tabs that are grooved. Rim diameter, 22–38 cm; wall thickness, 0.5–0.9 cm.
2. Incurving sided bowl with generally unrestricted orifice, interiorly thickened rim, and round lip (17.4%). One example has a sharp medial break, and two examples possess labial flanges. Rim diameter, 18–32 cm; wall thickness, 0.6–0.9 cm.
3. Flaring sided dish or plate with thickened or exteriorly everted rim and round lip (2.2%). Rim diameter, 24–42 cm; wall thickness, 0.6–0.9 cm.
4. Jar with short outcurving neck or insloping neck, exteriorly everted rim, and round lip (2.2%). Rim diameter, 18–27 cm; wall thickness, 0.7–0.9 cm; neck height, 1.2–2.8 cm.
*APPENDAGES: Foot.* There is one solid ovoid foot with parallel vertical groove-incisions around the exterior of the

foot. It is 6.2 cm in length but broken below its attachment to the vessel.

*INTRASITE DISTRIBUTION:* The type is defined on the basis of sealed levels of the Cocos phase material (Late Preclassic) in the South Square excavations (grid squares 20/30, 20/35, 25/35, 25/30) and in the North Square excavations (grid squares 40/30, 40/35, 45/35, 45/30). Laguna Verde Incised pottery continues throughout the Cocos Ceramic Complex without any apparent changes.

*INTERSITE DISTRIBUTION:* I have followed both Sabloff (1975) and Pring (1977) in differentiating a Grooved-incised Variety with preslip incising from the Laguna Verde Variety that has postslip and preslip elaborate fine-line incising. There appears to be some confusion in the naming of these varieties at other sites. At Uaxactun, the Laguna Verde Variety possesses both horizontal groove-incising and more elaborate designs (Smith 1955; Smith and Gifford 1966). The Laguna Verde Variety at Altar de Sacrificios contains only slanting lines on the exteriors of vessels (Adams 1971). At Tikal, Culbert differentiates between a simple-incised variety and a design-incised variety. At Barton Ramie, the unspecified variety (Gifford 1976) possesses both preslip groove-incising and postslip incising. At Becan, Ball (1977a) identifies an unspecified variety with only preslip groove-incising. Similarly, Robertson-Freidel (1980) identifies a grooved-incised variety at Cerros.

*TYPE:* Laguna Verde Incised.
*VARIETY:* Laguna Verde.
*ESTABLISHED AS A TYPE OR VARIETY:* Smith and Gifford (1966). This description is based on 3 rim sherds, 4 body sherds, and 2 whole vessels.
*GROUP:* Sierra.
*WARE:* Paso Caballo Waxy.
*COMPLEX:* Cocos.
*SPHERE AFFILIATION:* Chicanel.
*FREQUENCY:* 0.2 percent of the Cocos Ceramic Complex rim sherds (body sherds not included in the frequency percentage).
*ILLUSTRATION:* Figure 6.16.
*PRINCIPAL IDENTIFYING ATTRIBUTES:* Preslip and postslip fine-line incising in geometric or more elaborate designs; slip color and texture the same as Sierra Red: Sierra Variety.
*PASTE, TEMPER, AND FIRING:* Same as Sierra Red: Sierra Variety.
*SURFACE FINISH AND DECORATION:* Slip color and texture are the same as Sierra Red: Sierra Variety. The decoration on most examples is preslip, although one example has postslip incising. The incised designs are elaborate and often irregular and geometric. In three cases a broad band below the rim on the exterior contains a chevron design.
*FORMS*
1. One sherd is an incurving sided bowl with interiorly thick-

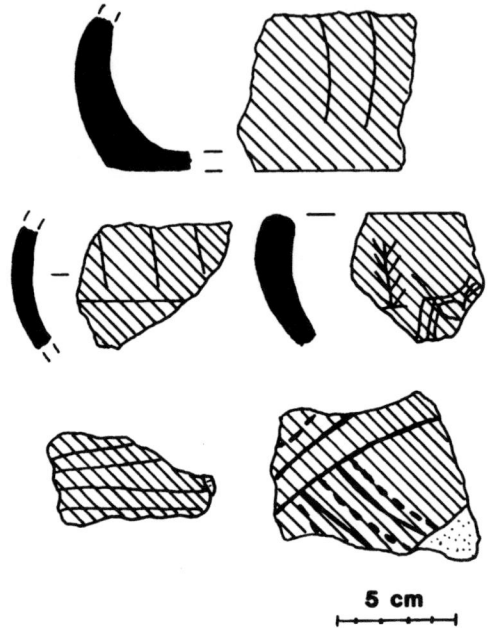

Figure 6.16. Laguna Verde Incised: Laguna Verde Variety.

ened rim and round lip. Rim diameter, 16 cm; wall thickness, 0.7 cm.
2. Two sherds are from slightly outcurving sided dishes or plates with exteriorly everted rim and round lip. The bases are slightly rounded. Rim diameter, 42 cm, 36 cm; wall thickness, 0.5–0.7 cm.
*APPENDAGES:* None noted.
*INTRASITE DISTRIBUTION:* Same as Laguna Verde Incised: Grooved-incised Variety.
*INTERSITE DISTRIBUTION:* See the discussion for Laguna Verde Incised: Grooved-incised Variety. Pring (1977) has identified the presence of the Laguna Verde Variety at Nohmul in northern Belize and suggests that this variety is closer to the originally defined variety from Uaxactun (Smith and Gifford 1966).

*TYPE:* Lagartos Punctated.
*VARIETY:* Lagartos.
*ESTABLISHED AS A TYPE OR VARIETY:* Smith and Gifford (1966). This description is based on 13 rim sherds and 2 body sherds.
*GROUP:* Sierra.
*WARE:* Paso Caballo Waxy.
*COMPLEX:* Cocos.
*SPHERE AFFILIATION:* Chicanel.
*FREQUENCY:* 0.5 percent of the Cocos Ceramic Complex rim sherds (body sherds not included in the frequency percentage).

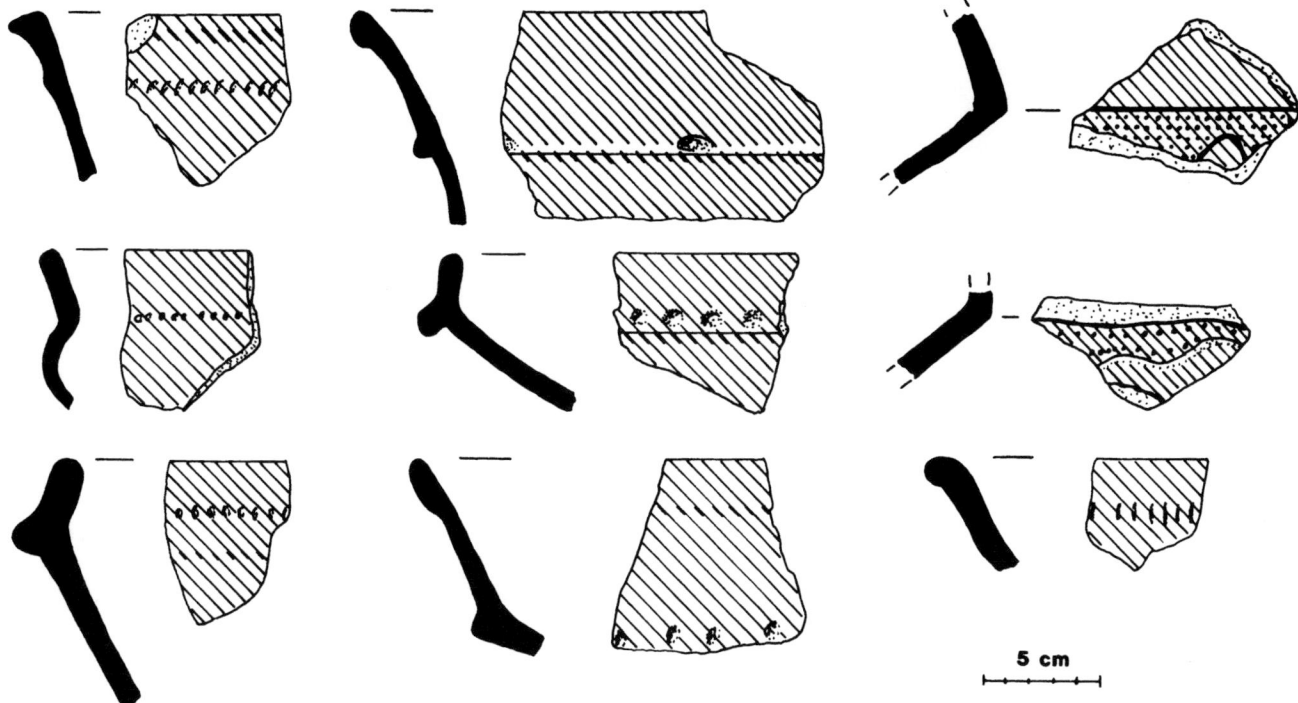

Figure 6.17. Lagartos Punctated: Lagartos Variety.

*ILLUSTRATION:* Figure 6.17.

*PRINCIPAL IDENTIFYING ATTRIBUTES:* Dot punctation on the exterior of vessel surfaces; slip color and texture the same as Sierra Red: Sierra Variety.

*PASTE, TEMPER, AND FIRING:* Same as Sierra Red: Sierra Variety.

*SURFACE FINISH AND DECORATION:* Slip color and texture same as Sierra Red: Sierra Variety. In general, the decoration involves a single row of deep dot punctations or shallower awl punctations on the exterior of vessels. The neck-body junctures of jars possess larger areas of punctation.

*FORMS*

1. Slightly recurving sided bowl with rounded base, direct or exteriorly folded rim, and round lip (33.3%). Rim diameter, 18–28 cm; wall thickness, 0.6–0.9 cm.
2. Incurving sided bowl with unrestricted orifice, exteriorly thickened rim, and round lip (26.7%). Rim diameter, 16–32 cm; wall thickness, 0.5–0.8 cm. Two examples have labial flanges.
3. Slightly outcurving to flaring necked jar (13.3%). There are no rim sherds of this form.
4. Outcurving sided bowl or dish with direct or exteriorly folded rim and round lip (13.3%). Both examples have medial ridges on which the punctation is placed. Rim diameter, 26 cm, 30 cm; wall thickness, 0.6–0.7 cm.
5. Incurving sided bowl with short vertical collar, interiorly thickened rim, and round lip (13.3%). Rim diameter, 14 and 18 cm; wall thickness, 0.6–0.7 cm.

*APPENDAGES:* None noted.

*INTRASITE DISTRIBUTION:* The type is defined on the basis of sealed levels of the Cocos phase material (Late Preclassic) in the South Square excavations (grid squares 20/30, 20/35, 25/35, 25/30) and in the North Square excavations (grid squares 40/30, 40/35, 45/35, 45/30). Lagartos pottery seems to continue throughout the Cocos Ceramic Complex without any apparent changes.

*INTERSITE DISTRIBUTION:* Pring (1977) has identified the sparse presence of this type at most sites in northern Belize. The Cuello type is similar to Lagartos Punctated at Uaxactun (Smith and Gifford 1966; Smith 1955), Altar de Sacrificios (Adams 1971), and Seibal (Sabloff 1975).

*TYPE:* Repollo Impressed.
*VARIETY:* Unspecified.
*ESTABLISHED AS A TYPE OR VARIETY:* Ball (1977). Pring (1977) identified one sherd of an Unspecified Variety. This description is based on 2 rim sherds and 1 body sherd.
*GROUP:* Sierra.
*WARE:* Paso Caballo Waxy.
*COMPLEX:* Cocos.
*SPHERE AFFILIATION:* Chicanel.
*FREQUENCY:* 0.1 percent of the Cocos Ceramic Complex rim sherds (body sherd not included in the frequency percentage).

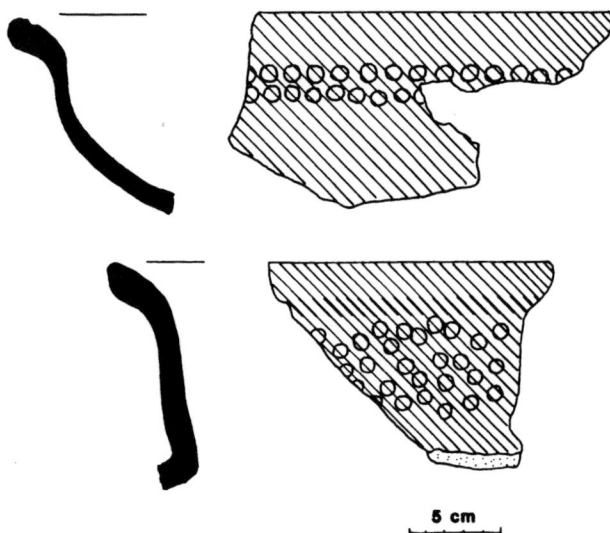

Figure 6.18. Repollo Impressed: Variety Unspecified.

*ILLUSTRATION:* Figure 6.18.
*PRINCIPAL IDENTIFYING ATTRIBUTES:* Decoration on vessel exteriors with reed-impressed circles; slip color and texture same as Sierra Red: Sierra Variety.
*PASTE, TEMPER, AND FIRING:* Same as Sierra Red: Sierra Variety.
*SURFACE FINISH AND DECORATION:* Slip color and texture same as Sierra Red: Sierra Variety. Decoration consists of reed-impressed horizontal rows of circles on the exterior of vessels, in all cases applied postslip but prefiring.
*FORMS*
1. Recurving sided bowl with exteriorly everted rim and round lip (2 examples). Rim diameter, no measurement and 22 cm; wall thickness, 0.6–0.9 cm.
2. Long outcurving necked jar with exteriorly everted rim and round lip (1 example). Rim diameter, 25 cm; wall thickness, 0.9 cm; neck height, 6 cm.
*APPENDAGES:* None noted.
*INTRASITE DISTRIBUTION:* The type is defined on the basis of sealed levels of the Cocos phase material (Late Preclassic) in the South Square excavations (grid squares 20/30, 25/30, 25/35, 20/35) and in the North Square excavations (grid squares 40/30, 45/30, 45/35, 40/35). The sample size is too small to determine any changes in the type through time.
*INTERSITE DISTRIBUTION:* The only other known occurrences of reed-impressed pottery for this time period are at Becan (Ball 1977a) and at Barton Ramie (Gifford 1976: 100).

*TYPE:* Union Appliquéd.
*VARIETY:* Unspecified.
*ESTABLISHED AS A TYPE OR VARIETY:* Type, Smith and Gifford (1966). Pring (1977) identified one sherd of an Un-specified Variety. This description is based on 8 body sherds, none of which are from identifiable forms.
*GROUP:* Sierra.
*WARE:* Paso Caballo Waxy.
*COMPLEX:* Cocos.
*SPHERE AFFILIATION:* Chicanel.
*FREQUENCY:* These 8 body sherds are not included in the frequency percentages.
*ILLUSTRATION:* Figure 6.19.
*PRINCIPAL IDENTIFYING ATTRIBUTES:* Appliquéd fillet around the exterior of vessels; secondary decoration of the fillet by deep punctations; slip color and texture same as Sierra Red: Sierra Variety.
*PASTE, TEMPER, AND FIRING:* Same as Sierra Red: Sierra Variety.
*SURFACE FINISH AND DECORATION:* Slip color and texture same as Sierra Red: Sierra Variety. Decoration consists of a thin appliquéd fillet (0.5–0.8 cm in width) probably attached at the neck-body juncture of jars. The fillet is decorated with deep dot punctations.
*FORMS:* The curvature of the body sherds suggests jar forms.
*APPENDAGES:* None noted.
*INTRASITE DISTRIBUTION:* The type is defined on the basis of sealed levels of the Cocos phase material (Late Preclassic) in the South Square excavations (grid squares 20/30, 25/30, 25/35, 20/35) and in the North Square excavations (grid squares 40/30, 45/30, 45/35, 40/35). The sample size is too small too suggest any possible changes of the type through time.
*INTERSITE DISTRIBUTION:* Appliquéd fillets occur on the monochrome red group at Uaxactun (Smith 1955) and on Hillbank Red at Barton Ramie (Gifford 1976: 103, Fig. 42w) during the Chicanel time period.

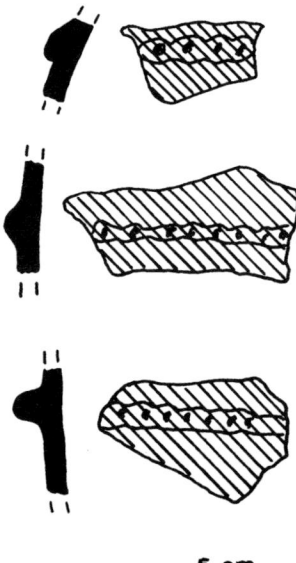

Figure 6.19. Union Appliquéd: Variety Unspecified.

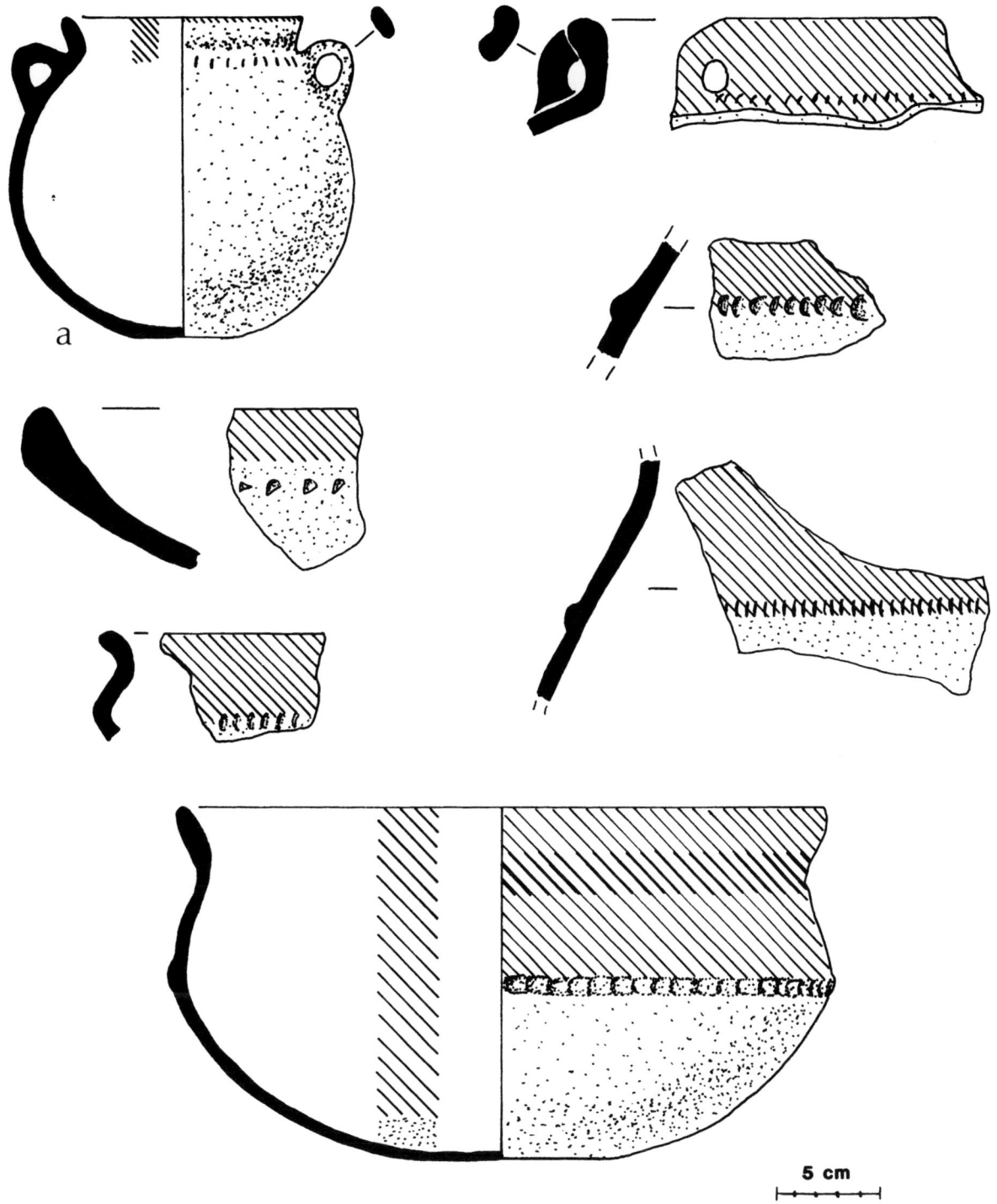

Figure 6.20. Puletan Red-and-unslipped: Puletan Variety.

*TYPE:* Puletan Red-and-unslipped.
*VARIETY:* Puletan.
*ESTABLISHED AS A TYPE OR VARIETY:* Pring (1977). Pring's description was based on 7 sherds, of which 6 were rims. This description is based on 22 rim sherds and 1 whole vessel.
*GROUP:* Sierra.

*WARE:* Paso Caballo Waxy.
*COMPLEX:* Cocos.
*SPHERE AFFILIATION:* Chicanel.
*FREQUENCY:* 0.9 percent of the Cocos Ceramic Complex rim sherds.
*ILLUSTRATION:* Figure 6.20.
*PRINCIPAL IDENTIFYING ATTRIBUTES:* Interior of the

vessel and just over the rim onto the exterior is slipped red; exterior of the vessel is largely unslipped; secondary decoration includes punctating, incising, and appliquéd ridges; color and texture of slip same as Sierra Red: Sierra Variety.

*PASTE, TEMPER, AND FIRING:* Same as Sierra Red: Sierra Variety.

*SURFACE FINISH AND DECORATION:* Slip color and texture same as Sierra Red: Sierra Variety. The slip was applied on the interior of vessels and just over the rim onto the exterior. The remainder of the exterior was left unslipped and a line of punctations, incisions, or an appliquéd ridge was placed where the slip ended.

*FORMS*

1. Incurving sided bowl with exteriorly folded or direct rim and round lip (91.6%). Rim diameter, 14–28 cm; wall thickness, 0.5–0.9 cm.
2. One sherd is from a slightly recurving sided bowl with direct rim and round lip. Rim diameter, no measurement; wall thickness, 0.5 cm.
3. One sherd and the whole vessel (Fig. 6.20a) are outcurving short necked jars with exteriorly folded rims and round lips. Rim diameter, 12 cm, 16 cm; wall thickness, 0.6 cm; neck height, 1.0 cm.

*APPENDAGES: Handles.* Both jars have simple single loop handles at opposite sides of the rim.

*INTRASITE DISTRIBUTION:* The type is defined on the basis of sealed levels of the Cocos phase material (Late Preclassic) in the South Square excavations (grid squares 20/30, 25/30, 25/35, 20/35) and in the North Square excavations (grid squares 40/30, 45/30, 45/35, 40/35). Puletan Red-and-unslipped pottery continues throughout the Cocos Ceramic Complex without any apparent changes.

*INTERSITE DISTRIBUTION:* Pring (1977) has identified the presence of the type at Colha and Chowacol in northern Belize. There are no other known comparisons.


*TYPE:* Puletan Red-and-unslipped.
*VARIETY:* Unnamed.
*ESTABLISHED AS A TYPE OR VARIETY:* Type, Pring (1977). Variety, present work. This description is based on 123 rim sherds, 4 body sherds, and 2 whole vessels.
*GROUP:* Sierra.
*WARE:* Paso Caballo Waxy.
*COMPLEX:* Cocos.
*SPHERE AFFILIATION:* Chicanel.
*FREQUENCY:* 5.0 percent of the Cocos Ceramic Complex rim sherds (body sherds not included in the frequency percentage).
*ILLUSTRATION:* Figure 6.21.
*PRINCIPAL IDENTIFYING ATTRIBUTES:* Interior of the vessel and just over the rim exteriorly, as well as the basal portion of some vessels, slipped red; remaining area of the vessel is left unslipped in a band around the exterior; secondary decoration with punctating, fluting, incising, and striating; color and texture of slip same as Sierra Red: Sierra Variety.

*PASTE, TEMPER, AND FIRING:* Same as Sierra Red: Sierra Variety.

*SURFACE FINISH AND DECORATION:* Slip color and texture the same as Sierra Red: Sierra Variety. Decoration is similar to the Puletan Variety, and I suspect that all this material should be included in one variety. Pring's (1977) description did not include the range of variability I encountered at Cuello and I have placed all doubtful material in the Unnamed variety. On some sherds the exterior just below the slipped rim is punctated or incised, and the unslipped surface may be striated or incised with parallel vertical lines. In other examples both the rim and basal portions of vessel exteriors are slipped red and the unslipped area is covered with crisscrossing incised lines. Pring (1977) mentions one example of Puletan Red-and-unslipped with striations, but he does not include striations in the identifying attributes for the Puletan Variety.

*FORMS*

1. Outcurving or flaring sided bowl or dish with exteriorly folded rim and round lip (41.5%). Rim diameter, 22–34 cm; wall thickness, 0.5–0.8 cm.
2. Incurving sided bowl with exteriorly folded or direct rim and round lip (13.8%). Two examples have sharp medial breaks with insloping upper portions. Rim diameter, 16–28 cm; wall thickness, 0.5–0.8 cm.
3. Short outcurving necked jar with direct or exteriorly folded rim and round lip (12.3%). Rim diameter, 16–22 cm; wall thickness, 0.5–0.8 cm; neck height, 1.8–2.4 cm.
4. Slightly recurving sided bowl with exteriorly folded rim and round lip (2.4%). Rim diameter, 18–24 cm; wall thickness, 0.6–0.8 cm.
5. Miniature outcurving or flaring sided dish with direct rim (30%). There are 40 examples of this form and in all cases the interiors are slipped and the exteriors are unslipped with faint irregular striations. The diameters of these vessels range from 6 cm to 14 cm. I have included these sherds in the Unnamed variety of Puletan Red-and-unslipped, although a separate red-and-striated type may be established if similar pottery is found elsewhere.

*APPENDAGES: Handles.* Two jars have simple loop handles; in both cases the jar has two handles attached on opposite sides of the vessel at the rim.

*INTRASITE DISTRIBUTION:* Same as Puletan Red-and-unslipped: Puletan Variety.

*INTERSITE DISTRIBUTION:* No known comparisons, though in concept and execution it is similar to the Pakluum Special: Black-and-unslipped and incised type at Becan (Ball 1977a), which Pring noted in his research (1977) as having criss-cross rhomboid incising.


*OTHER SIERRA CERAMIC GROUP POTTERY:* Unspecified.
*WARE:* Paso Caballo Waxy.
*COMPLEX:* Cocos.

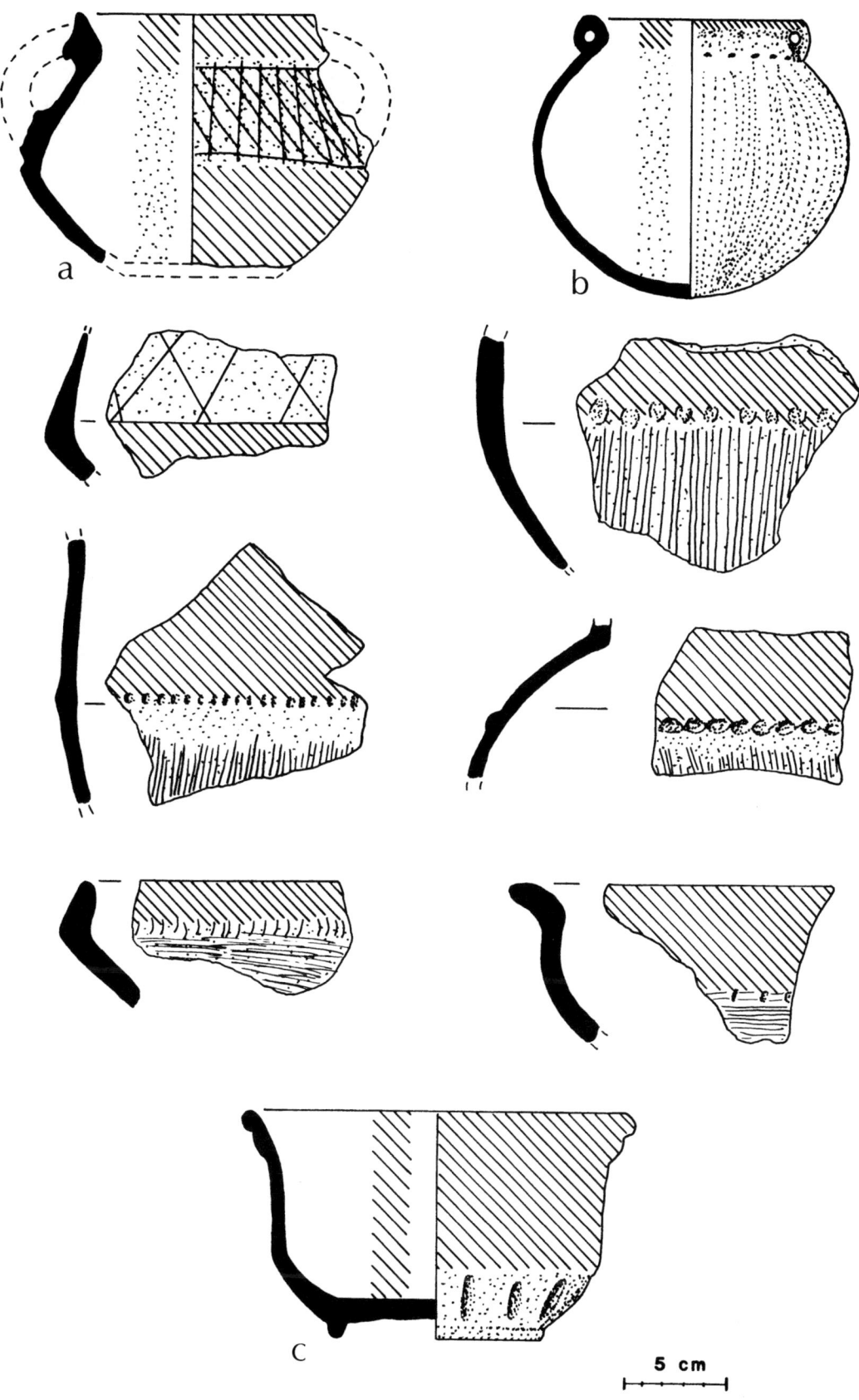

Figure 6.21. Puletan Red-and-unslipped: Unnamed variety.

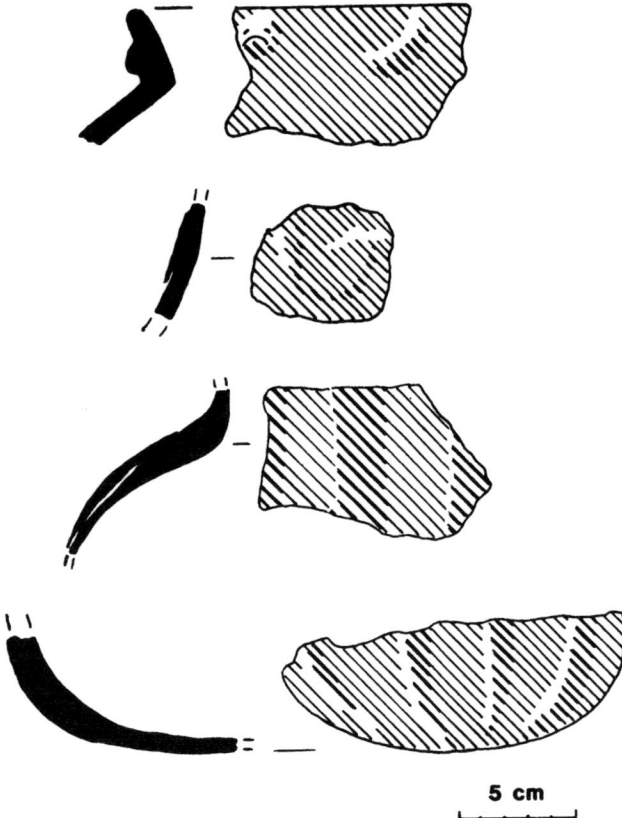

Figure 6.22. Sierra Ceramic Group pottery, unspecified, with modeling.

*SPHERE AFFILIATION:* Chicanel.
*FREQUENCY:* 0.1 percent of the Cocos Ceramic Complex rim sherds. This description is based on 2 rim sherds and 16 body sherds that are not included in the frequency percentage.
*ILLUSTRATION:* Figure 6.22.
*PRINCIPAL IDENTIFYING ATTRIBUTES:* See *Forms* below.
*PASTE, TEMPER, AND FIRING:* Same as Sierra Red: Sierra Variety.
*SURFACE FINISH AND DECORATION:* Slip color and texture same as Sierra Red: Sierra Variety; see *Forms* below.
*FORMS:* The two rim sherds are from outcurving or flaring necked jars. On one there is a small modeled face at the rim, and the other is modeled to give the appearance of a squash. The body sherds also are modeled to look like a squash, but some of the sherds are too small to properly identify. If more of this material is found, it may be necessary to establish a modeled type in the Sierra Ceramic Group.
*APPENDAGES:* None noted.
*INTRASITE DISTRIBUTION:* Same as Sierra Red: Sierra Variety.
*INTERSITE DISTRIBUTION:* Pring (1977) has also identified Unnamed Modeled sherds in the Sierra Ceramic Group.

*TYPE:* Polvero Black.
*VARIETY:* Polvero.
*ESTABLISHED AS A TYPE OR VARIETY:* Smith and Gifford 1966. This description is based on 44 rim sherds and 1 whole vessel.
*GROUP:* Polvero.
*WARE:* Paso Caballo Waxy.
*COMPLEX:* Cocos.
*SPHERE AFFILIATION:* Chicanel.
*FREQUENCY:* 1.8 percent of the Cocos Ceramic Complex rim sherds.
*ILLUSTRATIONS:* Figures 6.23a, 6.24.
*PRINCIPAL IDENTIFYING ATTRIBUTES:* Black to dark

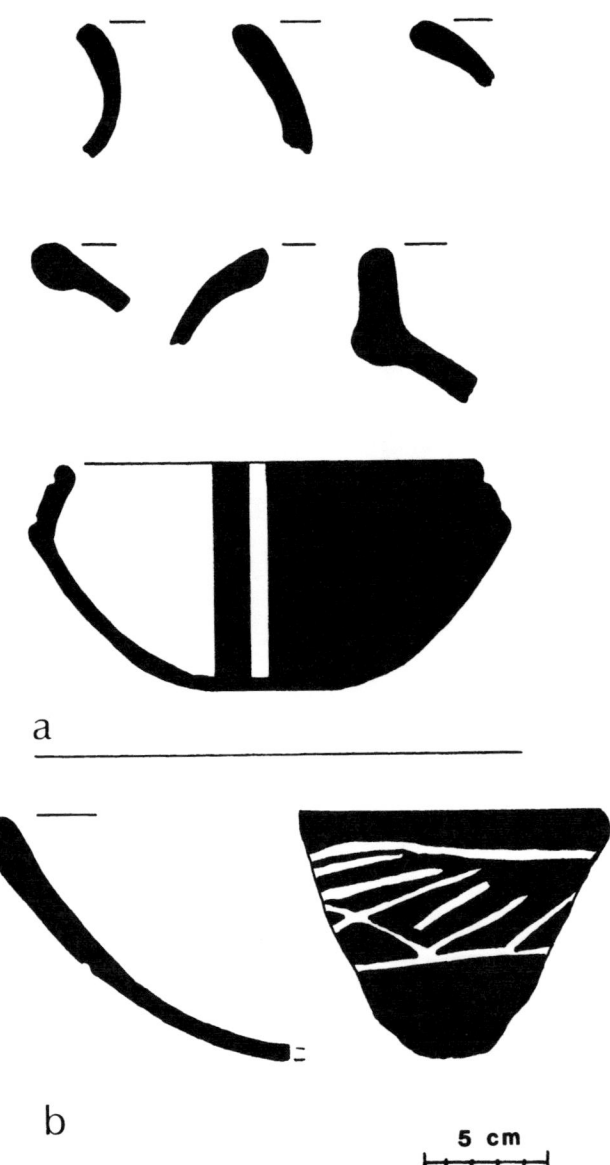

Figure 6.23. Polvero Ceramic Group pottery: *a*, Polvero Black: Polvero Variety; *b*, Lechugal Incised: Grooved-incised Variety.

gray glossy slip with a faintly waxy feel; outcurving sided bowls or dishes; a high percentage of forms have folded rims.

*PASTE, TEMPER, AND FIRING:* Paste color is variable, ranging from buff or light brown to dark brown or dark gray. Differential firing is common, producing a dark core. Paste texture is medium grained and all sherds possess carbonate inclusions. In addition, 5 percent of the sherds have sherd temper and 15 percent have a micaceous glitter.

*SURFACE FINISH AND DECORATION:* The surfaces of vessels are generally well-smoothed and the slip is a lustrous black, with only a faintly waxy feel. Color ranges from 5YR 2/1 (black) to, more commonly, 5YR 2/2 (dark reddish brown) and 2.5YR 2/2 (very dusky red). The slip shows some fire clouding and crackling, although markedly less than the Lopez Ceramic Complex pottery. One sorting problem results from the fact that Polvero Black often has reddish tinges to the slip and is not a true black. It is possible to mistake fire clouded Sierra Red sherds for Polvero Black.

*FORMS:* Three sherds of the Polvero Ceramic Group possess modeling. One is a bird's head modeled on the shoulder of a jar form (Fig. 6.24a). Another is a small face modeled at the rim of a round sided bowl (Fig. 6.24b). The third is an adorno from an unknown vessel form in the shape of a stylized face (Fig. 6.24c).

1. Outcurving sided bowl with slightly rounded base, exteriorly folded rim, and round lip (40.9%). Rim diameter, 16–26 cm; wall thickness, 0.5–1.0 cm.
2. Incurving sided bowl with generally unrestricted orifice, direct or interiorly folded rim, and round lip (27.3%). Rim diameter, 16–35 cm; wall thickness, 0.5–0.9 cm. One sherd possesses a narrow medial flange. Two sherds and the whole vessel are incurving bowls with sharp medial angles or a medial break. The whole vessel (Fig. 6.23a) is 18 cm in rim diameter, 9 cm in height, and vessel wall thickness is 0.6 cm. The vessel was ceremonially "killed" prior to burial.
3. Short outcurving necked jar with narrow mouth, direct or exteriorly folded rim, and round lip (13.6%). Rim diameter, 14–20 cm; wall thickness, 0.5–0.8 cm; neck height, 1.2–2.8 cm.
4. Outcurving sided bucket with exteriorly folded rim and round lip (6.8%). Rim diameter, 25–34 cm; wall thickness, 0.7–1.2 cm.
5. Flaring sided bowl with direct or exteriorly thickened rim and round lip (6.8%). Rim diameter, 15–26 cm; wall thickness, 0.5–0.8 cm.
6. Incurving sided bowl with restricted orifice (tecomate), interiorly folded rim, and round lip (4.6%). Rim diameter, 8–20 cm; wall thickness, 0.5–0.8 cm.

*APPENDAGES: Handle.* There is one loop handle from an unknown vessel form.

*Feet.* There are two solid ovoid feet from an unknown vessel form. They are small, about 3.0 cm in height and about 2.2 cm in diameter.

*INTRASITE DISTRIBUTION:* The type is defined on the basis of sealed levels of the Cocos phase material (Late Preclassic) in the South Square excavations (grid squares 20/30, 25/30, 25/35, 20/35) and in the North Square excavations (grid squares 40/30, 45/30, 45/35, 40/35). Polvero Black pottery continues throughout the Cocos Ceramic Complex

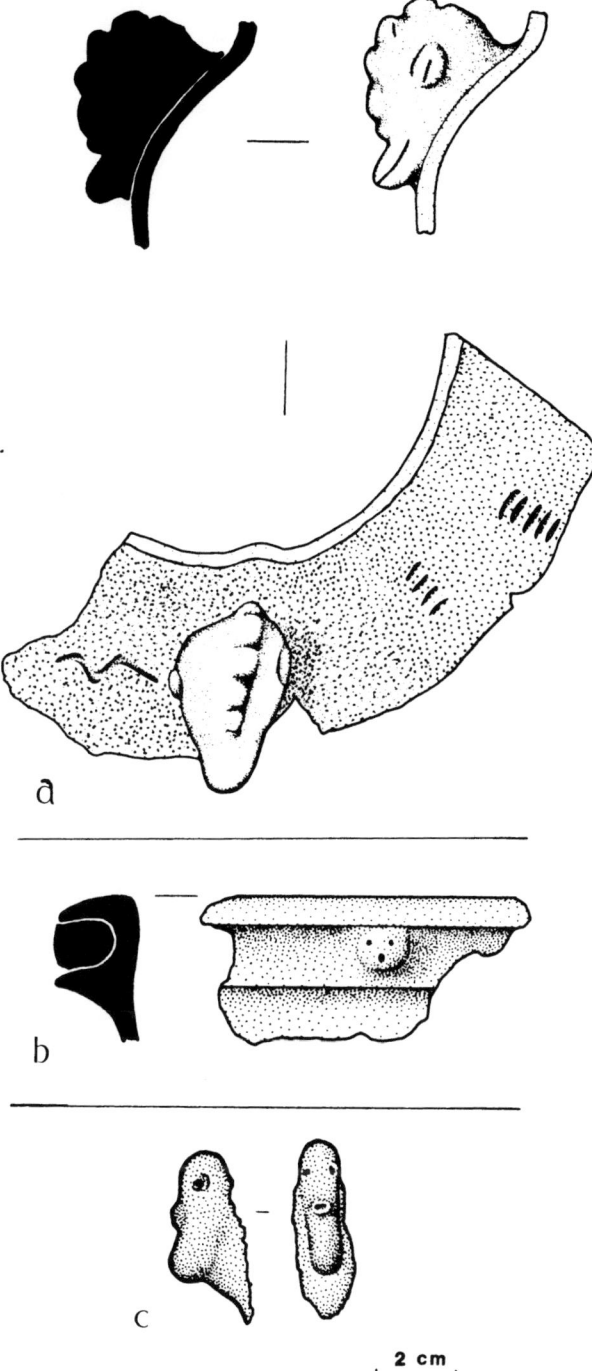

Figure 6.24. Polvero Ceramic Group pottery, unspecified, with modeling (slip color not indicated).

without any apparent changes. It is possible that the quality of the slip improves through time. By the end of the Late Preclassic it approaches the glossiness of Classic period black pottery, but as some of the material is eroded this change is not easily identifiable.

*INTERSITE DISTRIBUTION:* The Cuello pottery is similar to Polvero Black at most sites in the Maya Lowlands and, as at the other sites, is present only in small numbers.

*TYPE:* Lechugal Incised.
*VARIETY:* Grooved-incised.
*ESTABLISHED AS A TYPE OR VARIETY:* Type, Smith and Gifford (1966). Variety, Pring (1977). Pring's description was based on 11 sherds. This description is based on 14 rim sherds.
*GROUP:* Polvero.
*WARE:* Paso Caballo Waxy.
*COMPLEX:* Cocos.
*SPHERE AFFILIATION:* Chicanel.
*FREQUENCY:* 0.6 percent of the Cocos Ceramic Complex rim sherds.
*ILLUSTRATION:* Figure 6.23b.
*PRINCIPAL IDENTIFYING ATTRIBUTES:* Slip color and texture similar to Polvero Black; preslip groove-incising at the lip and on the exterior of vessels; incurving or round sided bowls.
*PASTE, TEMPER, AND FIRING:* Same as Polvero Black: Polvero Variety.
*SURFACE FINISH AND DECORATION:* For general comments, see Polvero Black: Polvero Variety. Slip color and texture are the same as Polvero Black. Decoration consists of preslip groove-incising in horizontal lines around the exterior of vessels and at the rim. There is also groove-incising of diagonal parallel lines that occasionally criss-cross.
*FORMS*
1. Incurving or round sided bowl with unrestricted orifice, direct or interiorly folded or thickened rim, and round lip (85.8%). Rim diameter, 16–25 cm; wall thickness, 0.4–0.8 cm. One of these sherds has a sharp medial angle or break.
2. Outcurving sided bowl or dish with exteriorly folded or thickened rim and round lip (14.2%). Rim diameter, 14–29 cm; wall thickness, 0.5–0.8 cm.
*APPENDAGES:* None noted.
*INTRASITE DISTRIBUTION:* The type is defined on the basis of sealed levels of Cocos phase material (Late Preclassic) in the South Square excavations (grid squares 20/30, 25/30, 25/35, 20/35) and in the North Square excavations (grid squares 40/30, 45/30, 45/35, 40/35). Lechugal Incised pottery continues throughout the Cocos Ceramic Complex without any apparent changes.
*INTERSITE DISTRIBUTION:* Following Pring (1977), the Cuello variety of Lechugal Incised has been designated "grooved-incised" to indicate the kind of incised decoration.

The Uaxactun variety of Lechugal Incised includes both groove-incising as well as fine-line incising (Smith 1955). At both Seibal (Sabloff 1975) and Altar de Sacrificios (Adams 1971) there is only a small sample of this type. The Macaw Bank Variety of Lechugal Incised at Barton Ramie (Gifford 1976) and the simple-incised variety of Lechugal Incised at Tikal are similar to the Cuello variety. Pring (1977) identified an impressed (Gallo) type, a punctated (Blackadore) type, and an appliquéd (Corriental) type in the Polvero Ceramic Group from northern Belize. None of these were found in my collection from Cuello.

*TYPE:* Flor Cream.
*VARIETY:* Unspecified.
*ESTABLISHED AS A TYPE OR VARIETY:* Type, Smith and Gifford (1966). Variety, present work. This description is based on 23 rim sherds, 2 body sherds, and 2 whole vessels.
*GROUP:* Flor.
*WARE:* Paso Caballo Waxy.
*COMPLEX:* Cocos.
*SPHERE AFFILIATION:* Chicanel.
*FREQUENCY:* 1.0 percent of the Cocos Ceramic Complex rim sherds (body sherds not included in the frequency percentage).
*ILLUSTRATION:* Figure 6.25.
*PRINCIPAL IDENTIFYING ATTRIBUTES:* Thin cream-colored slip that is lustrous and only faintly waxy; pale orange to pink paste.
*PASTE, TEMPER, AND FIRING:* The paste color is characteristically a pale orange or pink. Paste texture is generally fine grained and carbonate inclusions are present in about half of all sherds. Differential firing does not occur.
*SURFACE FINISH AND DECORATION:* The surface is covered with a thin cream-colored slip that often allows the paste color to show through the surface color because of its thinness. The color ranges from 5YR 7/2–7/4 (pinkish gray-pink), 5YR 8/2–8/3 (pinkish white to pink), 7.5YR 7/2–8/2 (pinkish-gray to pinkish white), and 10YR 7/1, 7/2, 8/2 (light gray-white). The slip is slightly lustrous and only faintly waxy. It is remarkably consistent in color over the surface of a single vessel or sherd, and although fire crackling or crazing occurs, there is no evidence of fire clouding. No decorated types of this ceramic group have been identified at Cuello, although one sherd possesses a punctated flange and one of the whole vessels has vertical shallow fluting around the exterior.
*FORMS*
1. Outcurving sided bowl with exteriorly thickened or folded rim and round lip (43.5%). Rim diameter, 14–28 cm; wall thickness, 0.4–0.8 cm. One of the whole vessels is this form (Fig. 6.25a). It was found in the rubbish deposited in the disused chultun, Feature 246. It is 14 cm in diameter, 9 cm in height, and vessel wall thickness is 0.6 cm.

2. Incurving sided bowl with generally unrestricted orifice, direct or interiorly thickened rim, and round lip (30.4%). Rim diameter, 16–28 cm; wall thickness, 0.4–0.8 cm. Three sherds of this form have medial ridges, and one has a medial flange. One of the whole vessels is an incurving sided bowl with a medial flange (Fig. 6.25b). It is 28 cm in diameter, 8 cm in height, and vessel wall thickness is 0.6 cm.
3. Incurving sided bowl with restricted orifice, direct or interiorly folded rim, and round or slightly pointed lip (17.4%). Rim diameter, 12–22 cm; wall thickness, 0.5–0.7 cm.
4. Narrow-mouthed jar with short outcurving neck, direct or exteriorly folded rim, and round lip (8.7%). Rim diameter, 14–16 cm; wall thickness, 0.6–0.8 cm; neck height, 1.5–1.8 cm.
5. One sherd belongs to a flaring sided vessel that is slipped on the interior and halfway down the exterior. The basal portion is unslipped. Rim diameter, no measurement; wall thickness, 0.6 cm.

*APPENDAGES: Spout.* There is one unsupported round spout, about 5.0 cm long and 1.8 cm in diameter.

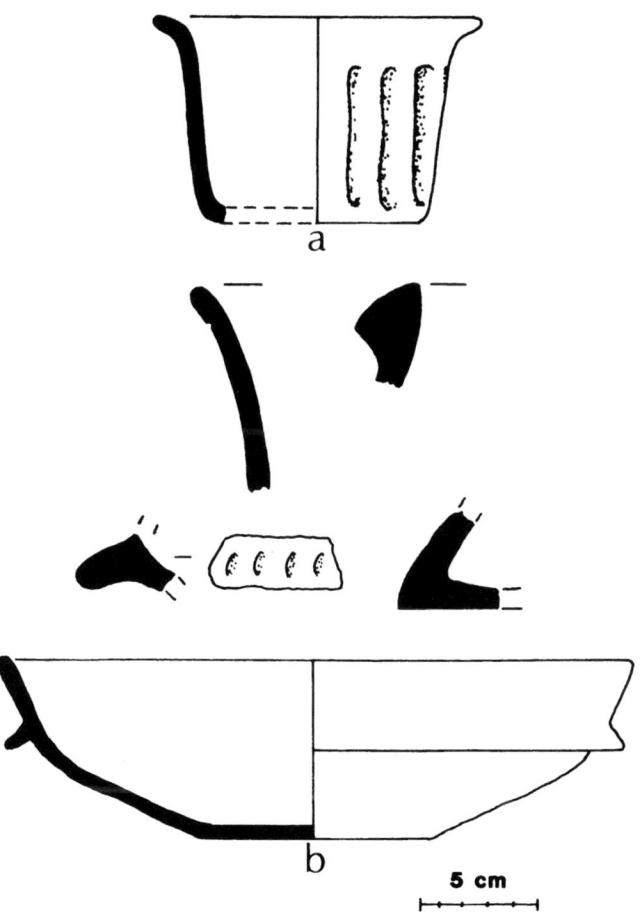

Figure 6.25. Flor Cream: Variety Unspecified.

*INTRASITE DISTRIBUTION:* The type is defined on the basis of sealed levels of Cocos phase material (Late Preclassic) in the South Square excavations (grid squares 20/30, 25/30, 25/35, 20/35) and in the North Square excavations (grid squares 40/30, 45/30, 45/35, 40/35). Flor Cream pottery continues throughout the Cocos Ceramic Complex without any apparent changes. It may get more abundant in later levels, but the sample size is too small to be certain. Pring (1977) originally identified a buff type, Cockscomb, but no cream type at Cuello. He does suggest that Cockscomb Buff may have some overlap with the cream types at other sites (at one end of its color range), although Cockscomb Buff tends to be browner, and that the vessel forms of Cockscomb Buff are similar to the vessel forms of Flor Cream (Pring 1977). I feel that the presence of Flor Cream at Cuello is unquestionable, and sherds Pring would have identified as Cockscomb Buff probably have been classified as Flor Cream or Chicago Orange.

*INTERSITE DISTRIBUTION:* The Cuello variety of Flor Cream is similar to the Flor Cream at Uaxactun (Smith 1955), at Barton Ramie (Gifford 1976), at Seibal (Sabloff 1975), at Altar de Sacrificios (Adams 1971), at Becan (Ball 1977a), and at Tikal.

*TYPE:* Matamore Dichrome.
*VARIETY:* Matamore.
*ESTABLISHED AS A TYPE OR VARIETY:* Pring (1977). Pring's description was based on 30 sherds and 8 whole vessels. This description is based on 78 rim sherds, 1 body sherd, and 2 whole vessels.
*GROUP:* Matamore.
*WARE:* Paso Caballo Waxy.
*COMPLEX:* Cocos.
*SPHERE AFFILIATION:* Chicanel.
*FREQUENCY:* 3.2 percent of the Cocos Ceramic Complex rim sherds (body sherd not included in the frequency percentage).
*ILLUSTRATIONS:* Figures 6.26, 6.30d.
*PRINCIPAL IDENTIFYING ATTRIBUTES:* Vessel areas slipped in two contrasting colors, with one color always red and the other black, cream, buff, or brown; slightly outcurving or flaring sided vessels.
*PASTE, TEMPER, AND FIRING:* Same as Sierra Red: Sierra Variety.
*SURFACE FINISH AND DECORATION:* The type is decorated by contrasting areas of the vessel slipped different colors, similar in effect to fire clouding. However, the division between different colored areas is so pronounced that I am in agreement with Pring (1977) that the effect is intentional. The slip texture is glossier than Sierra Red. One of the slip colors is always red, centered on 2.5YR 4/8 and 5/8, and the other color is either black (5YR 2/1), cream (2.5Y 8/2 white), or brown (2.5Y 5/4, 4/4 light olive brown, olive brown).

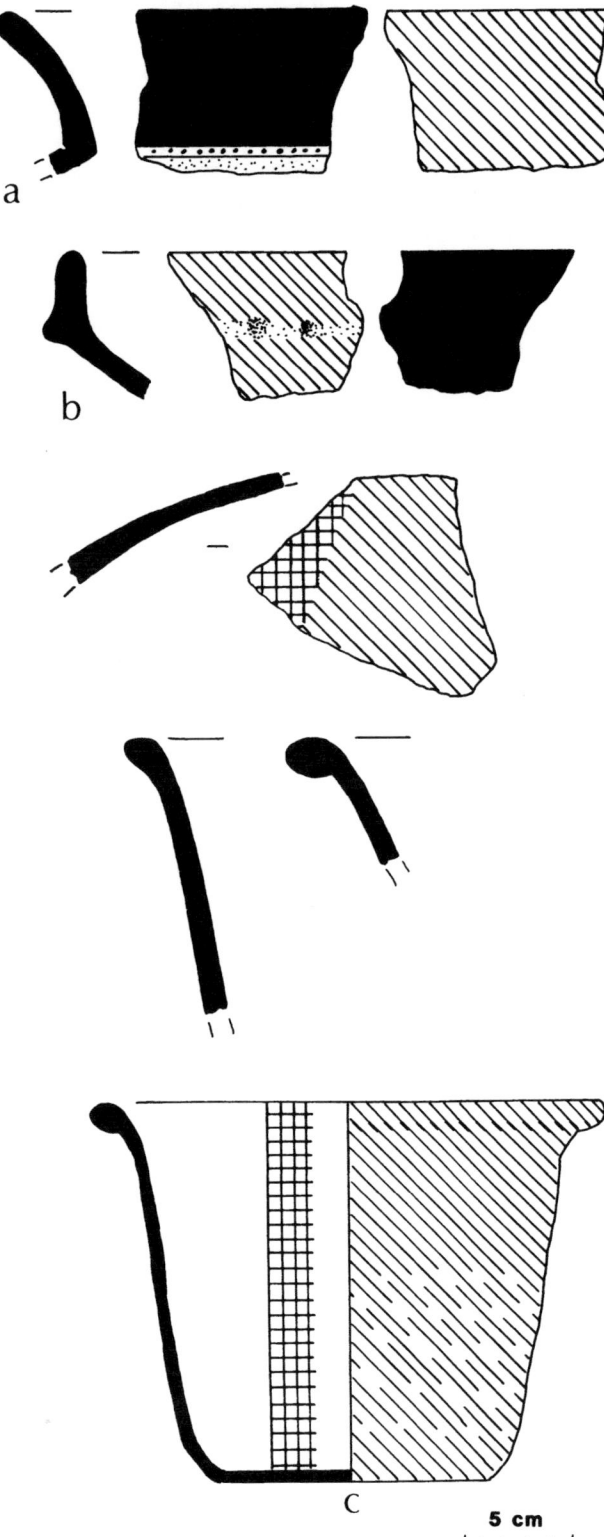

Figure 6.26. Matamore Dichrome: Matamore Variety.

Occasionally either the interior or exterior of the vessel is slipped red and the other side is black, cream, or brown, although more frequently irregular angular patches of different colors occur on both surfaces. The former sherds seem to occur in later Cocos levels. Pring (1977) also identified a Shipyard Variety of Matamore Dichrome that has a red and buff slip that is glossier than the Matamore Variety. I found little differentiation in any of the Matamore Dichrome sherds, all of which tend to be slightly glossy, and I have included all sherds in the Matamore Variety.

*FORMS*

1. Slightly outcurving sided or flaring sided bowl with exteriorly folded rim and round lip (73.1%). Rim diameter, 18–32 cm; wall thickness, 0.5–0.8 cm. One sherd has a medial ridge on this vessel form.
2. Incurving sided bowl with generally unrestricted orifice, direct or interiorly folded rim, and round lip (11.5%). Rim diameter, 12–25 cm; wall thickness, 0.5–0.9 cm. One sherd of this form has a medial flange with punctations (Fig. 6.26b), and a second is an incurving bowl with a sharp medial angle or break.
3. Narrow-mouthed jar with medium to long outcurving neck, direct or exteriorly folded rim, and round lip (9.0%). Rim diameter, 12–18 cm; wall thickness, 0.5–0.8 cm; neck height, 2.0–3.6 cm. One sherd of this form was additionally decorated with punctations at the neck-body juncture (Fig. 6.26a).
4. Slightly recurving sided bowl with exteriorly folded rim and round lip (3.8%). Rim diameter, 16–25 cm; wall thickness, 0.5–0.7 cm.
5. Vertical sided vessel with exteriorly folded or everted rim and round lip (2.6%). Rim diameter, no measurement; wall thickness, 0.5–0.7 cm.

*APPENDAGES:* None noted.

*INTRASITE DISTRIBUTION:* The type is defined on the basis of sealed levels of Cocos phase material (Late Preclassic) in the South Square excavations (grid squares 20/30, 25/30, 25/35, 20/35) and in the North Square excavations (grid squares 40/30, 45/30, 45/35, 40/35). Matamore Dichrome pottery continues throughout the Cocos Ceramic Complex without any apparent changes, with the possibility that dichrome slipping on opposite vessel sides may appear in the later Cocos levels only. The sample size of this type may be misrepresented as too small, because some of the less glossy fire-clouded sherds may have been classified as Sierra Red rather than as Dichrome. A conscious effort was made not to inflate the size of the Matamore Ceramic Group and doubtful sherds were placed in the Sierra Ceramic Group.

*INTERSITE DISTRIBUTION:* Robertson-Freidel (1980) has identified this type at Cerros in northern Belize. Pring (1977) has identified the type at Nohmul. There are no other known comparisons or identifications at other sites.

*TYPE:* Escobal Red-on-buff.
*VARIETY:* Unspecified.
*ESTABLISHED AS A TYPE OR VARIETY:* Type, Smith and Gifford (1966). Variety, Pring (1977). This description is based on 14 rim sherds and 1 body sherd.
*GROUP:* Escobal.

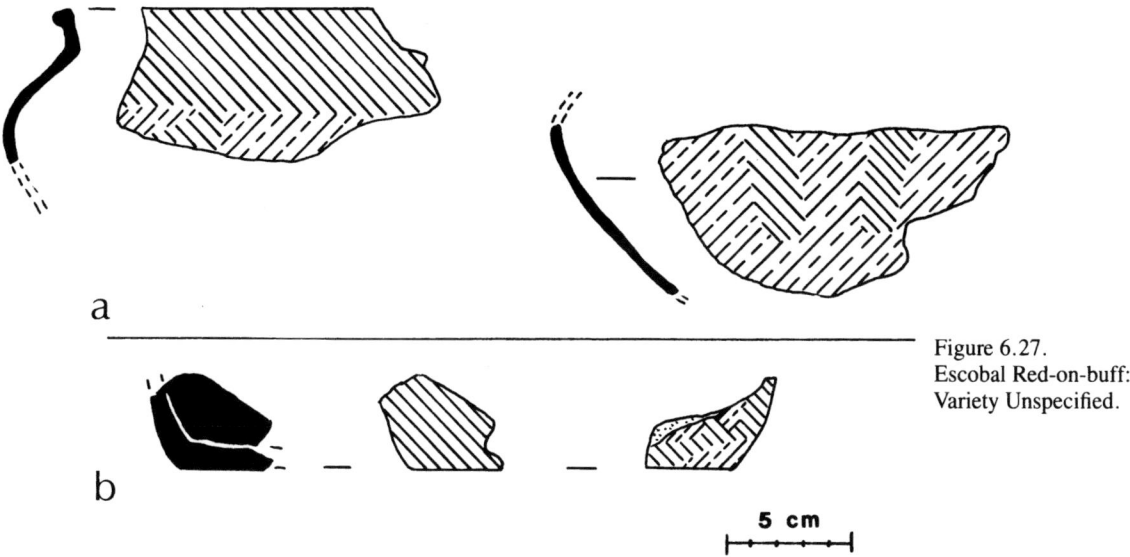

Figure 6.27. Escobal Red-on-buff: Variety Unspecified.

*WARE:* Paso Caballo Waxy.
*COMPLEX:* Cocos.
*SPHERE AFFILIATION:* Chicanel.
*FREQUENCY:* 0.6 percent of the Cocos Ceramic Complex rim sherds (body sherd not included in the frequency percentage).
*ILLUSTRATION:* Figure 6.27.
*PRINCIPAL IDENTIFYING ATTRIBUTES:* Creamy, thin buff underslip or wash; decoration with secondary red slip applied on vessel interior and on the exterior in geometric patterns; red slip similar to Sierra Red: Sierra Variety.
*PASTE, TEMPER, AND FIRING:* Paste color is variable, ranging from buff and tan to a darker brown. Differential firing is common, leaving a darker core. Paste texture is fine to medium grained and all sherds possess small carbonate inclusions.
*SURFACE FINISH AND DECORATION:* The surfaces of vessels are slipped a thin creamy buff with a color range centering on 5YR 7/3, 7/4, and 8/3 (pink). Over the slip, a red slip is applied on the interior of vessels and usually just over the rim exteriorly. The remaining exterior area is left primarily buff with vertical or diagonal red bands, dots, or blotches. The red slip is the same color as Sierra Red: Sierra Variety, principally 2.5YR 4/8, 5/8, 4/6, 5/6 (red). Jar forms tend to be unslipped on the interior.
*FORMS:* One unusual vessel base (Fig. 6.27b) is almost a square corner, with a red-brown interior and a buff exterior with red stripes on it.
1. Outcurving sided bowl or dish with direct or exteriorly folded rim and round lip (78.7%). Rim diameter, 22–35 cm; wall thickness, 0.6–0.8 cm.
2. Recurving sided bowl with slightly rounded base, exteriorly folded rim, and round lip (7.1%). Rim diameter, 28 cm; wall thickness, 0.7 cm.
3. Incurving sided bowl with slightly restricted orifice, interiorly folded rim, and round lip (7.1%). Rim diameter, 22 cm; wall thickness, 0.8 cm.
4. Short outcurving necked jar with exteriorly folded rim and square lip (7.1%). Rim diameter, 18 cm; wall thickness, 0.5 cm; neck height, 1.0 cm (see Fig. 6.27a).
*APPENDAGES:* None noted.
*INTRASITE DISTRIBUTION:* The type is defined on the basis of sealed levels of the Cocos phase material (Late Preclassic) in the South Square excavations (grid squares 20/30, 25/30, 25/35, 20/35) and in the North Square excavations (grid squares 40/30, 45/30, 45/35, 40/35). Elsewhere the type is considered a marker for the terminal part of the Late Preclassic, but at Cuello the sample is too small to confirm or refute this idea.
*INTERSITE DISTRIBUTION:* Pring (1977) has identified small quantities of the type at San Estevan and Nohmul in northern Belize. The Cuello type is a bit different from the type of the same name at other sites such as Uaxactun (Smith 1955), Barton Ramie (Gifford 1976), Becan (Ball 1977a), and Altar de Sacrificios (Adams 1971), where the exteriors are slipped red and the design appears on the interior of vessels.

*TYPE:* Chicago Orange.
*VARIETY:* Chucun.
*ESTABLISHED AS A TYPE OR VARIETY:* Pring (1977). Pring's description was based on 350 sherds, of which 30 were rims or large sherds indicating form. This description is based on 277 rim sherds.
*GROUP:* Chicago.
*WARE:* Fort George Orange.
*COMPLEX:* Cocos.
*SPHERE AFFILIATION:* Chicanel.
*FREQUENCY:* 11.0 percent of the Cocos Ceramic Complex rim sherds.
*ILLUSTRATION:* Figure 6.28a.
*PRINCIPAL IDENTIFYING ATTRIBUTES:* Thin orange or buff-orange nonlustrous slip or wash over a paste of a similar color; jar forms with outcurving necks.

*PASTE, TEMPER, AND FIRING:* Paste color is variable and ranges from a pale pinkish orange to tan, buff-orange, and brown. Paste color generally reflects surface color. Differential firing is common, leaving a dark core or one side of the vessel a darker color than the other. Paste texture is medium grained and all sherds possess carbonate inclusions that are large (up to 1.5 cm) and angular.

*SURFACE FINISH AND DECORATION:* Surface color is variable and, as stated above, is generally a reflection of paste color. This color range includes 5YR 5/6, 6/6, 7/6 (reddish yellow, yellowish red), 5YR 7/4 (pink), and 7.5YR 6/6–7/6 (reddish yellow). Fire clouding is common on about half of all sherds examined. The surface finish is achieved through the application of a thin wash or slip that erodes easily and is only occasionally lustrous. Completely oxidized sherds tend to have a lighter orange color than the incompletely oxidized material that is buff or brown. The Chucun Variety of Chicago Orange is difficult to differentiate from the Warrie Camp Variety on the basis of body sherds, and this is an as yet unresolved sorting problem. The forms of the two varieties are different in terms of rim and lip treatment, and the Chucun Variety tends to be slightly darker and browner in color. Pring (1977) originally identified a buff type, Cockscomb, but I feel that the orange and buff material forms a continuum and should be included in one type. The buff or buff-orange sherds are from incompletely oxidized orange vessels. However, it is possible that with future research and larger samples this distinction will prove important and a buff type may be identified more definitively. I have placed sherds similar to Cockscomb Buff in Chicago Orange and Flor Cream at Cuello.

*FORMS*
1. Wide-mouthed short outcurving necked jar with direct or exteriorly folded rim and round lip (53.8%). Rim diameter, 20–32 cm; wall thickness, 0.5–1.0 cm; neck height, 1.2–2.8 cm.
2. Outcurving sided bucket with exteriorly folded rim and round lip (20.6%). Rim diameter, 22–34 cm; wall thickness, 0.5–0.9 cm.
3. Long outcurving necked jar with direct or exteriorly folded rim and round lip (14.4%). Rim diameter, 18–30 cm; wall thickness, 0.6–1.2 cm; neck height, 3.5–4.8 cm.
4. Medium high vertical necked jar with direct or slightly thickened rim and round lip (6.5%). Rim diameter, 16–25 cm; wall thickness, 0.6–0.9 cm; neck height, 1.5–3.2 cm.
5. Incurving sided bowl with interiorly folded rim and round or slightly pointed lip (2.5%). Rim diameter, 14–24 cm; wall thickness, 0.6–0.9 cm.
6. Medium to long flaring necked jar with direct or exteriorly thickened or folded rim and round or beveled out lip (2.2%). Rim diameter, 18–35 cm; wall thickness, 0.7–1.2 cm; neck height, 2.5–4.8 cm.

*APPENDAGES: Handles.* There are eleven handles, associated with all the jar forms. Four are flat strap handles, of which one is incised to give the appearance of being three separate loops. Seven are round loop handles, of which one

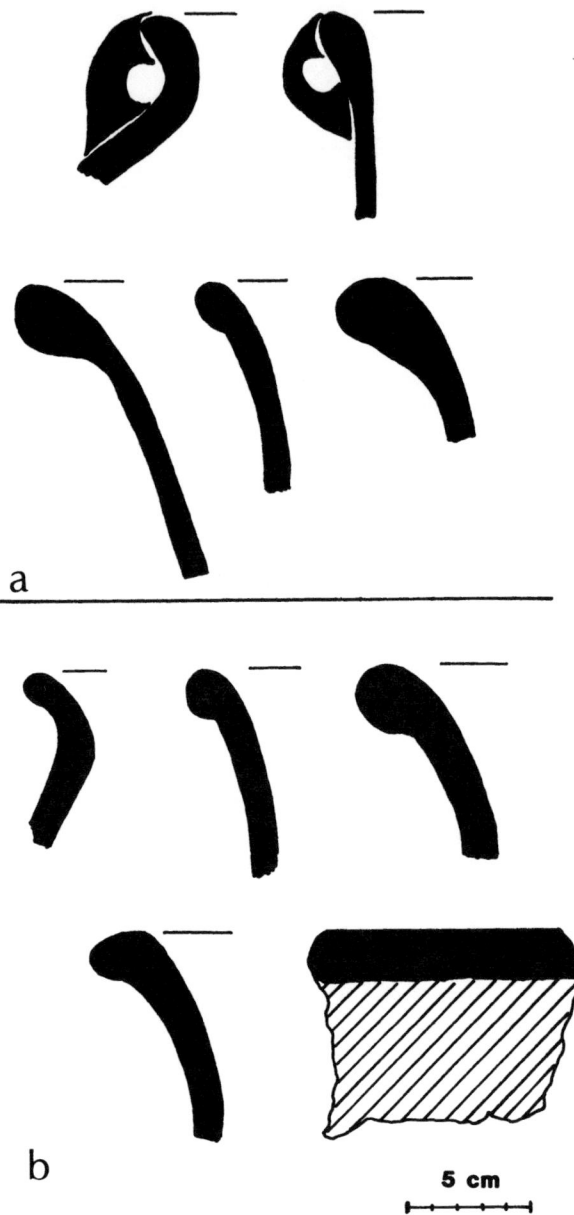

Figure 6.28. Chicago Ceramic Group pottery: *a,* Chucun Variety; *b,* Chucun Variety (Black-rimmed).

is incised to give the appearance of being two separate loops. The number of handles associated with this type may be elevated by the addition of handles from the Black-rimmed variety, because it is impossible to differentiate body sherds or appendages of these two varieties. I have included all the appendages in the Chucun Variety, though some may actually belong to the Black-rimmed variety.

*INTRASITE DISTRIBUTION:* This variety is defined on the basis of sealed levels of Cocos phase material (Late Preclassic) in the South Square excavations (grid squares 20/30, 25/30, 25/35, 20/35) and in the North Square excavations (grid squares 40/30, 45/30, 45/35, 40/35). Chucun Variety pottery continues throughout the Cocos Ceramic Complex without any apparent changes.

*INTERSITE DISTRIBUTION:* Pring (1977) identified the presence of this variety at Santa Rita. There are no specific comparisons for this time period, although Kuxche Orange: Kuxche Variety in the Tulix Ceramic Complex at Cerros (Robertson-Freidel 1980) appears on similar vessel forms and bears a modal similarity.

*TYPE:* Chicago Orange.
*VARIETY:* Chucun (Black-rimmed).
*ESTABLISHED AS A TYPE OR VARIETY:* Type, Pring (1977). Variety, present work. This description is based on 119 rim sherds.
*GROUP:* Chicago.
*WARE:* Fort George Orange.
*COMPLEX:* Cocos.
*SPHERE AFFILIATION:* Chicanel.
*FREQUENCY:* 4.8 percent of the Cocos Ceramic Complex rim sherds.
*ILLUSTRATION:* Figure 6.28b.
*PRINCIPAL IDENTIFYING ATTRIBUTES:* Thin orange or buff-orange nonlustrous slip or wash over paste of a similar color, same as Chicago Orange: Chucun Variety; decoration with a blackened rim band; jar forms with outcurving necks.
*PASTE, TEMPER, AND FIRING:* Same as Chicago Orange: Chucun Variety.
*SURFACE FINISH AND DECORATION:* For general comments, see Chicago Orange: Chucun Variety. Decoration consists of an irregular blackened rim band just over the rim interiorly and exteriorly. The black is probably achieved through the application of some organic material and looks like it has been thinly washed over the rim.
*FORMS*
1. Wide-mouthed jar with short outcurving neck, direct or exteriorly folded rim, and round lip (69.7%). Rim diameter, 22–32 cm; wall thickness, 0.7–1.0 cm; neck height, 1.5–2.8 cm.
2. Long outcurving necked jar with direct or exteriorly folded rim and round lip (17.6%). Rim diameter, 22–32 cm; wall thickness, 0.7–1.2 cm; neck height, 3.2–4.8 cm.
3. Outcurving sided bucket or large basin with exteriorly folded rim and round lip (5.9%). Rim diameter, 24–42 cm; wall thickness, 0.7–1.2 cm.
4. Wide-mouthed jar with short vertical or insloping collar, thickened rim, and round lip (5.1%). Rim diameter, 22–36 cm; wall thickness, 0.7–1.2 cm.
5. Incurving sided bowl with interiorly folded rim and round or slightly pointed lip (1.7%). Rim diameter, 14–19 cm; wall thickness, 0.7–0.9 cm.
*APPENDAGES:* There were no appendages included in this variety. Body sherds of the Chucun Variety are indistinguishable from those of Chucun (Black-rimmed) Variety, and some of the forms of the latter no doubt also had appendages. Handles have been described under the Chucun Variety.
*INTRASITE DISTRIBUTION:* See Chicago Orange: Chucun Variety.
*INTERSITE DISTRIBUTION:* See Chicago Orange: Chucun Variety for general comments. The Chucun (Black-rimmed) Variety has not been identified at any site other than Cuello. The Unnamed Black-on-orange in the Kuxche Ceramic Group at Cerros (Robertson-Freidel 1980) may be similar, although the Cerros variety has a more lustrous slip and is a deeper orange color.

## MORTUARY VESSELS

The largest sample of ceramic mortuary goods at Cuello comes from the Late Preclassic period. It provides good comparative data from the Early to Late facets of the Cocos Ceramic Complex, in contrast to the previous periods where the samples are too small to allow such comparisons. The South Square excavation Chicanel vessels generally are stratigraphically associated with a single mass burial. A later mass inhumation directly above the earlier one, the extreme complexity of the mass burial stratigraphy, and some stratigraphic discrepancies within the burial indicate that the lower mass burial probably represents the occurrence of more than one discrete event. In fact, the examination of the ceramics within the "mass burial" suggests that there are seventeen early facet vessels and six late facet vessels (Feature 128).

Eight of the mass burial vessels are Society Hall Red: Society Hall Variety, identified by their streaky red slip. These are mostly shallow dishes or deeper bowls that are varied in form, ranging in rim diameter from 31 cm to 62 cm and in height from 4.4 cm to 19 cm. Figure 6.12 illustrates typical vessel forms.

Sierra Red: Sierra Variety is represented by five vessels from the lower mass burial. Figures 6.6 through 6.8 provide examples of typical vessel forms. These monochrome red pots are even more varied in shape than the Society Hall vessels, and include a spouted jar resembling a teapot without a handle (Figure 6.29b), a miniature vessel with straight sides, and two outcurving sided bowls, one of which was found inverted over the head of one of the individuals in the mass burial (Fig. 6.29e). The fifth vessel, the most unusual form from Cuello, is an "amphora" jar with an outcurving long neck, three strap handles placed equidistant around the vessel and above the shoulder, and an extremely thickened foot support (Fig. 6.29a). I know of no other vessel of this shape from the Maya Lowlands.

Of the remaining Early Facet Chicanel vessels, two are Sierra Red: Ahuacan Variety. One is another spouted jar with a collar of incised and punctated designs just below its outcurving neck (Fig. 6.29d). The other is a composite silhouette vessel (Fig. 6.29c). Resembling this vessel in style, but with an extremely low shoulder and an exaggerated outcurving neck is an Ahchab Red-and-buff: Variety Unspecified vessel (Fig. 6.29f) from the same context.

The final ceramic vessel is a shallow dish with a decorated labial flange that may have been intended to represent the outline of a fish (Fig. 6.29g). According to this interpreta-

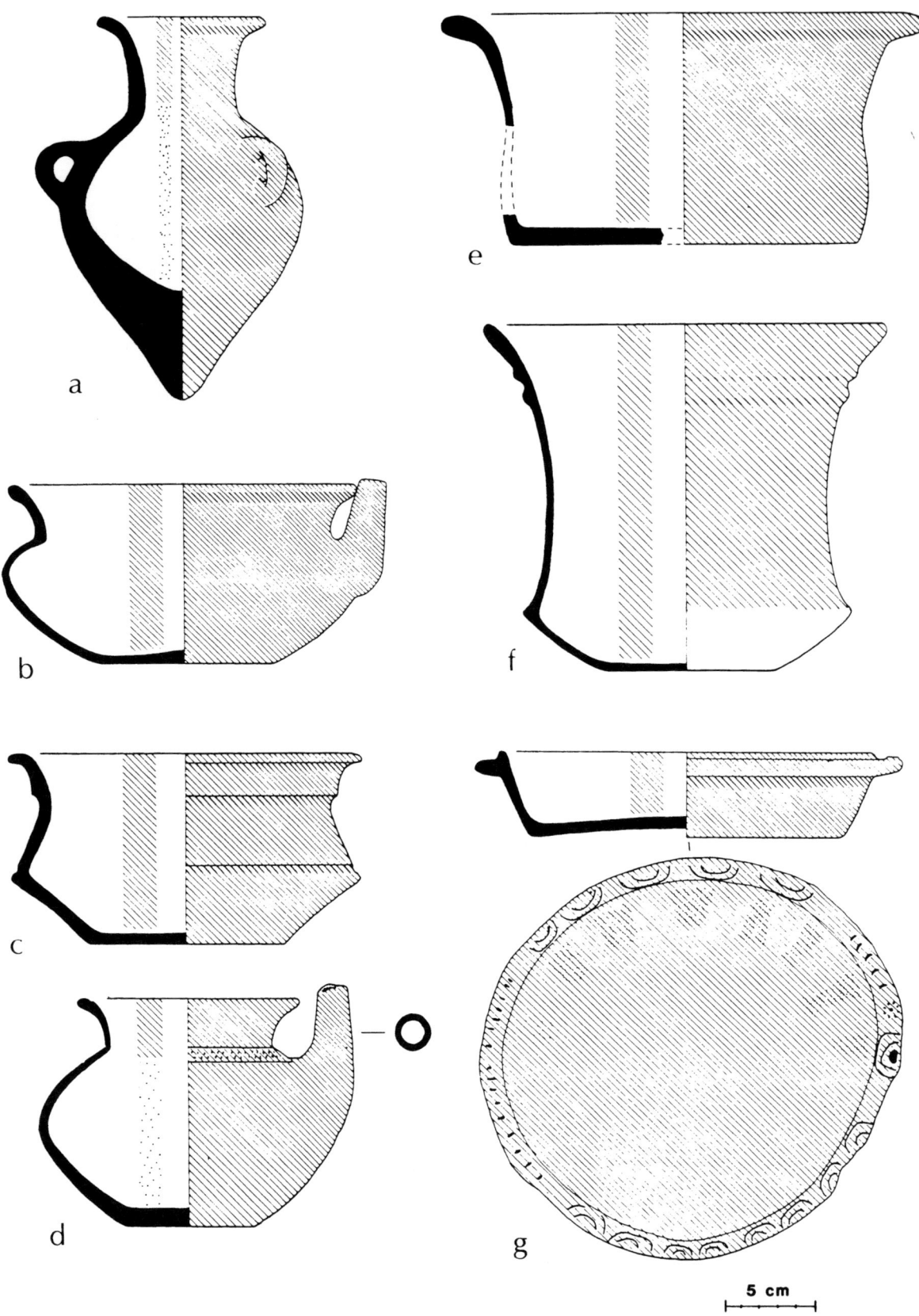

Figure 6.29. Whole vessels from the mass burial: *a, b, e*, Sierra Red: Sierra Variety; *c, d*, Sierra Red: Ahuacan Variety; *f*, Ahchab Red-and-buff: Variety Unspecified; *g*, Sierra Ceramic Group, unspecified, composite.

tion, the circle of punctations represents the eye, the short linear incisions opposite depict the tail, the semicircular incisions at top and bottom indicate the scales, and the indentation below the eye shows the mouth. The interior of this vessel appears to have been decorated with black organic paint, an uncommon technique in the Maya Lowlands for this time period.

The nonceramic items interred with the lower mass burial include some geometrically incised human bone tubes and a pierced shell. In addition to the whole vessels buried as grave goods, several pots were smashed prehistorically, and one had a small hole broken through the bottom implying ceremonial "killing." Associated individuals ranged in age from young children to mature adults and were usually in a flexed position with the knees against the chest.

The later mass inhumation (Feature 128) on the same spot as the earlier mass burial contained six vessels (Fig. 6.30). Five are bowls of Sierra Red: Sierra Variety and the sixth is a Matamore Dichrome: Matamore Variety bowl (Fig. 6.30d). In addition, this burial contained a partial Usulatan vessel from the highlands of Salvador, the only identified traded ceramic piece at Cuello.

The remainder of the Cocos vessels are from North Square excavation contexts and are associated largely with single individuals buried beneath or near Preclassic houses. Thirty-nine Cocos vessels were recovered from twenty-six North Square burials. Fourteen of these individual interments contained a single pot, six contained two pots each, and three had three vessels each. One of the double burials contained one pot and the other contained two. The triple burial contained a single pot.

Eleven vessels from North Square burials are Society Hall Red: Society Hall Variety. The range of forms is the same as that described for Society Hall vessels from the South Square excavations, including three shallow dishes, six deeper bowls, and two spouted jars. Five of the six bowls are "bucket" shaped, and three of these are quite large; the largest measures 40.8 cm in diameter and 30 cm in height. Eight of these Society Hall vessels are Middle Facet, and two of the buckets and a dish are Late Facet Chicanel.

Nineteen North Square vessels are Sierra Red: Sierra Variety. Unlike the Sierra Red material from the South Square, this assemblage contains no unusual vessel forms and consists of sixteen unremarkable dishes and bowls, one plain jar, and two spouted jars. Some of the bowls are incurving in contrast to the exclusively outcurving bowls of the Early Facet mass burial in the South Square excavation. Nine of the North Square Sierra Red burial vessels are Middle Facet, four are transitional Middle to Late, and six are Late Facet Cocos.

Dating to the Middle, transitional, and Late Facets are three Laguna Verde Incised: Grooved-incised Variety bowls (see Fig. 6.15a) from the North Square excavations. One has a medial flange with some incised decoration, one has a chevron incised band below its outcurving rim (similar to Fig. 6.15b), and the third has an outcurving rim with tab handles (Fig. 6.15c).

Two Puletan Red-and-unslipped jars from Middle Facet Cocos burials were found (Figs. 6.20a, 6.21b). A vessel of the Unnamed variety of Puletan Red-and-unslipped, dating from the Middle to late transitional facet, has a ring base and gouged indentations below the slipped portion of the vessel (Fig. 6.21c).

Other unusual vessels in Chicanel burials from the North Square excavation, all from the Middle Facet of the Cocos Ceramic Complex, include a Matamore Dichrome: Matamore Variety bucket (Fig. 6.26c), a restricted orifice bowl of Polvero Black: Polvero Variety (Fig. 6.23a) with a kill hole in the bottom, and a miniature strap handled jar of Richardson Peak Unslipped: Richardson Peak Variety (Fig. 6.1a). This late piece is particularly unusual because it is one of two unslipped vessels (Fig. 6.1a, b) in the entire Cocos ceramic assemblage from Cuello (one other incomplete unslipped vessel has been identified).

Other analyses (Pyburn 1981) of the burial ceramics suggest that there is no relationship among the sex, age, or location of burial and the number, type, or form of the vessels included as mortuary goods.

## THE STELA CACHE

By far the most unusual set of Cocos Ceramic Complex cache vessels unearthed at Cuello was found beneath the unmarked Stela 1, Feature 136 in the South Square excavations (see Fig. 1.5c). The stela is of local limestone, 80 cm long, 50 cm wide, and 20 cm thick, and it lacks adornment with the exception of a shallow horizontal groove across its rear face. This plain stela was erected in association with one of the final building phases of the small Cuello pyramid, Structure 35. (For a complete description of the archaeological excavations of the Cuello stela, see Hammond 1980 and 1982.) The stela most likely dates to about A.D. 100.

Beneath the stela was a cache containing a doughnut-shaped jade bead and three ceramic vessels (Fig. 6.31). One is a Sierra Red: Sierra Variety outcurving high necked jar that looks like a spoutless chocolate pot. It is badly eroded and may or may not have been slipped on its basal portion. Another vessel (Fig. 6.31b) is a round sided, restricted orifice bowl that was found inverted; it is decorated with the modeled head, tail, and wings of a parrot or macaw. It has been classified in the Sierra Ceramic Group, unspecified, with modeling, although its red, waxy slip is badly eroded. The third pot (Fig. 6.31c) is a medially ridged bowl with a faintly waxy, nonglossy trichrome slip of red and orange bands and a black-brown lip. The slip texture is characteristic of the Cocos Ceramic Complex, although the decoration is reminiscent of the polychromes of the later Floral Park and Tzakol ceramic spheres. No type designation has been given to this vessel because of its uniqueness in the Cuello collection.

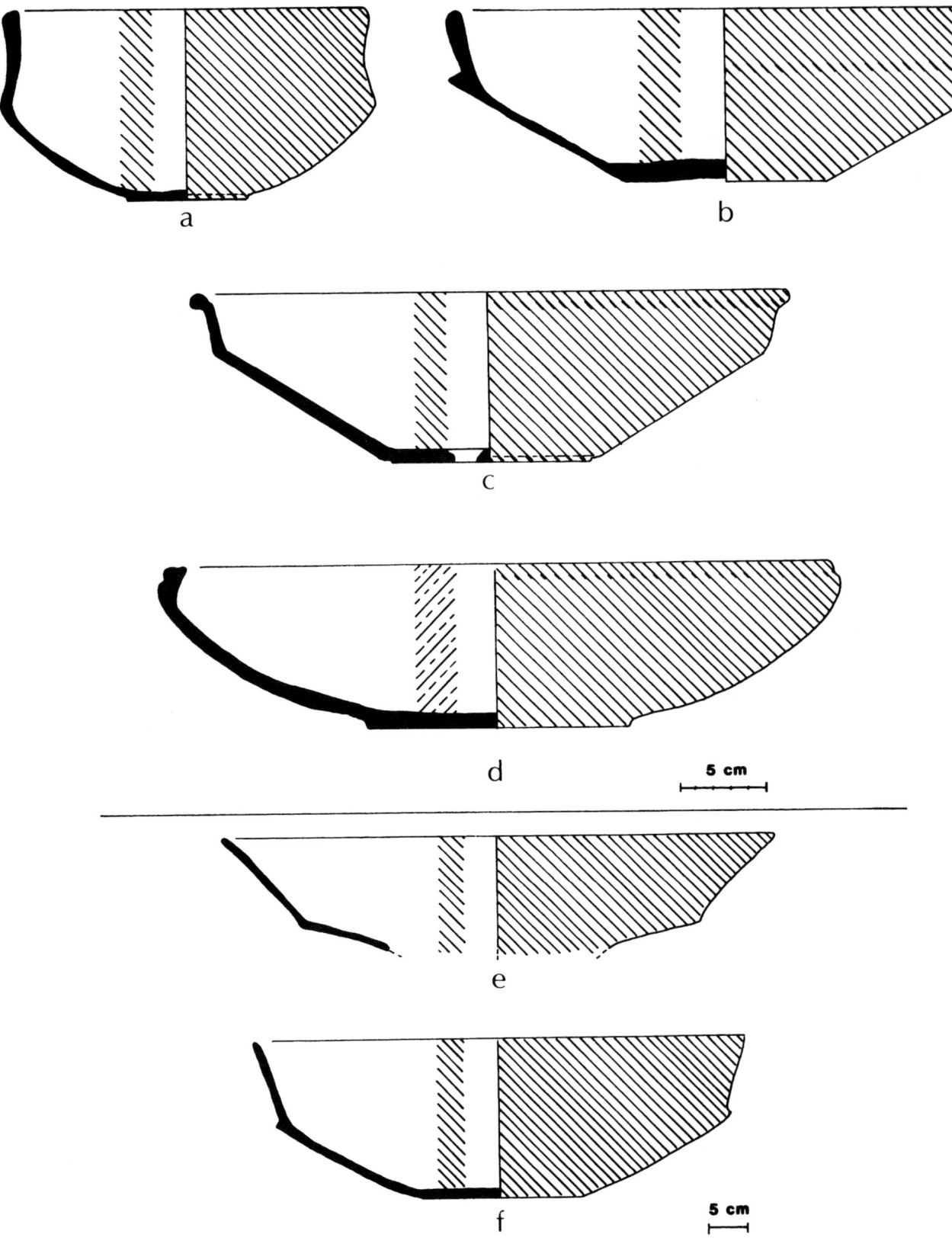

Figure 6.30. Whole vessels from Feature 128: *a–c, e, f,* Sierra Red: Sierra Variety; *d,* Matamore Dichrome: Matamore Variety. (*e, f,* different scale.)

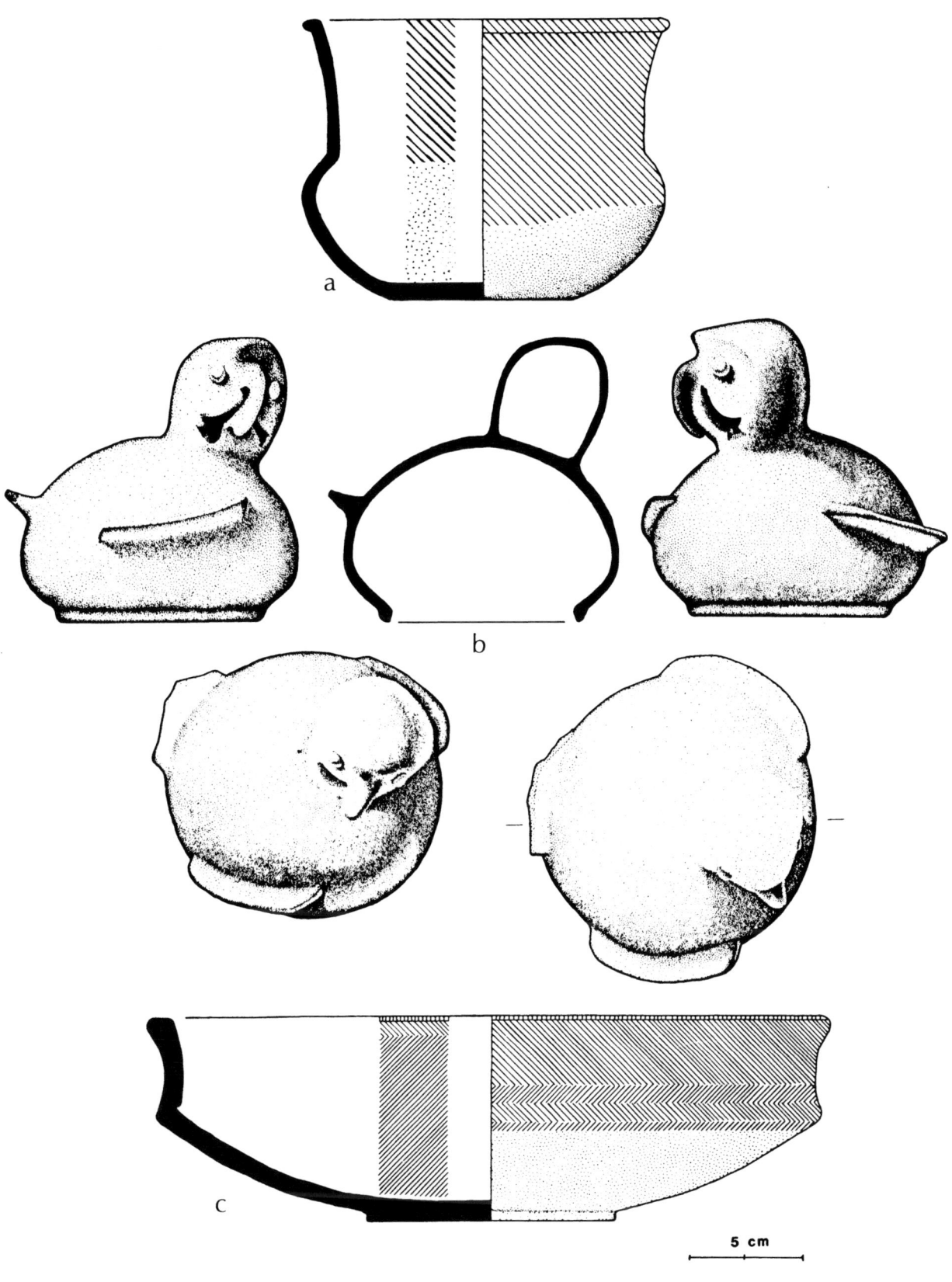

Figure 6.31. Whole vessels from the Stela cache: *a*, Sierra Red: Sierra Variety; *b*, Sierra Ceramic Group, unspecified, with modeling; *c*, Cocos Ceramic Complex trichrome.

CHAPTER SEVEN

# The Cuello Ceramic Sequence

The discovery of Early Preclassic pottery in the Maya Lowlands immediately precipitated speculation concerning the origins of ceramics in the Maya area and suggested to some that similarities existed between Central and South American ceramic complexes. Some of the similarities and differences between Swasey pottery and these geographically widespread complexes are discussed in an attempt to resolve and put to rest some of the questions concerning the relationships among Early Preclassic ceramic assemblages.

## EARLY CERAMIC COMPLEXES IN THE NEW WORLD

The earliest known pottery in the New World comes from South America. The earliest documented complex is the Valdivia phase on coastal Ecuador, dated to 3200 B.C. (Meggars, Evans, and Estrada 1965). Although modal similarities may be drawn between Swasey and Valdivia ceramics, much as between any two collections of pottery, such speculation concerning long range diffusion of ceramics is not undertaken here. Several reports on this topic already have been published (Ford 1969; Wauchope 1950; Sorenson 1955; and Meggars and Evans 1966). I suggest that many similarities found on pottery the world over are the result of working with a plastic medium that limits the possible kinds of forms and decoration rather than the result of diffusion.

Other early pottery from South America includes material from Puerto Hormiga, Colombia dated to between 3100 and 2500 B.C. (Reichel-Dolmatoff 1961, 1965); Rancho Peludo, Venezuela dated to between 2820 and 445 B.C. (Rouse and Cruxent 1963); the La Gruta phase material from Parmana, dated to between 2100 and 1600 B.C. (Roosevelt 1980: 195); and the Monagrillo culture from Parita Bay, Panama dated to 2140 B.C. (Willey and McGimsey 1954). Many of these early South American pottery complexes (with the exception of Rancho Peludo) are coeval, share a number of traits, and, therefore, have been described as part of a common tradition (Willey 1971: 273). Following chronologically, and with similar features, is the Monagrillo pottery from Panama, which shares with the early South American pottery and with the Swasey material an emphasis on simple incising and often modeling. One clear difference, however, is that much of the South American pottery contains fiber temper, and none of the Swasey pottery contains this material.

The Pox pottery of Guerrero and the Purron pottery of the Tehuacan Valley in Mexico first appear at a slightly later date than the South American ceramics. The Purron pottery dates to between 2300 and 1500 B.C. and the Pox pottery dates to about 2500 B.C. Both assemblages are alike in broad terms and, as mentioned previously, are much cruder than the Swasey material (MacNeish, Peterson, and Flannery 1970; Brush 1965).

After that time period, there is a gap in ceramic development in Mesoamerica, followed by the appearance of Early Preclassic pottery on the Pacific coast of Chiapas and Guatemala. The Barra pottery from Altamira, beginning about 1700 B.C. (Greene and Lowe 1967), bears little resemblance to the Swasey ceramics from Cuello. Similarly, other later material from Mesoamerica is notably different from the Swasey pottery. Examples are the ceramics from the San Lorenzo Tenochtitlan (Ojochi, Bajio, and Chicharras) phases (Coe and Diehl 1980), the Chiapa de Corzo Cotorra phase (Dixon 1959; Lowe and Agrinier 1960), and the Tehuantepec Lagunita phase (Zeitlan 1976).

Within the Maya Lowlands itself, Swasey pottery once again stands out as earlier and different from other known ceramic complexes. The closest ceramic similarities to Swasey pottery come from Mani, just north of the Puuc hills in Yucatan (Brainerd 1958). In his examination of the Becan material, Pring (1977) discovered a half-dozen sherds that belonged to the Swasey Ceramic Complex, and he also identified an early, glossy red type at the site of Dzibilchaltun. However, recent studies by Andrews (1986) suggest that the Mani ceramics are of a later date than the Swasey complex pottery. The earliest ceramic complex at Seibal, the Real, dates to between 900 and 600 B.C., as does the Xe Ceramic Complex from Altar de Sacrificios. Although slip textures and colors are different from the Swasey material, the ceramics from both Altar and Seibal share with the Cuello pottery similar vessel forms and decorative motifs (see Adams 1971; Sabloff 1975).

The earliest material from the site of San Jose in Belize is much later than the Swasey phase, although Thompson (1939) identified the "double cylinder" strap handle. The Jenney Creek pottery from Barton Ramie (Gifford 1976) has been dated similarly to a later phase and although the site is not far from Cuello, it shows little similarity to Cuello ceramics in the Early Preclassic. More work in the Maya

Lowlands is needed to place the Swasey pottery firmly within the chronological framework of regional ceramic developments.

## CERAMIC DEVELOPMENT AT CUELLO

The Swasey Ceramic Complex at Cuello contains the earliest pottery recovered so far in the Maya Lowlands, and it dates from about 2000 to 1500 B.C. In 1974, excavations by the Corozal Project at the site of Nohmul uncovered glossy red pottery in refuse deposits overlying bedrock that were obviously older than the Chicanel phase deposits, yet that pottery possessed none of the characteristics of Mamom ceramics (Hammond 1975). In 1975, Duncan Pring, ceramicist for the Corozal Project, began test excavations at the site of Cuello and unearthed a stratigraphic sequence placing this glossy red pottery earlier even than the Lopez Ceramic Complex of Mamom time (Hammond 1976; Pring 1977). Thus this early Swasey assemblage is defined on the basis of Pring's work from the 1975 and 1976 Cuello excavations and on my own analysis of material that largely derived from the 1980 excavations, supplemented by ceramics from the 1978 and 1979 field seasons. In addition, work by the Corozal Project in northern Belize suggests that Swasey pottery is present, in undetermined amounts, at San Estevan, Nohmul, and Santa Rita. Pring (1977) also has identified Swasey maerial at El Pozito and at Becan in Campeche, and Fred Valdez, Jr. and I have identified possibly late Swasey pottery at Colha in Belize (Kosakowsky and Valdez 1982).

Within the Swasey Ceramic Complex red slipped pottery is dominant, comprising almost 60 percent of the entire complex at any one time. Pring (1977) identified two monochrome red groups, Consejo and Ramgoat; Consejo ostensibly possessed a white underslip, distinguishing it from Ramgoat. Now that a larger sample than was available to Pring has been studied, I have chosen to lump these two groups together. The distinction between an underslip and a well-smoothed vessel surface is difficult, if not impossible, to make even microscopically. The two groups overlap in all respects and I have combined them, retaining the name Consejo for the red slipped pottery group in the Swasey Complex.

Consejo Red has a highly glossy red slip over either a well-smoothed surface or a white to buff-pink underslip. Incurved-recurved sided and vertical sided bowls, dishes, and plates predominate. Rims are direct with square or round lips. Preslip groove-incising is a common decoration, with one or two deep horizontal channels cut around the exteriors of vessels or with more elaborate vertical and diagonal designs. Postslip incising and other forms of decoration like punctation and appliqué modeling occur on one or two sherds but are rare. This more elaborate modeling usually is associated with unslipped exteriors of vessels. More commonly, either the interior or the exterior of the vessel is left with the underslip showing so that one surface of the vessel is red and the other cream or buff.

The orange Chicago Ceramic Group follows the monochrome red in sheer quantity (about 30 percent of the Swasey Ceramic Complex), although not in variety of ceramics. Originally, Pring (1977) differentiated a buff Tiger Ceramic Group separately from Chicago Orange. This additional research indicates that the buff and orange sherds form a continuum, with the incompletely oxidized sherds tending to buff and the completely oxidized sherds to orange. Again, I have chosen to lump these two groups because they overlap in all other respects (vessel form and site distribution) and have retained the name Chicago Orange. It is possible that with further analysis some differentiation between the buff-orange and orange pottery will be meaningful, but that does not appear to be the case now. Shapes include incurved-recurved sided bowls, dishes, and plates; tecomates; and jars with medium to high outcurving or flaring necks with thickened rims and square lips. The jar form often is associated with the "double cylinder" strap handle identified by Pring (1977). Chicago Orange pottery tends to have a thin, pale orange slip, or perhaps even a wash, over a pale orange paste of similar color, and only occasionally does it match the characteristic glossiness of other Swasey pottery groups.

The monochrome black group, Machaca, shares the same vessel forms with the red group, though it is low in frequency (a little less than 4 percent of the Swasey Ceramic Complex). Decoration, however, seems restricted to postslip incising in the form of parallel, thin, horizontal lines around the exterior of vessels, occasionally in conjunction with diagonally slanting parallel lines.

The unslipped group, Copetilla, consists largely of jars or bottle forms. There may be some typological overlap with Chicago Orange. Patchchacan Pattern-burnished has been placed within the Copetilla Ceramic Group, in keeping with Pring (1977). The decoration consists of cross-hatched lines filling rectangular or triangular zones and the pottery is similar to, though earlier than, the material from Mani, Yucatan (Brainerd 1958: 24).

As indicated previously, late Swasey material has been identified, largely by Pring (1977), at a number of sites in northern Belize, stretching into the states of Campeche and Yucatan in Mexico. The identification of such early pottery in the Maya Lowlands, in conjunction with MacNeish's (1980) current work on preceramic phases in northern Belize, suggests the possibility of an indigenous development of pottery making in this area of the Maya Lowlands. The Swasey pottery, however, significantly stands out as more technologically and stylistically developed than material of comparable age found elsewhere in Mesoamerica such as the Purron ceramics from the Tehuacan Valley and the Pox pottery from Guerrero (Brush 1965; MacNeish, Peterson, and Flannery 1970).

As Pring originally defined the Swasey Ceramic Complex, it spanned a period of time lasting about a thousand or more years. Furthermore, he stated ". . . the complex appears to span a long period of time with surprisingly few innovations or developments" (Pring 1977: 366). After examination of a larger sample, I have been able to identify enough ceramic change to warrant redefining his terminal Swasey as a separate ceramic complex, the Bladen.

The Bladen Ceramic Complex begins about 1500 B.C. and ends about 1000 or 900 B.C. Once again, monochrome reds dominate the complex (about 56 percent). Consejo continues as the monochrome red group, but there is a decrease in the number of vessels with square lips and direct rims, which are replaced with exteriorly thickened rims and round lips. There is also an increase in the number of flaring and outcurving sided vessels. Decoration consists primarily of groove-incising, and postslip incising is apparently no longer in fashion on monochrome reds. Modeling and punctation, though still occurring rarely, appear more frequently than in the Swasey complex, usually on unslipped vessel exteriors, and there is a continuation of the dichrome effect by leaving one side of the vessel with the underslip showing.

Chicago Orange continues as the next most abundant group (24 percent) as it did in the Swasey Ceramic Complex. However, orange sherds now are decorated by postslip incising, in combinations of horizontal lines and diagonal parallel lines on the exteriors of vessels. Incising is sometimes combined with modeling to create a stylized face. Vessel forms include incurved-recurved sided dishes and bowls and medium outcurving or flaring necked jars with both direct and thickened rims and round or square lips. Although the "double cylinder" strap handle continues, associated with the Chicago Ceramic Group, it is gradually replaced by a loop handle with incisions that in effect mock the "cylinder" strap handles.

While the black and unslipped groups continue virtually unchanged (although they, too, exhibit the increased emphasis on round lips), two new groups first appear in the Bladen Ceramic Complex. The cream Quamina Ceramic Group, although small in quantity (about one percent of the Bladen Ceramic Complex), consists of three types: Quamina Cream, Tower Hill Red-on-cream, and Tower Hill Red-on-cream with resist decoration. Quamina Cream has vessel forms similar to the red Consejo Ceramic Group. Tower Hill Red-on-cream is characterized by broad bands of red that leave rectangular areas of the cream underslip exposed, and it is largely restricted to an incurved-recurved sided bowl form (almost cuspidor in shape) with exteriorly thickened rim and round lip.

The second group that appears in the Bladen Ceramic Complex is orange-brown Honey Camp, comprising about 15 percent of the Bladen complex at any one time. It is marked by an orange to brown surface (the brown apparently produced by a thin wash or organic smudging) that is so well smoothed that it is difficult to tell whether or not the pottery is slipped. Decoration consists of fine-line, postslip incising in parallel lines on the exterior of vessels. Vessel forms include thin-walled flaring sided dishes or bowls with direct rims and round or square lips, and the jar forms overlap with Chicago Orange. Orange-brown pottery has been identified at other sites in the Maya Lowlands (Gifford 1976) as well as in the highlands at Chalchuapa (Sharer 1978; Sharer and Gifford 1970), but the Bladen orange-brown occurs on different vessel forms and has different decorations. The Jocote Orange-brown of both the Tok Ceramic Complex at Chalchuapa and the Jenney Creek Ceramic Complex at Barton Ramie is usually decorated by punctated or impressed fillets on outcurving necked jars.

When examining other Mesoamerican ceramic complexes of the same time period as Bladen, once again the dissimilarities are more noteworthy than the similarities. Modally the Bladen Ceramic Complex bears some resemblances to the Jenney Creek Ceramic Complex at Barton Ramie (Gifford 1976), the Eb complex at Tikal, the Xe complex at Altar de Sacrificios (Adams 1971), the Real complex at Seibal (Sabloff 1975), the Bolay complex at Colha (Kosakowsky and Valdez 1982), and it has been placed tentatively within the Xe Ceramic Sphere.

While relationships between the Bladen complex and other terminal Early Preclassic ceramic complexes are uncertain, it is abundantly clear that Bladen pottery leads directly into the succeeding Lopez Ceramic Complex pottery at Cuello, both stratigraphically as well as typologically. As Pring (1977) discovered, the Lopez Ceramic Complex is perhaps the most difficult to identify because of its stratigraphic position. Lopez deposits were sandwiched between Swasey, Bladen, and Late Preclassic material, thus providing few temporally unmixed collections. The Lopez complex dates from about 1000 or 900 to 400 B.C.

In the Lopez Ceramic Complex, monochrome red pottery of the Joventud Ceramic Group continues to be dominant, comprising about 40 percent of the complex at any one time. Joventud pottery is characterized by a thick, soft, and markedly waxy, nonglossy slip. The color is fairly consistent (dark red) with a tendency to fire crackling and crazing rather than clouding. Outcurving sided dishes with direct rims and round lips are the most numerous forms, and the group is marked by the presence, in small quantities, of thin-walled tecomates and bottles. Almost all decoration is in the form of preslip groove-incising, especially around the rim on the interior of outcurving dishes. The "double-line break" motif is especially common. Chamfering, impressing, punctating, and modeling also are present in small numbers.

The black Chunhinta Ceramic Group and the cream Pital Ceramic Group follow Joventud closely in terms of vessel forms and decoration. Pottery of a third group, Muxanal, is similar in form and incised decoration, but it is additionally decorated with red on a cream slip. An underslip that is cream or white in color is covered by a red slip on the exterior surface that consists of dots, circles, or vertical bands, and the interior is a solid red. This decoration occurs on both outcurving sided dishes and the upper portions of medial angle vessels.

The two remaining groups, Richardson Peak (unslipped)

and Chicago (orange), have similar vessel forms but are easily distinguishable from one another. Chicago Orange continues in the Lopez Ceramic Complex, although it is no longer decorated and is usually restricted to jar forms. The "double cylinder" strap handle is replaced by simple loop handles. Richardson Peak Unslipped is similarly largely restricted to jar forms, but vessel walls tend to be thicker than those of Chicago Orange and the pottery has a coarse paste and a rough unslipped exterior. In addition, Pring (1977) originally identified a buff group, Machiquila, as well as some other minor types that are not present in my typology because the sample was too small for accurate classification.

Once again, ceramic complexes from areas outside the Maya Lowlands that are chronologically equivalent to the Lopez Ceramic Complex show some modal similarities. The "double-line break" motif appears at sites in the highlands of Salvador and the Gulf Coast Lowlands. The Cuadros, Jocotal, and Conchas phase ceramics from Coastal Guatemala, 1000 to 300 B.C. (Coe and Flannery 1967); the Dili phase ceramics from Chiapa de Corzo, 850 to 600 B.C. (Greene and Lowe 1967); the Nacaste phase ceramics from San Lorenzo Tenochtitlan, 900 to 700 B.C. (Coe and Diehl 1980); and the Tok, Colos, Kal, and Chul phase ceramics from Chalchuapa, 1200 to 300 B.C. (Sharer 1978) all overlap modally with the Lopez material at Cuello.

Within the Maya Lowlands, the ceramic picture continues to be somewhat confusing. The Lopez Ceramic Complex falls securely within the Mamom Ceramic Sphere, although the dates from Cuello are a bit earlier than those from other Lowland sites, and some markers of the Mamom horizon are absent at Cuello such as Mars Orange and Palma Daub. Clearly, the Lopez complex shares traits with the Mamom at Uaxactun (Smith 1955), the San Felix at Altar de Sacrificios (Adams 1971), the Escoba at Seibal (Sabloff 1975), the late Eb at Tikal, the late Jenney Creek at Barton Ramie (Gifford 1976), the Acachen at Becan (Ball 1977a), the Ah Pam and Yancotil at Yaxha-Sacnab (Rice 1979), and the early Chiwa from Colha (Adams and Valdez 1980). A more complete discussion of these relationships is presented by Pring (1977).

Thus, the Middle Preclassic period from approximately 900 to 400 B.C. is clearly an important one for understanding processes of culture change in the Maya Lowlands. Unlike the longer sequence at Cuello, most sites in the area have ceramic histories that first begin during this time period, and for this reason many researchers have been concerned with the origins of Maya ceramics in the Lowlands. It is not within the scope of this study to discuss whether or not ceramic production is indigenous to the Maya Lowlands or if it came from one source or from multiple areas outside the Lowlands. Traditionally these discussions are based upon weak modal similarities of Early and Middle Preclassic ceramics from the Lowlands with ceramics from other regions. Instead, suffice it to say that the Middle Preclassic is a period during which there is some apparent progress toward ceramic homogeneity in the Maya Lowlands, although regionalization is still rampant. In fact, Ball (1977b) has suggested that the Middle Preclassic represents a period of time when dispersed groups were gradually filling in the geographical gaps in the Lowland area.

The Late Preclassic at Cuello begins at about 400 B.C. with the Cocos Ceramic Complex and ends about A.D. 250. Although the preceding Middle Preclassic period is characterized by few known northern Belize sites with Mamom Ceramic Sphere pottery, the Late Preclassic represents a significant change; almost every known site has Chicanel Ceramic Sphere pottery, and furthermore it is virtually the same from site to site.

At Cuello, the Cocos Ceramic Complex is marked by the dominance of the monochrome red group, as in earlier ceramic complexes. The red Sierra Ceramic Group contains a large number of types and varieties, and the changes in the distribution of these types through time suggest that there are three facets to the Cocos complex.

In the Early Facet, the red Sierra Ceramic Group is dominated by the presence of Sierra Red: Ahuacan Variety and Ahchab Red-and-buff, two types originally identified by Culbert at Tikal. The main vessel form is a flat based, outcurving or flaring sided dish or bowl with direct rim and round lip. Society Hall Red, characterized by a thin slip applied with streaky horizontal markings, appears in the Early Facet. Other types in the Sierra Ceramic Group are decorated by a wide range of techniques, including groove-incising, punctating, appliquéing, impressing, and modeling.

The black Polvero Ceramic Group and the cream Flor Ceramic Group follow the monochrome red in terms of vessel form, although they seem to lack the wide variety of decorative techniques. The final major monochrome type is Chicago Orange, which continues in a similar manner from the preceding complexes, although now vessels are thicker walled and a black-rimmed variety first appears. Chicago Orange shares a number of vessel forms with the unslipped type, Richardson Peak, though the latter is rougher in surface texture.

The Middle Facet of the Cocos Ceramic Complex is marked by the appearance of Sierra Red: Sierra Variety and an increased emphasis on round sided bowls, flaring sided dishes and bowls with interiorly folded rims, and medial angle vessels. Secondarily, these forms are decorated with flanges or ridges placed near the medial break or lip of the vessel. In general, however, flanges are not particularly popular until later in the complex, and even then are small in number. Sierra Red: Big Pond Variety, a glossy version of Sierra Red, also appears in the Middle Facet. The other monochrome groups are virtually unchanged in this Middle Facet, although they, too, exhibit an increase in the numbers of new vessel forms, in accordance with the Sierra Ceramic Group.

A new dichrome group, Matamore, also appears in the Middle Facet of the Cocos Ceramic Complex. The dichrome effect is achieved by slipping either the interior or exterior of the vessel red and the other side black or, more commonly, buff. Pring (1977) felt that, although this effect may have been caused by fire clouding, it was a deliberate decoration and as the slip texture is glossier than Sierra Red, he defined a new group. Based upon a larger sample size, I am in agreement with Pring.

The Late Facet of the Cocos Ceramic Complex is marked by the addition of yellowish and brownish varieties of Society Hall Red and the use of a streaky technique on Society Hall to create intentional dichromes and trichromes. In addition, there is a scanty representation of Sapote Striated in the Sapote Ceramic Group.

Originally, the Cocos Ceramic Complex was divided by Pring (1977) into two facets: an early, longer facet, followed by a shorter one marked by the appearance of his Sierra Red: Xaibe Variety (now called Society Hall Red) and by a greater percentage of medial angle and flanged vessels. The larger sample now obtained from Cuello, however, provides enough detail to divide the Cocos Ceramic Complex into the three facets described above.

Within the Maya Lowlands, the Cocos Ceramic Complex from Cuello fits securely within the Chicanel Ceramic Sphere. During the early part of the Late Preclassic, the Cuello ceramics share similar features with the Chicanel pottery from Uaxactun (Smith 1955), the Chuen and Cauac pottery from Tikal, the Cantutse pottery from Seibal (Sabloff 1975), the late Plancha and Salinas pottery from Altar de Sacrificios (Adams 1971), the Barton Creek and Mount Hope pottery from Barton Ramie (Gifford 1976), the Pakluum pottery from Becan (Ball 1977a), the Ixtabai and C'oh pottery from Cerros (Robertson-Freidel 1981), and the Blossom Bank pottery from Colha (Adams and Valdez 1980). In addition, Chicanel pottery from Santa Rita, Nohmul, San Estevan, El Pozito, and Lamanai, all in northern Belize, is similar to the Cocos Ceramic Complex material, at least in the Early and Middle facets.

Certain features found on the pottery from these other sites are not found on the Cuello pottery in any large quantity. For example, while the flange is a relatively important decorative feature on the Chicanel pottery from Uaxactun (Smith 1955), it is virtually absent on the Cuello ceramics. However, in general, the Chicanel Ceramic Sphere marks a time of increasing cultural homogeneity throughout the Maya Lowlands.

Toward the end of the Late Preclassic there is a divergence in this apparent ceramic homogeneity, with different sites heralding the beginnings of the Classic Period in different ways. At Cuello, while there is evidence that new forms and advances in slip control and firing were introduced and utilized along side the more traditional Preclassic pottery, there is an apparent absence of Floral Park (Willey and others 1965) features on Platform 34. The markers of the Floral Park Ceramic Sphere—Usulatan style of decoration with its resist painted, parallel wavy lines, and mammiform tetrapod supports—are present in fairly large numbers at other northern Belize sites such as Cerros, Lamanai, Nohmul, Barton Ramie, and Colha (a major lithic manufacturing and exporting center). It seems likely that during this Late Preclassic period of expansion, population growth, and increased communication, particularly in the Peten core of the Maya Lowlands, sites that were located on nodal river and trade networks in northern Belize would exhibit close ceramic ties to the Peten and to each other. The manufacture and use of Floral Park ceramics, and later on Early Classic pottery, probably occurred first at those northern Belize sites located along these networks while bypassing Cuello, a minor center, until later in time. During the final facet of the Cocos Ceramic Complex at Cuello, the pottery continues to be fairly traditional, with only conservative changes in vessel form and decoration.

The transition from the Preclassic period to the Classic period at Cuello at about A.D. 250 does not appear to be especially dramatic, at least in terms of the ceramics. This observation may be true throughout northern Belize, even at sites where there is a strong Floral Park presence. It is likely that what many researchers have interpreted as an absence of an Early Classic population in Belize is better interpreted as an absence of traditional Early Classic ceramic markers until much later in time than their appearance in the Peten core of the Maya Lowlands. At Cuello and other sites, Chicanel ceramics continued to be manufactured and used well into the Early Classic period, reminding us of the heterogeneity occurring in the Maya Lowlands at the same time that all communities were undergoing similar processes of growth and change on their paths to the increased social complexity of the Early Classic. Throughout prehistory, however, Cuello remained a small center, unique because it is the only archaeological site yet discovered in the Maya Lowlands with such early radiocarbon dates. It is likely that as more research is conducted in the Maya Lowlands and more early sites are located and described, Cuello will slip back into obscurity and take its place as just one of many small but growing centers of the Preclassic period.

# References

Adams, Richard E. W.
  1971  The Ceramics of Altar de Sacrificios. *Papers of the Peabody Museum of Archaeology and Ethnology, Harvard University*, 63(1). Cambridge: Harvard University.
Adams, Richard E. W., and Fred Valdez, Jr.
  1980  The Ceramic Sequence of Colha, Belize: 1979 and 1980 Seasons. In *The Colha Project Second Season 1980 Interim Report*, edited by Thomas R. Hester, Jack D. Eaton, and Harry J. Shafer. Center for Archaeological Research, The University of Texas at San Antonio and Centro Studie Recerche Ligabue, Venezia. San Antonio: University of Texas.
Andrews, E. Wyllys, V
  1986  Olmec Jades from Chacsinkin, Yucatan and Maya Ceramics from La Venta, Tabasco. In Research and Reflections in Archaeology, Essays in Honor of Doris Stone, edited by E. Wyllys Andrews V, pp. 11–49. *Middle American Research Institute Publication* 57. New Orleans: Tulane University.
Ball, Joseph W.
  1977a  The Archaeological Ceramics of Becan, Campeche, Mexico. *Middle American Research Institute Publication* 43. New Orleans: Tulane University.
  1977b  The Rise of the Northern Maya Chiefdoms: A Socioprocessual Analysis. In *The Origins of Maya Civilization*, edited by R. E. W. Adams, pp. 101–132. Albuquerque: University of New Mexico Press.
Brainerd, George W.
  1958  The Archaeological Ceramics of Yucatan. *The Anthropological Records* 19. Berkeley: University of California Press.
Brew, John O.
  1946  Archaeology of Alkali Ridge, Southeastern Utah. *Papers of the Peabody Museum of American Archaeology and Ethnology* 21. Cambridge: Harvard University.
Brush, Charles F.
  1965  Pox Pottery: Earliest Identified Mexican Ceramics. *Science* 149: 194–195.
Coe, Michael, and Richard A. Diehl
  1980  *In the Land of the Olmec*. Austin: University of Texas Press.
Coe, Michael, and Kent V. Flannery
  1967  Early Cultures and Human Ecology in South Coastal Guatemala. *Smithsonian Institution Contributions to Anthropology* 3. Washington: Smithsonian Institution Press.
Dixon, Keith A.
  1959  Ceramics from Two Preclassic Periods at Chiapa de Corzo, Chiapas, Mexico. *Papers of the New World Archaeological Foundation* 5. Provo: New World Archaeological Foundation.
Dunnell, Robert C.
  1971  Comment on Sabloff and Smith. *American Antiquity* 36: 115–118.

Ford, James A.
  1969  A Comparison of Formative Cultures in the Americas, Diffusion or the Psychic Unity of Man. *Smithsonian Institution Contributions to Anthropology* 2. Washington: Smithsonian Institution Press.
Ford, James A.
  1954  On the Concept of Types. *American Anthropologist* 56(1): 42–54.
Gifford, James C.
  1960  The Type-Variety Method of Ceramic Classification as an Indicator of Cultural Phenomena. *American Antiquity* 25(3): 341–347.
  1976  Prehistoric Pottery Analysis and the Ceramics of Barton Ramie in the Belize Valley. *Memoirs of the Peabody Museum of Archaeology and Ethnology* 18. Cambridge: Harvard University.
Greene, Dee, and Gareth Lowe
  1967  Altamira and Padre Piedra, Early Preclassic Sites in Chiapas, Mexico. *Papers of the New World Archaeological Foundation* 20. Provo: New World Archaeological Foundation.
Hammond, Norman
  1975  (Editor) *Archaeology in Northern Belize. Cambridge University Corozal Project 1974-1975 Interim Report*. Cambridge: Centre for Latin American Studies, Cambridge University.
  1976  (Editor) *Archaeology in Northern Belize. Cambridge University Corozal Project 1976 Interim Report*. Cambridge: Centre for Latin American Studies, Cambridge University.
  1978  (Editor) *Cuello Project 1978 Interim Report*. New Brunswick: Archaeology Research Program, Rutgers University.
  1980  Early Maya Ceremonial at Cuello, Belize. *Antiquity* 54: 176–190.
  1982  A Late Formative Period Stela in the Maya Lowlands. *American Antiquity* 47(2): 396–403.
Hammond, Norman, and Charles H. Miksicek
  1981  Ecology and Economy of a Formative Site at Cuello, Belize. *Journal of Field Archaeology* 8: 259–269.
Kosakowsky, Laura J.
  1982  A Preliminary Summary of Formative Ceramic Variability at Cuello, Belize. *Ceramica de Cultura Maya* 12: 26–42. Philadelphia: Temple University.
  1983  *Intrasite Variability of the Formative Ceramics from Cuello, Belize: An Analysis of Form and Function*. Doctoral dissertation, University of Arizona, Tucson. Ann Arbor: University Microfilms.
Kosakowsky, Laura, and Fred Valdez, Jr.
  1982  Rethinking the Northern Belize Formative Ceramic Chronology. Paper presented at the 1982 annual meeting of the Society for American Archaeology, Minneapolis.

Lowe, Gareth, and P. Agrinier
　1960　Mound 1, Chiapa de Corzo, Chiapas, Mexico. *Papers of the New World Archaeological Foundation* 7. Provo: New World Archaeological Foundation.

MacNeish, Richard S., F. A. Peterson, and Kent V. Flannery
　1970　*The Prehistory of the Tehuacan Valley*, Vol. 3, *Ceramics*. Austin: University of Texas Press.

MacNeish, Richard S., S. J. Wilkerson, and A. Nelken-Terner
　1980　*First Annual Report of the Belize Archaic Archaeological Reconnaissance*. Andover: Robert F. Peabody Foundation for Archaeology.

Matheny, Raymond
　1970　The Ceramics of Aguacatel, Campeche, Mexico. *Papers of the New World Archaeological Foundation* 27. Provo: New World Archaeological Foundation.

Meggars, Betty J., and Clifford C. Evans
　1966　A Transpacific Contact in 3000 B.C. *Scientific American* 214: 28–35.

Meggars, Betty, Clifford Evans, and Emilio Estrada
　1965　Early Formative Period of Coastal Ecuador: the Valdivia and Machalilla Phases. *Smithsonian Institution Contributions to Anthropology* 1. Washington: Smithsonian Institution Press.

Miksicek, Charles H.
　1978　Preliminary Results of the 1978 Archaeobotanical Field Work at Cuello. In *Cuello Project 1978 Interim Report*, edited by N. Hammond, pp. 67–72. New Brunswick: Rutgers University, Archaeological Research Program.

Pring, Duncan
　1977　*The Preclassic Ceramics of Northern Belize*. Doctoral dissertation, London University, England. Ann Arbor: University Microfilms.

Pyburn, Anne
　1981　The Significance of Similarity. Manuscript on file with the Department of Anthropology, University of Arizona, Tucson.

Reichel-Dolmatoff, G.
　1961　Puerto Hormiga: Un Complejo Prehistorico Marginal de Colombia. *Revista Colombiana de Anthropologia* 10: 349–354. Bogota.
　1965　Excavaciones Arqueologicas en Puerto Hormiga. *Ediciones de la Universidad de los Andes*. Bogota: Universidad de los Andes.

Rice, Prudence
　1979　Ceramic and Nonceramic Artifacts of Lakes Yaxha-Sacnab, El Peten, Guatemala. Part I, The Ceramics: Section A, Introduction and the Middle Preclassic Ceramics of Yaxha-Sacnab, Guatemala. *Ceramica de Cultura Maya* 10: 1–36. Philadelphia: Temple University.

Ricketson, Oliver G., and Edith B. Ricketson
　1937　Uaxactun, Guatemala. Group E 1926–1931. *Carnegie Institution of Washington Publication* 477. Washington: Carnegie Institution.

Robertson-Freidel, Robin A.
　1980　*The Ceramics from Cerros: A Late Preclassic Site in Northern Belize*. Doctoral dissertation, Harvard University, Cambridge, Mass. Ann Arbor: University Microfilms.

Roosevelt, Anna C.
　1980　*Parmana. Prehistoric Maize and Manioc Subsistence along the Amazon and Orinoco*. New York: Academic Press.

Rouse, Irving, and J. M. Cruxent
　1963　Venezuelan Archaeology. *Caribbean Series* 6. New Haven: Yale University.

Sabloff, Jeremy A.
　1975　Excavations at Seibal: Ceramics. *Memoirs of the Peabody Museum of Archaeology and Ethnology* 13(2). Cambridge: Harvard University.

Sabloff, Jeremy A., and Robert E. Smith
　1969　The Importance of Both Analytic and Taxonomic Classification in the Type: Variety System. *American Antiquity* 34(3): 278–285.

Sharer, Robert
　1978　*The Prehistory of Chalchuapa, El Salvador*, Vol. 3, *Ceramics*, Philadelphia: University of Pennsylvania Press.

Sharer, Robert J., and James C. Gifford
　1970　Prehistoric Ceramics from Chalchuapa, El Salvador and Their Relationships with the Maya Lowlands. *American Antiquity* 35(4): 441–462.

Smith, Robert E.
　1955　Ceramic Sequence at Uaxactun, Guatemala. *Middle American Research Institute Publication* 20. New Orleans: Tulane University.
　1971　The Pottery of Mayapan: Including Studies of Ceramic Material from Uxmal, Kabah and Chichen Itza. *Papers of the Peabody Museum of Archaeology and Ethnology* 66, Cambridge: Harvard University.

Smith, Robert E., and James C. Gifford
　1966　Maya Ceramic Varieties, Types and Wares at Uaxactun: Supplement to Ceramic Sequence at Uaxactun. *Middle American Research Institute Publication* 28. New Orleans: Tulane University.

Smith, Robert E., Gordon R. Willey, and James C. Gifford
　1960　The Type: Variety Concept as a Basis for the Analysis of Maya Pottery. *American Antiquity* 25(3): 330–341.

Sorenson, John L.
　1955　A Chronological Ordering of the Mesoamerican Preclassic. *Middle American Research Records* 2(3): 41–70.

Thompson, J. Eric
　1939　Excavations at San Jose, British Honduras. *Carnegie Institution of Washington Publication* 506. Washington: Carnegie Institution.

Wauchope, Robert
　1950　A Tentative Sequence of Preclassic Ceramics in Middle America. *Middle American Research Records* 1: 211–250. New Orleans: Tulane University.

Willey, Gordon R.
　1971　An Archaeological Frame of Reference for Maya Culture History. In *Desarrollo Cultural de Los Maya*, edited by E. Vogt and A. Ruz Lhuillier, pp. 137–187. Mexico.

Willey, Gordon R., and Charles McGimsey
　1954　The Monagrillo Culture of Panama. *Papers of the Peabody Museum of Archaeology and Ethnology* 49(2). Cambridge: Harvard University.

Willey, Gordon R., T. Patrick Culbert, and Richard E. W. Adams
　1967　Maya Lowland Ceramics: A Report from the 1965 Guatemala City Conference. *American Antiquity* 32(3): 289–315.

Willey, G. R., W. R. Bullard, Jr., J. B. Glass, and J. C. Gifford
　1965　Prehistoric Maya Settlements in the Belize Valley. *Papers of the Peabody Museum of Archaeology and Ethnology* 54. Cambridge: Harvard University.

Wright, James V.
　1967　Type and Attribute Analysis: Their Application to Iroquois Culture History. In *Iroquois Culture History and Prehistory: Proceedings of the 1965 Conference on Iroquois Research*, edited by E. Tooker, pp. 99–100. Albany: New York State Museum and Science Service.

Zeitlan, R. N.
　1976　Long Distance Exchange and the Growth of a Regional Center on the Southern Isthmus of Tehuantepec, Mexico. Paper presented at the 1976 annual meeting of the Society for American Archaeology, St. Louis.

# Index

Aac Red-on-buff
   at Tikal, 33
   at Yaxha-Sacnab, 33
Abelino Red
   at Altar de Sacrificios, 16
Acachen Ceramic Complex
   at Becan, 51, 91
Achiotes Ceramic Group, 10, 24
Achiotes Unslipped
   at Altar de Sacrificios, 14, 24
   at Seibal, 14, 24
Ahchab Red-and-buff: Unspecified Variety, 10, 54, 57–58, 59, 83, 91
Ah Pam Ceramic Complex
   at Yaxha-Sacnab, 27, 28, 91
Ahuacan Variety (Sierra Red), 10, 12, 54, 57, 58, 83, 84, 91
Altamira site, Guatemala
   Barra ceramics, 14, 88
Altar de Sacrificios site, Guatemala, 9, 14, 16, 17, 18, 19, 20, 21, 24, 26, 27, 28, 30, 31, 32, 33, 36, 38, 43, 45, 46, 47, 48, 49, 51, 62, 68, 70, 71, 78, 79, 81, 88, 90, 91, 92
Amphora, 83, 84
Andrews, E. Wyllys V, 15, 88
Angle, on vessels, 44, 50, 59, 62, 63, 64, 66, 68, 69, 74, 77, 78, 80. *See also* Flange; Ridge
Animal representations. *See* Decoration, on vessels
Appendages, on vessels. *See* Foot; Handle; Spout
Appliquéd decoration, on vessels, 9, 10, 11, 12, 44, 47, 50, 54, 72, 74, 78, 89, 91
Architectural phases
   at Cuello, 7
Architecture. *See* House platforms; Masonry structures; Platform 34; Pole and thatch structures; Pits, slab-lined; Pyramid; Structure 35

Backlanding Incised:
   Backlanding Variety, 10, 13, 17, 40
   Grooved-incised Variety, 10, 13, 17–18, 26, 40
Ball, Joseph W., vii, 51, 70, 71, 91
Barquedier Grooved-incised: Barquedier Variety, 10, 23, 25–26, 40
Barranco Red-on-cream, 9, 10, 48
Barton Creek Ceramic Complex
   at Barton Ramie, 92
Barton Ramie site, Belize, 9, 26, 28, 37, 38, 43, 45, 47, 48, 49, 62, 63, 64, 67, 70, 72, 78, 79, 81, 88, 90, 91, 92
Basal angle. *See* Angle, on vessels
Basal flange. *See* Flange, basal
Basal ridge. *See* Ridge, basal
Base, of vessel
   concave, 60, 61, 64, 66, 67
   flat, 16, 24, 25, 29, 33, 34, 38, 39, 40, 42, 43, 44, 47, 48, 49, 60, 61, 62, 84
   ring, 62, 75
   rounded, 39, 40, 62, 64, 70, 71, 75, 77, 81
   *See also* Foot, on vessels
Becan site, Mexico, 16, 18, 43, 45, 46, 47, 48, 49, 51, 62, 70, 72, 74, 79, 81, 88, 89, 91, 92
Belize, 1. *See also* Barton Ramie site; Belmopan; Caledonia site; Cerros site; Colha site; Chowacol site; El Pozito site; Kichpanha site; Lamanai site; Lubaantun site; Nohmul site; Orangewalktown; San Estevan site; San Jose site; Santa Rita site
Belize Glossy Ware, 8, 9, 12
Belmopan, Department of Archaeology, vii, 9, 46
Big Pond Variety (Sierra Red), 10, 54, 59–63, 91
Black Rock Variety. *See* Joventud Red
Blackadore Punctated, 10, 78
Bladen Ceramic Complex
   architectural phases, 7
   burial ceramics, 38–40
   ceramic groups, 23
   dating of, 9, 90
   relationship to other site complexes, 90
   summary of attributes, 90
   type descriptions, 23–38
Blossom Bank Ceramic Complex
   at Colha, 92
Bobo Red-and-unslipped, 9, 10, 46
Bolay Ceramic Complex
   at Colha, 25, 35, 90
Bomba Red-and-unslipped: Bomba Variety, 28
Botanical remains, vii, 3
Bottle-shaped vessels, 14, 15, 16, 22, 23, 24, 25, 35, 42, 43, 52, 89, 90
Bound to Shine Variety (Society Hall Red), 10, 12, 67–68, 69
Bowl
   incurving, 14, 16, 17, 18, 20, 22, 24, 25, 26, 27, 29, 31, 32, 33, 34, 35, 36, 37, 39, 43, 44, 46, 47, 48, 49, 51, 52, 55, 57, 59, 64, 66, 70, 71, 74, 76, 77, 78, 79, 80, 81, 82, 83, 85, 91 (*see also* Tecomate)
   incurving with collar, 16, 19, 21, 25, 26, 31, 36, 37
Bowl or dish
   flaring, 14, 16, 17, 18, 19, 20, 21, 24, 25, 26, 27, 30, 31, 32, 35, 36, 37, 38, 39, 42, 43, 44, 47, 50, 52, 56, 57, 59, 61, 66, 67, 74, 79, 80, 90, 91
   miniature, 55, 74, 83, 85
   outcurving, 14, 17, 18, 20, 24, 26, 27, 28, 31, 32, 34, 35, 37, 39, 52, 55, 57, 59, 61, 64, 66, 69, 71, 74, 77, 78, 79, 80, 81, 83, 84, 85, 91 (*see also* Bucket)
   recurving, 14, 15, 16, 17, 18, 19, 20, 21, 24, 25, 26, 27, 29, 30, 31, 32, 34, 35, 36, 37, 38, 39, 44, 45, 46, 49, 50, 52, 57, 59, 60, 66, 67, 71, 72, 73, 74, 76, 80, 81, 84, 89, 90 (*see also* Cuspidor)
   vertical, 15, 16, 17, 18, 19, 20, 21, 24, 26, 27, 30, 31, 32, 35, 37, 39, 42, 43, 45, 52, 80
Brainerd, George, 15, 43
Bridged spout, 59
Bucket, 57, 59, 60, 67, 80, 82, 85. *See also* Bowl, outcurving
Burial vessels, 5, 38–40, 83–86
Burials, 3, 4, 5, 38–40, 83–86. *See also* Mass burial
Burnishing, on vessels, 14, 15, 16. *See also* Pattern-burnishing, on vessels

Cabro Red
   at Cerros, 63
Calcutta Incised: Grooved-incised Variety, 10
Caledonia site, Belize, 43, 51
Canquin Black-on-red, 10, 19, 29, 33
Cantutse Ceramic Complex
   at Seibal, 92
Capaz Variety. *See* Chunhinta Black
Carbonate temper. *See* Paste inclusions, carbonate
Cauac Ceramic Complex
   at Tikal, 92
Cave, Loltun, 15
Ceramic complex
   definition of, 8
   names of, 10, 11, 12
Ceramic group
   definition of, 8
   frequencies of, 13, 23, 41, 54
   names of, 10, 11, 12, 13, 23, 41, 54
Ceramic sphere
   definition of, 8
Ceramic type
   definition of, 7
   naming of, 7–8
Ceramic variety
   definition of, 7
   definitions of Unnamed and Unspecified, 8
   naming of, 7–8
Ceramic ware
   definition of, 8
   names of, 10, 11, 12, 13, 23, 41, 54
Cerros site, Belize, 9, 56, 59, 63, 67, 70, 80, 83, 92
Chacalte Incised:
   Chacalte Variety, 10, 13, 20–21, 31, 37, 40
   Yo Creek Variety, 10, 12, 30–31, 40
Chacchinic Red-on-orange-brown, 10, 28
Chalchuapa site, El Salvador, 33, 37, 38, 90, 91
Chamfering, on vessels, 11, 41, 45, 46, 90

Chiapa de Corzo site, Mexico, 33, 88, 91
Chicago Ceramic Group
	in Bladen Ceramic Complex, 10, 23, 34–36, 37, 40, 90
	in Cocos Ceramic Complex, 10, 54, 81–83, 91
	in Lopez Ceramic Complex, 10, 41, 52–53, 91
	in Swasey Ceramic Complex, 10, 13, 20, 21–22, 89
Chicago Orange:
	Chicago Variety, 10, 13, 14, 21–22, 34, 35, 36, 40, 52
Chiwa Ceramic Complex
	at Colha, 91
"Chocolate" pot, 57, 60, 67, 83, 84, 85. *See also* Jar
Chompipi Incised, 21, 36, 38
Chowacol site, Belize, 43, 56, 63, 67, 74
Chucun varieties. *See* Chicago Orange
	Chucun Black-rimmed Variety, 10, 54, 82, 83
	Chucun Variety, 10, 54, 79, 81–83, 91
	Nago Bank Variety, 10, 11, 23, 34–35, 36, 37, 38, 39, 40, 52, 90
	Warrie Camp Variety, 10, 12, 41, 52–53, 82
Chuen Ceramic Complex
	at Tikal, 58, 92
Chultun
	at Cuello, 5, 78
Chunhinta Black:
	Capaz Variety, 47
	Chunhinta Variety, 10, 41, 47, 48
Chunhinta Ceramic Group, 10, 41, 47–48, 90
Cockscomb Buff, 10, 79, 81
Cockscomb Ceramic Group, 10, 79
Cocos Ceramic Complex
	architectural phases, 7
	burial vessels, 83–86
	ceramic groups, 54
	dating of, 9, 91
	relationship to other site complexes, 92
	stela cache, 85, 87
	summary of attributes, 91–92
	type descriptions, 54–83
Coe, Michael, 15, 32
C'oh Ceramic Complex
	at Cerros, 92
Colha site, Belize, 9, 16, 22, 25, 32, 35, 42, 43, 51, 53, 56, 62, 63, 67, 68, 74, 89, 90, 91, 92
Colombia. *See* Puerta Hormiga site
Color symbols, key to, 8
Comistun Incised
	at Seibal, 34
Complex. *See* Ceramic complex
Composite vessels, 11, 23, 28, 29
Conchas Phase, Guatemala, 91
Consejo Ceramic Group
	in Bladen Ceramic Complex, 10, 13, 23, 24–30, 40, 90
	in Swasey Ceramic Complex, 10, 13, 15–19, 40, 89
Consejo Red:
	Consejo Variety, 10, 13, 15–16, 17, 18, 19, 24, 25, 27, 29, 40
	Estrella Variety, 10, 11, 23, 24–25, 26, 27, 29, 39, 40
Copetilla Ceramic Group, 13–15, 23–24, 40, 89
Copetilla Unslipped:
	Copetilla Variety, 10, 13–14, 15, 21, 22, 24, 40
	Gallon Jug Variety, 10, 11, 23–24, 39, 40

Copper Bank Incised: Copper Bank Variety, 10, 23, 37–38
Corozal Orange Ware, 8, 9, 11
Corriental Appliquéd, 10, 11, 78
Cotton Tree Incised: Cotton Tree Variety, 10, 23, 35–36, 37, 38, 39, 40
Cowpen Incised: Cowpen Variety, 10, 11, 36
Crazing or crackling of vessel slip, 31, 42, 43, 47, 48, 57, 59, 77, 78, 90
Crisanto Black, 20
Cuadros Phase, Guatemala, 33, 91
Cudjoe Composite:
	Cudjoe Variety, 11, 23, 28, 29
	Unnamed variety, 11, 23, 28–29
Culbert, T. Patrick, vii, 9, 18, 19, 57, 70, 91
Cuspidor, 57, 90. *See also* Bowl or dish, recurving
Cylinder handle. *See* Handles on vessels

Decoration, on vessels
	animal representations, 33, 46, 51, 77, 83, 84, 85, 87
	geometric, 14, 15, 17, 18, 19, 20, 21, 25, 26, 28, 29, 30, 31, 32, 33, 34, 35, 36, 37, 38, 39, 43, 44, 45, 47, 48, 49, 50, 52, 57, 69, 70, 71, 72, 73, 74, 75, 76, 77, 78, 79, 80, 81, 83, 84, 85, 89
	human representations, 31, 38, 46, 51
	*See also* Appliquéd decoration
Deprecio Incised:
	Grooved-incised Variety, 11, 41, 47–48
	Unspecified Variety, 11, 47
Desvario Chamfered: Desvario Variety, 11, 41, 45–46
Dichrome slip, on vessels, 13, 18, 19, 23, 26, 27, 28, 29, 32, 33, 34, 41, 48, 49, 50, 51, 54, 57, 58, 68, 69, 79, 80, 81, 89, 90, 91, 92
Diehl, Richard A., 15
Dish or plate
	flaring, 55, 61
	outcurving, 43, 44, 46, 47, 48, 49, 50, 51, 61, 70, 90
	*See also* Bowl or dish
Double cylinder handle. *See* Handles, double cylinder
"Double-line break" motif, on vessels, 44, 45, 90
Double slip, on vessels, 15–19, 24–30, 31–34, 49–51, 57–58, 62–63
Dzibilchaltun site, Yucatan, Mexico, 16, 88

Early Classic
	in Mesoamerica, 1, 92
Early Preclassic
	dating of, 1, 2
	in Mesoamerica, 88–90
	structures at Cuello, 2–3
	*See also* Bladen Ceramic Complex; Swasey Ceramic Complex
Eb Ceramic Complex
	at Tikal, 18, 19, 27, 28, 90, 91
Ecuador, 15, 88
El Pozito site, Belize, 14, 16, 22, 28, 32, 35, 43, 51, 89, 92
El Salvador. *See* Chalchuapa site
Escoba Ceramic Complex
	at Seibal, 91
Escobal Ceramic Group, 10, 11, 54, 80–81
Escobal Red-on-buff: Unspecified Variety, 10, 11, 54, 80–81
Established type and variety
	definition of, 8
Estero Red-and-unslipped, 11, 28

Estrada, Emilio, 15
Estrella Variety (Consejo Red), 10, 11, 23, 24–25, 26, 27, 29, 39, 40
Evans, Clifford, 15
Everted rim. *See* Rim, vessel
Excavations, at Cuello, 2–6

Feet. *See* Foot, on vessels
Fillet, appliquéd or modeled, 72, 73, 90
Fingernail or thumbnail punctating, 29, 46, 51, 52, 64, 67, 90, 91. *See also* Impressing, on vessels
Fireburn Red-and-cream:
	Fireburn Variety, 10, 11, 23, 26–27, 40
	Unnamed variety, 10, 11, 23, 27–28, 40
Fire clouding, on vessels, 13, 16, 31, 35, 36, 42, 47, 48, 52, 55, 57, 59, 77, 79, 82, 92
Flange
	basal, 59, 62, 64
	labial, 46, 57, 58, 59, 69, 83
	medial, 59, 62, 64, 77, 78, 79, 80, 85, 91, 92
	*See also* Angle; Ridge
Flannery, Kent V., 32
Flor Ceramic Group, 10, 11, 54, 78–79, 91
Flor Cream: Unspecified Variety, 11, 54, 78–79, 82
Floral Park Ceramic Sphere, 85, 92
Flores Waxy Ware, 11, 41, 42–51
Fluting, on vessels, 74, 78
Foot, on vessels
	mammiform tetrapod, 92
	ovate, solid, 49, 69, 77
	round, hollow, 25, 35, 37, 43, 53, 59
	round, solid, 59
Forms, of vessels. *See* Bottle-shaped vessels; Bowl; Bowl or dish; Bucket; Chocolate pot; Cuspidor; Dish or plate; Jar; Tecomate; Vessel form measuring
Fort George Orange Ware, 8, 9, 11, 13, 21, 23, 34, 35, 41, 52, 54, 81–83
Frequency distribution, of pottery
	definition of, 8
	of ceramic groups, 13, 23, 41, 54

Gadrooning, on vessels, 34, 39
Gallo Impressed, 10, 11, 78
Gallon Jug Variety (Copetilla Unslipped), 10, 11, 23–24, 39, 40
Gifford, James C., 42, 44, 45, 47, 48, 49, 56, 58, 59, 64, 69, 70, 72, 76, 78, 80
Groove-incising, on vessels, 10, 13, 17–18, 23, 25, 26, 40, 41, 43, 44, 45, 47, 48, 49, 54, 69, 70, 78, 85, 89, 90, 91. *See also* Incising, on vessels
Group. *See* Ceramic Group
Guatemala. *See* Altamira site; Altar de Sacrificios site; Conchas Phase; Cuadros Phase; Jocotal Phase; Seibal site; Tikal site; Tilapa Red-on-white; Uaxactun site; Yaxha-Sacnab site
Guerrero, Mexico. *See* Pox ceramics
Guitara Incised:
	Grooved-incised Variety, 11, 41, 43–45
	Guitara Variety, 11, 45

Haleb Red-on-cream
	at Tikal, 18, 19
Hammond, Norman, vii, 2
Handles, on vessels
	double cylinder, 14, 22, 24, 35, 37, 88, 90, 91
	incised loop, 24, 35, 42, 53, 82

loop, 24, 25, 27, 35, 37, 42, 53, 57, 59, 67, 73, 74, 75, 77, 82, 91
nubbin, 53, 59
quadruple cylinder, 14, 22
strap, 42, 59, 67, 82, 83
triple cylinder, 22
Hillbank Red
at Barton Ramie, 72
Honey Camp Ceramic Group, 11, 23, 36–38, 40, 90
Honey Camp Orange-brown: HoneyCamp Variety, 11, 23, 36–37, 40, 90
House platforms, at Cuello, 2–6
Huetche Ceramic Group
at Seibal, 34
Huetche White, 32
Human representations. *See* Decoration, on vessels
Human sacrifice, at Cuello, 4. *See also* Mass burial

Impressing, on vessels, 9, 10, 11, 12, 28, 46, 51, 54, 71–72, 78, 90, 91. *See also* Fingernail or thumbnail punctating; Reed-impressing
Incising, on vessels, 10, 11, 12, 13, 17, 20, 21, 23, 26, 28, 30–31, 34, 35, 36, 37, 38, 39, 40, 41, 45, 46, 48, 49, 51, 54, 69, 70, 74, 83, 84, 85, 89, 90. *See also* Groove-incising, on vessels; Handles, incised loop
Ixtabai Ceramic Complex
at Cerros, 92

Jar
flaring necked, 14, 16, 21, 24, 34, 35, 39, 42, 53, 55, 56, 58, 59, 68, 71, 76, 82, 89, 90
medium to long necked, 14, 16, 21, 24, 35, 37, 42, 43, 52, 55, 56, 57, 59, 60, 72, 80, 82, 83, 85, 89, 90
outcurving necked, 16, 21, 24, 25, 26, 34, 35, 37, 38, 39, 41, 42, 43, 52, 55, 56, 57, 58, 59, 63, 67, 68, 69, 71, 72, 74, 76, 77, 79, 80, 81, 82, 83, 84, 85, 89, 90
short to medium necked, 14, 21, 24, 25, 26, 35, 37, 38, 39, 41, 42, 52, 55, 56, 59, 60, 67, 73, 74, 77, 79, 81, 82, 83, 84, 85, 90
vertical to insloping necked, 14, 24, 35, 41, 42, 53, 55, 69, 82, 83
Jenney Creek Ceramic Complex
at Barton Ramie, 26, 88, 90, 91
Jocote Ceramic Group
at Barton Ramie, 37, 90
at Chalchuapa, 37, 90
at Cuello, 9, 11
Jocotal Phase, Guatemala, 91
Jolote Variety. *See* Joventud Red
Joventud Ceramic Group, 9, 11, 41, 42–47, 53, 90
Joventud Red:
Black Rock Variety, 43
Jolote Variety, 43
Joventud Variety, 43
Mocho Variety, 43
Palmasito Variety, 11, 41, 42–43, 44, 45, 46, 50, 57
Unspecified Variety, 43
Juaya Resist: Juaya Variety
at Chalchuapa, 33

Kichpanha site, Belize, 46
"Kill-holes," in vessels, 77, 85
Kuxche Ceramic Group
at Cerros, 83
Kuxche Orange: Kuxche Variety
at Cerros, 83

Labial eversion. *See* Flange, labial
Labial flange. *See* Flange, labial
Lagartos Punctated: Lagartos Variety, 11, 54, 70–71
La Gruta phase, Parmana, South America, 88
Laguna Verde Incised:
Grooved-incised Variety, 11, 54, 69–70, 85
Laguna Verde Variety, 11, 54, 70
Lagunita Phase, Mexico, 88
Lamanai site, Belize, 92
Late Preclassic
dating of, 1
in Mesoamerica, 91–92
structures at Cuello, 4–6
*See also* Cocos Ceramic Complex
Lazaro Variety (renamed San Lazaro Variety). *See* Muxanal Red-on-cream
Lechugal Incised:
Grooved-incised Variety, 11, 54, 78
Macaw Bank Variety, 78
Simple-incised Variety, 78
Lip, on vessel
beveled, 14, 24, 35, 42, 43, 53, 56
grooved, 63
pointed, 14, 16, 20, 21, 22, 24, 25, 31, 32, 37, 39, 43, 44, 79, 82
round, 14, 16, 17, 18, 19, 20, 21, 22, 23, 24, 25, 26, 27, 28, 29, 30, 31, 32, 34, 35, 36, 37, 38, 39, 40, 42, 43, 44, 45, 46, 47, 48, 49, 50, 52, 53, 55, 56, 57, 58, 59, 63, 64, 67, 68, 69, 70, 71, 72, 74, 77, 78, 79, 80, 81, 82, 83, 89, 90, 91
square, 13, 14, 15, 16, 17, 18, 19, 20, 21, 22, 23, 24, 26, 35, 40, 55, 89, 90
Loltun Cave, 15
London Red-and-unslipped, 11
Loop handle. *See* Handles, incised loop; Handles, loop
Lopez Ceramic Complex
architectural phases, 7
ceramic groups, 41
dating of, 9, 90
relationship to other site complexes, 91
summary of attributes, 90–91
type descriptions, 41–53
Lubaantun site, Belize, 49

Machaca Black:
Machaca Variety, 11, 13, 20, 30, 40
Wamil Variety, 11, 12, 23, 30, 40
Machaca Ceramic Group, 11, 13, 20–21, 23, 30–31, 37, 40, 89
Machalilla Burnished Line
in Ecuador, 15
Machiquila Buff, 11, 52
Machiquila Ceramic Group, 9, 11, 52, 91
MacNeish, Richard S., 89
Mammiform feet, on vessels, 92. *See also* Foot, on vessels
Mani Cenote, Yucatan, Mexico, 14, 15, 25, 88, 89
Mars Orange Ware, 53, 91
Masonry structures, at Cuello, vii, 4, 5
Mass burial, 4, 83, 84, 85

Matamore Ceramic Group, 10, 11, 54, 79–80, 91
Matamore Dichrome:
Matamore Variety, 11, 54, 58, 59, 79, 80, 84, 85
Shipyard Variety, 10, 12, 80
Matheny, Ray, 28
Maya Lowlands, ceramics from, 88–92
Mayapan site, Mexico, 62
Measurement procedures, for Cuello pottery, 8–9
Medial angle. *See* Angle
Medial flange. *See* Flange, medial
Medial ridge. *See* Ridge, medial
Meggars, Betty, 15
Melinda Punctated, 9, 11, 46
Mexico. *See* Becan site; Chiapa de Corzo site; Dzibilchaltun site; Guerrero; Mani Cenote site; Mayapan site; Monte Alban site; Olmec heartlands; Pox ceramics; Tehuantepec; Tres Zapotes site
Mica. *See* Paste inclusions, mica
Middle Preclassic
dating of, 1, 3
in Mesoamerica, 90–91
structures at Cuello, 3–4
*See also* Lopez Ceramic Complex
Miniature vessels, 55, 74, 83, 85
Mocho Variety. *See* Joventud Red
Modeling, on vessels, 13, 19, 23, 29, 30, 36, 41, 46, 48, 51, 54, 76, 85, 90, 91
Monagrillo culture, Panama, 88
Monte Alban site, Mexico, 15
Mottling, of vessel slip, 43, 48
Mount Hope Ceramic Complex
at Barton Ramie, 63, 92
Munsell color readings, 7, 8
Muxanal Ceramic Group, 11, 41, 49–51, 90
Muxanal Red-on-cream:
Comprimido Variety, 51
San Lazaro Variety (formerly Lazaro Variety), 11, 12, 41, 48, 49–51
Unspecified Variety, 27, 28

Nabanche Ceramic Complex
at Dzibilchaltun, 16
Nago Bank Variety (Chicago Orange), 10, 11, 23, 34–35, 36, 37, 38, 39, 40, 52, 90
Nohmul site, Belize, 9, 14, 16, 32, 43, 51, 53, 56, 62, 63, 67, 70, 80, 81, 89, 92
Nomenclature, ceramic, 7–8
North square, at Cuello
ceramics from, 54, 55, 56, 59, 63, 67, 68, 70, 71, 72, 74, 77, 78, 79, 80, 81, 82
excavations in, 1, 4–6
Nubbin handle. *See* Handles, nubbin

Olmec Heartlands, Gulf Coast, Mexico, 45, 91
Orangewalktown, Belize, 1
Organic paint, on vessels, 84
Ossory Red-on-orange, 11
Ovate foot. *See* Foot, ovate

Paila Ceramic Group, 11
Paint, organic, 84
Pakluum Ceramic Complex
at Becan, 92
Pakluum Special: Black, unslipped and incised, 74
Palma Daub, 91
Palmasito Variety (Joventud Red), 11, 41, 42–43, 44, 45, 46, 50, 57
Panama. *See* Parita Bay
Parita Bay, Panama
Monagrillo Culture, 88

Parmana site, South America
    La Gruta Phase, 88
Paso Caballo Waxy Ware, 11, 57–81
Paso Danto Incised: Unspecified Variety, 11, 41, 49
Paste inclusions
    carbonate, 13, 15, 20, 21, 31, 35, 36, 42, 47, 48, 49, 52, 55, 56, 57, 58, 59, 63, 78, 81
    crushed sherds, 42, 57
    mica, 15, 55, 56, 59, 63
Paste, temper, and firing analytical techniques, 8
Patchchacan Pattern-burnished: Patchchacan Variety, 11, 14–15, 89
Patos Appliqued, 9, 11, 47
Pattern-burnishing, on vessels, 11, 12, 13, 14–15, 89. *See also* Burnishing
Pettville Red-and-cream:
    Pettville Variety, 10, 12, 13, 18–19, 26, 27, 40
    Unnamed variety, 10, 12, 13, 19, 27, 40
Pico de Oro Incised, 17, 18
Pinol Black-on-red, 9, 12, 47
Pinola Creek Incised, 26
Pital Ceramic Group, 9, 12, 41, 48–49, 51, 52, 90
Pital Cream:
    Pital Variety, 49
    Unspecified Variety, 12, 41, 48–49
Pits, slab-lined, 5
Plancha Ceramic Complex
    at Altar de Sacrificios, 92
Plate. *See* Dish or plate
Platform 34, at Cuello, vii, 1–6
Pole and thatch structures, 2–6
Polvero Black: Polvero Variety, 12, 54, 76–78, 85
Polvero Ceramic Group, 12, 54, 76–78, 91
Polychrome pottery. *See* Trichrome vessel
Pox ceramics, Mexico, 88, 89
Principal identifying attributes
    definition of, 8
Pring, Duncan, vii, 7–24, 26, 28–36, 41–49, 51–55, 59, 63, 64, 67, 70–74, 76, 78–83, 88, 89, 91, 92
Puerto Hormiga site, Colombia, 88
Puletan Red-and-unslipped:
    Puletan Variety, 12, 54, 73–74, 85
    Unnamed variety, 12, 54, 74, 75, 85
Punctating, on vessels, 9, 10, 11, 13, 19, 23, 29, 46, 51, 52, 54, 64, 67, 70, 71, 72, 74, 78, 83, 84, 89, 90, 91. *See also* Fingernail or thumbnail punctating
Purron ceramics, Mexico, 88, 89
Pyramid, vii, 1, 2, 4, 5. *See also* Structure 35

Quamina Ceramic Group, 12, 23, 30–34, 40, 90
Quamina Cream: Quamina Variety, 12, 23, 30–32, 34, 40, 90

Rancho Peludo site, Venezuela, 88
Ramgoat Red, 12, 16, 89
Real Ceramic Complex
    at Seibal, 16, 17, 19, 26, 30, 31, 88, 90
Reed-impressing, on vessels, 51, 54, 71, 72, 90, 91. *See also* Fingernail or thumbnail punctating; Impressing; Punctating
Repasto Black-on-red, 12
Repollo Impressed: Unspecified Variety, 12, 54, 71–72
Resaca Impressed, 9, 12, 46
Resist decoration, on vessels, 12, 23, 33, 58, 90
Rice, Prudence, 51
Richardson Peak Ceramic Group, 9, 41, 54, 55, 56, 90

Richardson Peak Unslipped:
    Richardson Peak Variety (Cocos), 12, 42, 55–56, 85, 91
    Richardson Peak Variety (Lopez), 12, 41–42, 90, 91
    Unspecified Variety, 9
Ridge
    basal, 59, 64
    medial, 59, 64, 66, 67, 68, 71, 79
    *See also* Angle; Flange
Rim, vessel
    direct, 14, 15, 16, 17, 18, 19, 20, 21, 22, 24, 25, 26, 27, 29, 30, 31, 32, 33, 34, 35, 36, 37, 38, 39, 40, 42, 43, 44, 45, 46, 47, 48, 49, 50, 52, 53, 55, 59, 64, 67, 68, 71, 74, 77, 78, 79, 80, 81, 82, 83, 89, 90, 91
    everted, exteriorly, 17, 26, 27, 42, 43, 44, 46, 47, 48, 49, 50, 52, 57, 59, 63, 64, 67, 68, 69, 70, 72, 80
    everted, interiorly, 38, 63
    folded, exteriorly, 14, 16, 22, 24, 25, 26, 28, 31, 32, 34, 35, 37, 41, 42, 43, 44, 45, 48, 49, 50, 52, 53, 55, 56, 57, 58, 59, 63, 64, 67, 68, 71, 74, 77, 78, 79, 80, 81, 82, 83
    folded, interiorly, 16, 19, 25, 26, 32, 43, 44, 48, 49, 53, 57, 58, 59, 63, 68, 77, 78, 79, 80, 81, 82, 83
    thickened, exteriorly, 13, 14, 16, 21, 23, 24, 25, 26, 27, 30, 37, 39, 40, 41, 44, 46, 47, 50, 53, 55, 56, 68, 69, 71, 77, 78, 82, 83, 89, 90
    thickened, interiorly, 13, 14, 17, 18, 19, 20, 21, 22, 23, 24, 26, 27, 29, 31, 35, 36, 37, 40, 47, 55, 59, 68, 69, 70, 71, 78, 79, 82, 83, 89
Rio Nuevo Glossy Ware, 8, 9, 12, 13, 15, 17, 18, 19, 20, 23, 24, 25, 26, 27, 28, 29, 30, 31, 32, 33
Robertson (-Freidel), Robin, vii, 63, 70, 80

Sabloff, Jeremy, 7, 8, 49, 70
Salinas Ceramic Complex
    at Altar de Sacrificios, 92
Sample size, of ceramics, 7
San Antonio Golden-brown, 68
San Estevan site, Belize, 9, 14, 16, 32, 42, 43, 46, 49, 51, 53, 56, 63, 67, 81, 89, 92
San Felix Ceramic Complex
    at Altar de Sacrificios, 91
San Jose site, Belize, 14, 88
San Lazaro Variety (Muxanal Red-on-cream), 11, 12, 41, 48, 49–51
San Lorenzo Tenochtitlan site, Mexico, 15, 88, 91
Santa Rita site, Belize, 9, 14, 16, 42, 43, 51, 56, 62, 83, 89, 92
Sapote Ceramic Group, 12, 54, 55, 92
Sapote Striated: Unspecified Variety, 12, 54, 55, 92
Seibal site, Guatemala, 9, 14, 16, 17, 18, 19, 20, 21, 24, 26, 27, 28, 30, 31, 32, 34, 36, 38, 43, 45, 46, 47, 48, 49, 62, 71, 78, 79, 88, 90, 91, 92
Shapes, of vessels. *See* Forms, of vessels
Sherd temper. *See* Paste inclusions, crushed sherds
Shipyard Variety (Matamore Dichrome), 10, 12, 80
Sierra Ceramic Group, 10, 12, 54, 57–76, 80, 91
Sierra Red:

Ahuacan Variety, 10, 12, 54, 57, 58, 83, 84, 91
Big Pond Variety, 10, 54, 59–63, 91
Sierra Variety, 7, 43, 54, 57, 58–62, 63, 64, 69, 70, 71, 72, 74, 76, 77, 79, 80, 83, 84, 85, 92
Xaibe Variety (now Society Hall Red), 12, 64, 92
Sierra Variety. *See* Sierra Red
Smith, Robert E., 42, 44, 45, 47, 48, 49, 56, 58, 59, 64, 69, 70, 72, 76, 78, 80
Smudging, on vessels, 13, 19, 29, 36, 48, 83, 90
Society Hall Red:
    Bound to Shine Variety, 10, 12, 67–68, 69
    Society Hall Variety (formerly Sierra Red: Xaibe Variety), 12, 54, 64–67, 68, 83, 84, 85, 90, 92
    Unnamed dichrome, 12, 68–69
Society Hall Variety. *See* Society Hall Red
South America, 88
South square, at Cuello
    ceramics from, 13, 14, 15, 16, 20, 22, 23, 24, 25, 26, 27, 28, 30, 31, 32, 33, 35, 36, 37, 38, 41, 42, 43, 45, 46, 47, 48, 49, 51, 53, 54, 55, 56, 57, 58, 59, 63, 67, 68, 70, 71, 72, 74, 77, 78, 79, 80, 81, 82
    excavations in, 1, 2–4
Sphere. *See* Ceramic sphere
Spouts, on vessels
    circular, bridged, 59
    circular, unsupported, 22, 25, 35, 37, 38, 39, 46, 57, 59, 60, 63, 65, 67, 79, 83, 84
    ovate, unsupported, 43, 46, 53
Stela, at Cuello, 4, 85, 87
Stopper Brown, 12
Stopper Ceramic Group, 12
Strap handle. *See* Handles, on vessels
Striations, on vessels, 12, 54, 55, 56, 74, 92
Structure 35, vii, 1, 2, 4, 5
Supports, on vessels. *See* Base; Foot, on vessels
Swasey Ceramic Complex
    architectural phases, 7
    ceramic groups, 13
    dating of, 9, 89
    relationship to other site complexes, 88–89
    summary of attributes, 89
    type descriptions, 13–22

Tabs, on vessel rim, 69. *See also* Flange; Ridge
Tecomate, 25, 26, 44, 52, 77, 89, 90. *See also* Bowl, incurving
Tehuacan Valley, Mexico
    Purron ceramics, 88, 89
Tehuantepec, Mexico
    Lagunita Phase, 88
Temper. *See* Paste inclusions
Thompson, J. Eric S., 88
Thumbnail punctating. *See* Fingernail punctating
Tiger Buff, 12, 21
Tiger Ceramic Group, 12, 21, 89
Tikal site, Guatemala, 9, 18, 19, 27, 28, 33, 43, 45, 46, 47, 48, 57, 58, 62, 67, 70, 79, 90, 91, 92
Tilapa Red-on-white, 32–33
Tok Ceramic Complex
    at Chalchuapa, 33, 90
Toribio Red-on-cream, 19, 33
Tower Hill Red-on-cream:
    Tower Hill Variety, 12, 23, 32–33, 40, 90
    Unnamed (resist) variety, 12, 23, 33, 90

Tres Zapotes site, Veracruz, Mexico, 14
Trichrome vessel, 85, 87
Tulix Ceramic Complex
  at Cerros, 63, 83
Type. *See* Ceramic type
Type-variety classification, 7
Tzakol Ceramic Sphere, 85
Tzec Ceramic Complex
  at Tikal, 57, 58

Uaxactun site, Guatemala, 9, 14, 43, 45, 46, 47, 48, 49, 51, 62, 70, 71, 72, 78, 79, 81, 91, 92
Uaxactun Unslipped Ware, 12, 41, 54, 55, 56
Union Appliquéd: Unspecified Variety, 12, 54, 72
Unnamed variety. *See* Ceramic variety, unnamed

Unspecified Variety. *See* Ceramic variety, unspecified
Usulatan pottery, 85, 92

Valdez, Jr., Fred, vii, 22, 28, 89
Valdivia site, Ecuador, 88
Vaquero Creek Red, 63
Variety. *See* Ceramic variety
Venezuela. *See* Rancho Peludo site
Vessel form, measuring of, 8–9. *See also* Forms, of vessels

Wamil Variety (Machaca Black), 11, 12, 23, 30, 40
Ware. *See* Ceramic ware
Warrie Camp Variety (Chicago Orange), 10, 12, 41, 52–53, 82

Xaibe Variety (renamed Society Hall Red), 12, 64, 92
Xe Ceramic Complex
  at Altar de Sacrificios, 16, 17, 19, 26, 27, 30, 31, 88, 90
Xe Ceramic Sphere, 24, 26, 27, 28, 90

Yalmanac Impressed: Unspecified Variety, 28
Yancotil Ceramic Complex
  at Yaxha-Sacnab, 91
Yaxha-Sacnab site, Guatemala, 27, 28, 32, 33, 43, 47, 48, 49, 51, 91
Yo Creek Variety (Chacalte Incised), 10, 12, 30–31, 40
Yotolin Pattern-burnished, 11, 12, 14–15

## ABSTRACT

Excavations at the site of Cuello in Belize, which began in the early 1970s and ended in 1980, demonstrated an unusually old and previously unknown ceramic sequence for the Lowland Maya area. The site was occupied from the Early Preclassic (Formative) at about 2000 B.C. until the Late Preclassic at about A.D. 250 to 300 when the area under study was largely abandoned, although other areas of the site continued to be occupied.

The analysis of the pottery from Cuello utilizes the traditional type-variety classification system to order the ceramics chronologically. The Cuello typology spans a period of time beginning in the Early Preclassic with the Swasey Ceramic Complex and ending in the Late Preclassic with the Cocos Ceramic Complex.

While few other sites in the Maya Lowlands have been identified as belonging within the Swasey Ceramic Sphere, a number of sites do contain late Early Preclassic pottery of the Xe Ceramic Sphere, equivalent to the Bladen Ceramic Complex at Cuello. Like most Maya sites occupied during the Middle Preclassic, Cuello belongs within the Mamom sphere of ceramics and within the Chicanel sphere for the Late Preclassic. This monograph describes and summarizes the ceramic sequence at Cuello and relates that sequence to the wider spheres of ceramics and interaction during the Preclassic period in northern Belize.

## SUMARIO

Excavaciónes al sitio de Cuello, comenzando en 1974 y terminando en 1980, demonstro una secuencia cerámica muy vieja y previamente desconocida. El sitio fue occupado desde el Preclásico Temprano, acerca de 2000 A.C. hasta el Preclásico Tardo, acerca de 250 al 300 D.C., cuando un parte del sitio fue abandonado.

El análisis de las cerámicas de Cuello utiliza la sistema tradicional, "tipo-variedad," para se organiza las cerámicas en un orden cronológico. Las cerámicas de Cuello empiezan con el "Complejo Swasey" en el Preclásico Temprano, y terminan en el Preclásico Tardo con el "Complejo Cocos."

Hay unos pocos sitios en las Tierras Bajas de los Maya con las cerámicas Swasey, pero hay mas sitios con las cerámicas de la "Esfera Xe"; el mismo del "Complejo Bladen" a Cuello. Cuello esta en la "Esfera Mamom" en el Preclásico Medio, y en la "Esfera Chicanel" en el Preclásico Tardo; el mismo de la mayor parte de las Tierras Bajas de los Maya.

Este libro describe la relación de Cuello a las otras esferas cerámicas en otros sitios en el Preclásico.